# Lord *of the* Elements

*Interweaving Christianity and Nature*

BASTIAAN BAAN

Floris
Books

Translated by Matthew Dexter

First published in Dutch under the title *De Heer der elementen*
by Christofoor Publishers, Zeist in 2006
First published in English by Floris Books in 2013
Third printing 2018

 Also available as an eBook

British Library CIP Data available
ISBN 978-086315-959-6
Printed in Great Britain by TJ International

# Contents

# Preface

This book is the result of intense interaction. First of all I owe the impressions needed for writing it to my interaction with nature. From an early age I experienced a familiar and indispensable relationship with nature. With or without words, I had an ongoing conversation with nature. Added to that came an interest in chemistry and alchemy. What interested me in each area of research was always the world behind the sense-perceptible phenomena

Over the years I had the good fortune to meet many people who had gained experience and new insights in this field and had developed new methods. The biologist Frits Julius taught me to look with fresh eyes at 'familiar' natural phenomena. My teacher Dick van Romunde gave indications on how to observe plants in a phenomenological way. Meetings and conversations with Friedrich Benesch, Annie Gerding-Le Comte, Ingeborg Lüdeling and Maria Thun became inspirations for a strengthened, deepened and Christianized experience of nature. All these people have made invaluable contributions to the field of nature observation.

In the 1980s I began lecturing and holding conferences on nature beings, initially with Maria Thun, who has amassed a wealth of knowledge and experience in this field. Surveying the available literature on the subject, I found little on the history of the different views of nature beings, and even less on the relationship between nature and Christianity.

Preparation of lectures for a year-long course presented an opportunity for initial research into these themes. They were given for a group of seven students and discussed afterwards, and I owe these students many relevant questions, suggestions and valuable material.

Readers who are not familiar with anthroposophy may wonder at the prominence of the insights of Rudolf Steiner, the founder of anthroposophy. This, naturally, has to do with my own outlook. However, other authors from quite different perspectives have acknowledged Steiner's unique place in this area of research. The biologist Sigrid Lechner-Knecht writes in *Die Hüter der Elemente*, an aphoristic book on nature spirits in different cultures, that of all authors on this subject, Rudolf Steiner has dealt with it in the most exhaustive and differentiated way 'in a meticulous and scientifically researched system.' She discusses his views extensively.

Another author from a quite different perspective, Tanis Helliwell, also mentions the unique position of Rudolf Steiner, when she describes a conversation with an Irish nature spirit, a leprechaun. Her book on meetings with nature spirits was published in many different countries. In daily life, Tanis Helliwell works as a consultant for businesses, universities and government. She has been clairvoyant and clairaudient since childhood. In conversations with a leprechaun, the nature spirit told her that a hundred years ago a man gathered a group of nature beings who are now cooperating with human beings. For the first time in centuries the separation between humans and nature spirits was overcome. The leprechaun tells Tanis Helliwell the name of this man: it is Rudolf Steiner.

I owe a great debt of gratitude to my wife Æola Baan for help in further developing the lectures. She supported this endeavour in every possible way and helped me write the book. Jolanda Gevers Leuven meticulously prepared the manuscript. And there were three people who were able to judge and correct the manuscript from their own fields of expertise: Dick van Romunde from the perspective of his discipline (physics, chemistry and phenomenology), Maarten Udo de Haes, a priest in the Christian Community, with regard to the anthroposophical and Christological themes, Feike Weeda, a student of theology, from the perspective of scientific theology.

# 1 What is Matter?

The origin and appearance of matter is an infinitely wide area of research, where we have only made a few inroads. The paradox of this research into matter is that, although we have penetrated deeper than ever into the world of the smallest particles, this realm becomes increasingly mysterious and inaccessible. This is true for physicists as well as chemists, who have discovered ever more about the nature of matter. Even the most brilliant of these scientists have to admit that matter is an enigma. A physicist who had penetrated deeply into the field of electronics was forced to admit, 'Something unknown is doing we don't know what.' There appears to be a true enigma at the heart of the world in which we lead our everyday lives.

When discussing the realm of atoms, physician and Nobel laureate Werner Heisenberg would not talk of things and facts, but of trends and possibilities: 'In our experiments with atomic *processes* we are dealing with things and facts, with phenomena as real as the phenomena of everyday life. However, atoms and elemental particles *themselves* do not have the same level of reality. They are a world of trends or possibilities, rather than a world of things and facts.'[1]

Never in the history of humankind have we penetrated so deeply into the realm of matter; and never before were we so deeply connected with, and chained to the physical world. We can try to distance ourselves from this materialism, but we are all part of this reality – a reality which is often so overwhelming that many people experience matter as the only reality. Like it or not, we are all caught in the 'morass' of materialism. Our every fibre is bound to the material world, without our realizing what we are doing: 'Something unknown is doing we don't know what.'

Most people in our time are aware, consciously or unconsciously, of the strong powers of attraction emanating from the material world.

Most people experience the lure of the world which can be so strong that we are in danger of losing ourselves in it.

An alchemical image from the sixteenth century manuscript *Splendor Solis* illustrates, in all its simplicity, what the world of matter means to the human being, how we are caught in it, and the fact that there is another world which attracts us too (Figure 1). The alchemists called this: 'Morass Man' (in the original German, *Moormensch)*. A human being stuck up to his knees in a morass, in the mud. He is almost black from head to toe. The black mud clinging to him reaches up to his neck. The head is red and covered in a kind of membrane which prevents him from looking around. One arm is red too and hangs by his side. The other arm is white, it is raised up and points to an angel with a star on her head, at the edge of the morass. The angel holds a red mantle in her hands: the mantle of the transformation of matter, or transmutation as the alchemists called it. The angel waits at the edge to receive the Morass Man and pull him out of the world which chains him to matter, to draw him away from the death of matter. Two worlds in their utmost extremes: the morass in which man, who still desires to return to the world of his origins, is held fast; on the other hand the angel who liberates the man from his bondage to matter.

In ancient times it was known that not only the human being lives in this tension between 'morass' and 'angel,' matter and spirit, but that creation as a whole is stretched between these extremes, now drawn to the material world, now to the spiritual. This is how Paul expresses it in his Epistle to the Romans (8:19-22):

> For the creation waits with eager longing for the revealing of the sons of God; for the creation was subjected to futility, not of its own will but by the will of him who subjected it in hope; because the creation itself will be set free from its bondage to decay and obtain the glorious liberty of the children of God. We know that the whole creation has been groaning in travail together until now.

The whole creation – the world of the elements, the world of created beings, stones, plants and animals – has a deep, subconscious

Figure 1. The Morass Man. From the manuscript, *Splendor Solis, c.* 1530. Berlin, Kupferstichkabinet. Cod. 78 D 3.

longing for 'the revealing of the sons of God,' which means us human beings. From the beginning of creation the human being has played a key role in the world. The angel draws Morass Man out of the weight of matter, but the human being influences the realms of the hierarchies too, by his deeds and behaviour.

Paul expresses this in a very forceful way: 'Do you not know that we are to judge angels?' (1Cor.6:3). We human beings draw even the hierarchies along in the wake of our development – or our further degeneration. When man remains stuck in the morass of materialism, the angel has no option but to follow and accompany him.

Since olden times it was known that the genius, the guardian angel, has to accompany the human being entrusted to him, wherever he goes. The influence of human beings on all the realms of nature is more visible and demonstrable. We only have to look around to see the decisive influence human beings have on the life and survival of the natural world; that humans are more and more becoming a crucial factor in this respect. Biologists, ecologists and environmentalists daily remind us of this. Surveying the media one is left with the impression that this conviction is now shared by most of society, after decades of doubt and debate about the importance of man's role in the further development of the earth.

In September 2004, *National Geographic* published a whole issue on this theme: 'Threatened earth: The consequences of global warming.' This series of articles no longer deals with predictions, but with hard facts. The main article begins with the following list of facts:

Carbon dioxide concentration increasing. Seas warming up. Temperatures rising. Glaciers melting. Arctic ice caps thinning. Sea levels rising. Lakes drying up. Dry spells increasing. Permafrost melting. Wildfires increasing. Lakes freezing over later. Ice shelves breaking off. Winters milder. Animal migrations changing. Mountain streams drying up. Spring coming sooner. Birds nesting earlier. Coral reefs bleaching. Autumn beginning later. Diseases spreading.

And for all these issues the influence of the human being is no longer in doubt, has been proven. All in all a very worrying situation, a situation none of us can escape, of which we are all part. In the following chapters I want to approach this theme in several different ways.

The gospels give an example of one approach, the archetype of the religious dimension. The evangelists describe an occasion where the elements are unleashed and people suffer a multitude of fears. This occasion can acquire a new meaning, especially in our threatened world, different from earlier times. Christ and his disciples were crossing a lake. Suddenly a storm rose up, deeply disturbing the waters.[2] In despair and mortal fear in the face of such overpowering forces of nature, the disciples clung to the Christ and roused him from his sleep: 'Save, Lord; we are perishing.'

Now something quite astonishing happened, whose significance and scope we have hardly begun to penetrate. 'Then he rose and rebuked the winds and the sea; and there was a great calm. And the men marvelled, saying, "What sort of man is this, that even winds and sea obey him?"' (Matt.8:25–27). They did not find an answer to this question. As yet they were not able to. But there was deep awe in their question: what kind of a man is this who can penetrate the world of the elements so deeply that even the wind and the waves obey him?

The more we penetrate into the world of matter, the more enigmatic this world becomes. But anyone attempting to find a religious dimension in solving this enigma will sooner or later have to ask, like the disciples: 'Who is he?' In the following poem I have made this crucial question my theme.


*He rebuked the winds*

Stormwind over waves
Rain drowning the harvest
Lightning splitting the trees
Surf maiming the coast –

They do not stop before for my heart,
They break into my house.
Spurred on by ancient violence
I am never and nowhere at home

Until I enter the place
Dedicated to Him.
There is a silence here,
Beyond the storm of time.

Who is He, that his words
Can chain the winds and waters?
Who is He that the storm in my soul
Will only listen to Him?

Christ is the Lord of the Elements. This was the epithet early Irish
Christians gave him. In Chapter 3 we will explore this in more depth.
Through the ages, this fact has received relatively little attention from
traditional Christianity. One could call it a blind spot of theology.
Both the Catholic and the Protestant tradition distrust nature as a
source of revelation (the Book of Nature). The blessed human being
stands at the centre of creation. As lord and master of creation he has a
responsibility towards his Creator – but not always explicitly towards
the realms of nature which are placed below him. The idea that nature
might be ensouled by spiritual beings is unimaginable within this
worldview. That would be deemed superstition – or worse. Anyone
concerned with ideas like this seeks to know 'more than is good for
a human being.' In short: religion and nature were kept well apart.
A classical example of this separation is the Chancellor in Goethe's
*Faust* (II, Act I), who exclaims:

Mind and Nature – don't speak to Christians so.
That's why they burn atheists, below,
Such speech is dangerous, all right,
Nature is sin, and Mind's the devil.
It harbours within it, Doubt, that evil,
Their misshapen hermaphrodite.

Everything to do with nature seems somehow taboo in traditional
Christianity. In a recent dissertation on Monachism, John van Schaik
concluded that Christianity has not developed a theology of nature.[3]
Is this perhaps a lack in Christianity?

In the Old and New Testament there are some clues, some hints at a theology of nature. But there are fragments too in certain streams of esoteric Christianity. The Celtic church called Christ Lord of the Elements.

In nearly all pre-Christian religions and in streams of Christianity up until the nineteenth century, it is evident that the world of matter arises out of the world of spirit, and that the problem of the origin and appearance of matter is a religious one. In most cultures around the world – the Pueblo and Navaho Indians in North-America, the Aztecs in Mexico or the animist cultures of South-East Asia – time and again we find that the problem of the origin of matter is related to the existence of a divine being which creates the physical world.

We will study the theme of the origin and emergence of matter with the help of a few historic examples. They will have to be fragmentary but will give food for thought on the relationship between spirit and matter – and on the relationship between Christ and the elements.

When we look at the Greek philosophers, we notice that they posit certain phases in creation. First there is a primordial being, a spiritual being which places the world-soul outside itself, and then makes the step towards the 'earth-body,' to the material world. We encounter this progression of spirit, soul and body, from the earliest forms of philosophy onward. Everything arises out of the one spirit. According to Heraclitus, *c.* 500 BC the physical world arises out of fire. To understand this we must first of all understand the mindset of the ancient Greeks, which was not abstract. 'Fire' for the Greeks was a spiritual being. With fire, Heraclitus did not mean a visible flame, but the invisible warmth which 'incubates' the creation and brings it into being. It is a divine warmth, hatching as it were the 'world egg,' so that this divine warmth gradually brings forth the etheric and later the physical elements.

For the ancient Greeks, fire, water, air and earth were not yet what we think of as the elements: above all they were qualities. Fire has the quality of something which contains warmth and dryness. Air has the qualities warm and damp. Water the qualities of moist and cold. Earth the qualities of cold and dry. The ancient Greeks imagined the elements to be qualities rather than visible substances. Gradually, out of these qualities, out of the etheric substance, the visible elements arise. 'Water' to the ancient Greeks meant everything fluid. According to Heraclitus creation came about slowly in this gradual densification of spiritual fire to physical fire, to air, to water, to earth. At the same time, he says, everything continues to fluctuate between densification and rarefaction. Heraclitus' most famous dictum is *panta rhei,* 'everything flows.' Everything flows continually between spiritualization and materialization.

The philosopher Plotinus (204–270 AD), the most important of the Neo-Platonists, also believes the world has arisen out of the One, who unites all opposites within himself. Out of the world-spirit the world-soul arises, which is drawn between the spiritual and the material world. Once again this archetypal image of spirit, soul and body.

We must make an effort to understand the thinking of these ancient philosophers and theologians to fully comprehend what they mean by this 'creation-emanation.' What we express in words and concepts was to these first thinkers a reality, a being.

Valentinus *c.* 100 AD, founder of the gnostic schools in Rome and Alexandria, tried to find a connection between Genesis (the seven days of creation) and the Prologue of St John's Gospel ('In the beginning was the Word'). He explores a possible bridge between paganism and Christianity. It is worth the effort trying to follow his attempt to achieve this. He writes: The nameless Godhead begins his creation – we might say: his creation before the creation – with a archetypal pair which he places outside himself.

Valentinus names this pair *bythos* (abyss) and *sigè. Sigè* is an expression from the Greek mysteries, meaning a holy silence.[4] Before he creates, God is like a silent abyss: *sigè-bythos.* In this state *bythos* is the male aspect of the Godhead, and *sigè* the female. The early Christians believed that from the very beginning, that is before the creation as described in Genesis, God had a male and a female aspect. When the archetypal pair, the silence and the abyss, has been placed outside the Godhead, the desire arises in God to manifest himself, to reveal himself. This may seem strange, but perhaps as humans we can understand the Creator by comparing him with an artist who becomes silent, outwardly and inwardly, before creating something. However, from the inner world where the Godhead resides, a desire arises to become manifest.

God does this first of all in the *nous* (spirit, reason, intellect). God 'thinks' himself, becomes conscious of himself. And according to the

Greek philosophers we humans were given a little spark of this. Beside that God places *aletheia* (truth) outside himself. This Greek word is derived from *a-letheia*, which means 'not having passed through the river Lethe,' the river of unmindfulness, of oblivion. When we consider the concept of 'truth,' we refer to a spiritual content which has not passed through oblivion before birth. We remember something from before its birth. In the Greek word this meaning is clearly expressed. In the third phase of emanation the third pair come into being. God wishes to speak and creates the *logos* and *zoë* (life). Only now does the logos (the word of creation) sound forth. God was silent before he created.

In the trinity of these pairs of concepts we can recognize aspects of the Christian Trinity. God is silent in a limitless abyss: the primordial ground. That is the realm of the Father, from which all comes forth. Then God thinks himself and places truth outside of himself. That is the aspect of the Holy Spirit, the thinking aspect, the *nous.* And finally he speaks his word and creates life, *zoë.* That is the third aspect of the Godhead: the Son who speaks out.

These first Christian philosophers can engender deep respect in us, when we realize how vivid and differentiated their thinking on Creation was. Valentinus describes a total of thirty beings who form the foundation of physical creation. He calls these eons, because they arise out of an evolution in time. Twenty-nine eons long, God is busy in his 'workshop,' out of sight, creating. His creating still takes place in the supersensible, in spiritual realms. Only in the thirtieth eon does it become visible and tangible what has been created earlier in spiritual realms. For ancient Greek, Roman and Persian thinkers an eon was not only a measure of time, but also a being. A being encompassing an era, as a regent. For twenty-nine eons God forms his creation in the spirit, before he actually places the creation outside himself during the thirtieth eon, and matter is created.

These apparently unfamiliar ideas are actually referred to in the Letter to the Hebrews (1:2). 'But in these last days he [God] has spoken to us by a Son, whom he appointed the heir of all things, through whom also he created the world.'

With these ideas in mind, the beginning of the Old Testament reads differently: 'In the beginning God created the heavens and the earth. The earth was without form and void, and darkness was upon

the face of the deep ... And God said, "Let there be light"; and there
was light.' Within these few sentences an infinite span of time lies
hidden, a succession of spiritual creations.

However, Genesis, too, makes a distinction between a spiritual
and a physical creation. The Bible begins with a spiritual creation and
then, as if nothing has happened, it appears as if creation begins all
over again.

In the first chapter the seven days of creation are described, and
then in the second chapter, history seems to begin anew (Gen.2:4–7):

> These are the generations of the heavens and the earth when
> they were created. In the day that the LORD God made the
> earth and the heavens, when no plant of the field was yet in
> the earth and no herb of the field had yet sprung up – for the
> LORD God had not caused it to rain upon the earth, and there
> was no man to till the ground; but a mist went up from the
> earth and watered the whole face of the ground – then the
> LORD God formed man of dust from the ground, and breathed
> into his nostrils the breath of life; and man became a living
> being.

The first chapter of Genesis describes a spiritual creation, and in
the second chapter this transforms itself into a physical process of
creation. God is a being with the capacity to work spiritually and
then to express himself in the physical world, in nature. The words of
the Creed in the Christian Community, 'An almighty divine being,
spiritual, physical,' relate to this.

In the Middle Ages most philosophers and mystics took for granted
that creation arose out of the spirit. The mystic Hildegard von Bingen
(1098–1179) described this process in words and concepts, but was
also able to transform her visions into visible images of the process
of creation. When Hildegard was 65 she had her last great vision of
the 'activity of God,' 'a view, an insight so deeply mysterious and
overwhelming that my whole body trembled, and which caused me,
being in poor health, to fall ill.'

It took the next ten years of her life, from 1163 to 1173, to dictate
or write the impressions of this vision. This work became known as
*De Operatione Dei, (On the Activity of God.)* She describes her vision

– which is not only a 'picture' (imagination) and an inspiration, but is also a spiritual touching, (intuition) – as follows:

> I beheld a mysterious and miraculous view. My entire soul was shocked by this and the sensations of my body were extinguished. Like gentle raindrops it streamed from the breath of God into the knowledge of my soul, in the same manner in which the Holy Spirit radiated upon John the Evangelist, when he lay on the bosom of Christ, and received from his heart the awe-inspiring Revelation.

In this slightly strange description she points to the origin of the Revelation of John, the Apocalypse. It arose at the Last Supper when John lay at the bosom of Jesus. That is the moment of germination of the Revelation of John, when heart speaks to heart. Now it was Hildegard who was initiated in the same way as John the Evangelist. Here we have a very precise description of inspiration: a divine being communicates itself to a human being, not only in pictures (imaginations), or in words (inspirations), but all-embracingly.

In this vision the essence and meaning of the first words of the Gospel of St John are revealed. These words contain an awe-inspiring potency – certainly in the original Greek. When John first dictated them to his scribe, the man fell down as if dead, unable, literally and figuratively to remain standing. But these inspired words do not relinquish their meaning straight away. It takes an 'inspired listener.'

In her vision Hildegard von Bingen enters the sphere where the words of the Prologue of John originated. This sphere communicates itself to her, 'as the rain of the spirit streams out onto John.' Out of the inspiration and imagination she receives, she describes how the Creator goes about his labours like an artist.

> In the primordial beginning, he said, was the word. The word, which was without beginning before the creatures, and which shall be without an end, let all creatures come into being. And he created his works in his likeness, the way an artist makes his work radiant with beauty. What he had foreseen for an eternity arose in visible appearance ... Each word of this gospel, dealing with the beginning of God's work

[the Prologue of John] was taught me face to face, and I let
it be explained to me. I saw that this explanation must be
the beginning of another scripture, not yet revealed. In this
scripture many questions on the mysterious creation of God
must be examined.

At that moment a new revelation arose from the inspiration of the
Prologue of John. A scripture which had not been written yet. It took
her ten years to write this work, *De Operatione Dei.*

The visions of the origin of creation were given by Hildegard in
two images. The first can be found in the book *Scivias,* the second,
written nearly thirty years later, in *De Operatione Dei.*

In the first vision, Hildegard sees the world egg, a kind of mandorla
(aureole), in which the whole cosmos is encapsulated: fire, the stars,
the moon, the clouds, the four winds, the water, the air, and finally
the earth (Figure 2). Everything is cherished by the fire of the
godhead: the golden flames surrounding creation. For Hildegard
von Bingen the world has changed the moment she received this first
vision. The world veils and reveals God at the same time.

The earth is at the centre of the cosmic egg – here represented by
the four elements, water (blue-white wave), earth (green hills), air
(black triangle) and fire (golden triangle). 'For the elements of the
earth have been created for human beings, with the intention to serve
them.' (Hildegard in *Scivias.)*

The vision becomes even more humanly recognizable when
Hildegard sees the world wheel (Figure 3). In the lower left-hand
corner we see Hildegard von Bingen. In the middle we see three
standing figures. At the top of the image the face of the Godhead
appears. Below that a being of (spiritual) fire, encompassing the
whole of creation with its body of flames. It is the expression of God's
love, which envelopes creation with a ring, a cloak of glowing love.
In the middle the human being. Hildegard describes him as follows:

In the centre of this gigantic wheel there appeared the figure
of a human being. His skull reached upward, the soles of his
feet reached downwards, into the spheres of strong white
and shining air. At its right were the fingertips of the right
hand, on the left those of the left hand, streched out in both

Figure 2. The Cosmic Egg. From Hildegard von Bingen's *Scivias*.

directions, to the circumference of the circle. In precisely
this manner the figure held its arms streched out in both
directions.

Hildegard deliberately describes this imagination of the human
being in the four directions of space, as a cross. Around this figure she
beholds countless animals direct their breath in the direction of the
human being. The seven planets and the stars, too, give their forces
to the human being: 'All the planets radiated in the direction of the
animals, and through these at the human figure.'

Golden beams radiated from the Creator towards all parts of
creation: to the human being; to the world of stars; the world of the
air; to water and finally to the centre, to the earth. We see the four
elements: fire, air, water and earth. And everything in creation, the
visible as well as the invisible world ultimately lets its forces stream
towards this one human being who is the centre of creation. The
winds, the animals, the fiery figure itself: the forces flow from all
directions towards the human being, who is the quintessence of the
four essences of creation. The four elements appear in the human
being. For Hildegard von Bingen 'fire' resides in the marrow of the
bones, the most mysterious and hidden part of our body, where
blood is produced. The air is in the voice and breath; water in the
veins; earth in the bones, where fire and earth meet. But the human
being, the centre of creation is the one who can make or break
creation.

> In the centre of the universe stands the figure of man. He is
> more important than all the other creatures of the earth. His
> figure is small, but the power of his soul is tremendous. His
> head held high, his feet in the depths, he moves the elements
> of the heights and of the depths.

The human being and the four elements are mysteriously connected
with the whole of creation, like communicating vessels. Everything
man thinks, speaks and does has consequences for creation. 'Heaven
and earth complain about human beings,' said Hildegard. They react
to the ever continuing Fall and they feel that creation is no longer
whole. Strife and unrest among humans cause confusion among the

Figure 3. Universal Man. From Hildegard von Bingen's *De Operatione Dei*.

elements. But at the same time the elements look up at the human being and wait for redemption through man.

> The elements drink in everything belonging to the nature
> of man, in the same way as the human being takes in the
> elements from nature; for the human being lives with the
> elements, and they with him ... Therefore it is written: Heaven
> and earth complain about mankind. For the restless battle
> in his labours so often brings confusion to the elements. It
> is as though a human being were holding a net in his hands
> and moving it. In the same way the human being brings the
> elements into motion, so that they transmit man's actions
> according to their atmosphere. (From *Causae et curae.*)

Hildegard von Bingen no longer talks about an abstract world of the spirit, like the physics of the Greek philosophers, but about a being with a name: the Lord of the Elements. The human being lives within creation as *homo quadratus:* fourfold man, who carries the whole of creation, the world of the four elements within himself, and who can bring creation to its fullfilment or to its destruction.

In this chapter I have discussed theological texts offering spiritual concepts that can help, up to a point, to understand the process of creation. Hildegard von Bingen does not speak in theological concepts, she describes powerful visionary images. In the next chapter we will explore a third path which led to insights into creation: the mysteries.

# 2 The Path Through the Elements in the Mysteries

The path which led through the elements in the ancient mysteries was, of course, a mystery. It has been said that the mysteries were the best kept secret of antiquity. We only have a few indications of what went on behind the firmly closed doors of mystery centres. The neophytes, the newly initiated, were sworn to absolute secrecy, to what was called *a-rhetos* (unspoken, secret, holy). Everything that went on behind the doors of mystery centres was connected with the unsayable. The rites were *apo-rhetos,* which means forbidden, secret, unmentionable. We would say, 'trespassers will be prosecuted.' Anyone who had not undergone the necessary preparations had to remain outside and there was no way they could acquire the spiritual insight which was granted in the mysteries. These insights were taboo. What we know of them are only a few, probably corrupted, fragments from antiquity. These fragments only conjure up more questions and riddles.

Based on the fragments which have survived, I will attempt to reconstruct the path through the elements in the mysteries as best as I can. I will have to quote other, comparable experiences, from nature religions on the one hand, where even today the path through the elements is travelled, and where people can describe from their own experiences what they go through. On the other hand I will have co call upon anthroposophy to help us understand the path through the elements. And finally I want to explore the 'entrance' to the experince of initiation, an area we all know to a certain extent, because we all have had certain elemental experiences in nature.

## Classical initiation

We have a short description – almost a formula – by the Greek
Platonist philosopher Apuleius of the path through the elements
in the ancient mysteries. It is one of the very few texts offering a
glimpse behind the scenes of the mysteries. This work of Apuleius,
*Metamorphosis*, was written in about AD 150. However, the text
still leaves us with many questions. In the evening, after a time of
asceticism and purification, the neophyte was led into the temple by
the mystagogue, the supervisor. There the actual initiation took place,
which Apuleius describes succinctly:

> I arrived at the boundary of death and I stepped onto the
> threshold of Persephone.[1] At midnight I beheld the sun in a
> shining white radiance. The gods above and the gods below, I
> beheld face to face. I worshipped them in close proximity.

It is impossible to describe the immense journey of initiation in a
more succinct, more mysterious way. When the neophyte arrives at
the threshold of Persephone – that is, the threshold of the underworld
and at the same time the threshold between life and death – he passes
through the elements.

Most historians assume that beyond the threshold the neophytes
were subjected to all sorts of mechanical trickery. Hans Kloft, for
example, in his otherwise well researched work *Mysterienkulte der
Antike,* drops his descriptive perspective and begins to fantazise:
'We can certainly assume an ingenious application of all available
technical aids, such as we find today in the hall of mirrors and the
secret cabinets at fun fairs.'

This shows how misunderstanding and speculative assumptions
about what happened behind the temple doors can easily arise in
our times.

Anyone speaking from real experience, knows that 'beyond the
threshold' refers to experiences free from the body. The Greek
historian Plutarch wrote: 'The mysteries deal with life after death
and the state of the soul after death. The candidates experience the
same as souls after death.' These experiences are no longer connected
with physical objects, nor in the ordinary sense related to the physical

elements. However, the physical elements *are* the point of departure from which the neophyte breaks through the physical world into the spiritual realms beyond the threshold, to experience the awe-inspiring world of the elements. We all know that these elements possess hidden, overwhelming powers: we see them unleashed in storms and other violent natural phenomena. Beyond the threshold of the physical world the neophyte experiences that the four elements are connected to spiritual beings who encounter him face to face and demand: What kind of a being is this who dares to penetrate into our realm?' It is impossible to cross this threshold 'illegally,' without a passport, as it were.

What happens if someone does manage to cross the threshold unprepared is described by Goethe (1749–1832) in a confrontation with the spirit of the elements in the first scene of *Faust.* This scene, of Faust being confronted by the Spirit of the Earth, is autobiographical. It was the very first scene of the play Goethe wrote. He indicated that after practising alchemy and magic he experienced such a crossing of the threshold himself, when he was about thirty. We know that around that age, Goethe read the *Aurea Catena Homeri,* The Golden Chain of Homer, a famous eighteenth century book on alchemy. It contains certain images on which the alchemist, the Rosicrucian, would meditate. If you really grow into these images they can lead you across the threshold, into the spiritual world. Even Karl Julius Schröer, the Goethe-scholar, is quite clear this is not some 'hall of mirrors at a funfair.' He wrote: 'These experiences [of Faust with the Spirit of the Earth] are an expression of the fact that Faust enters a different state of consciousness, free from the body.'

What does Faust experience when he opens this book and allows these images for meditation to work on him? Incidentally, in Goethe's play they are images from Nostradamus, not from the *Aurea Catena Homeri.*

When Faust has meditated on the symbolic image of the macrocosmos he lives into the second image. A huge being called the Spirit of the Earth is summoned up, and appears behind Faust. When Goethe directed the play himself he had a colossal face rise up behind Faust, veiled in mist, surrounded by fire: the elements of water and fire and, within the mist, of air. When the image of the Spirit of the Earth is addressed, it describes itself in quite an extraordinary way:

In life's tide currents, in action's storm,
Up and down, like a wave, Like the wind I sweep!
Cradle and grave,
A limitless deep, An endless weaving to and fro,
A restless heaving of life and glow,
So shape I, on Destiny's thundering loom,
The Godhead's live garment, eternal in bloom.[2]

Perhaps without realizing it the Spirit of the Earth has taken us through the four elements. *Cradle and grave:* the world of earth, of 'ashes to ashes, dust to dust.' *A limitless deep:* the element of water. How better to describe the element of air, than *an endless weaving to and fro?* And with *a restless heaving of life and glow* there is the fourth element, fire. Thus the being describes itself, as it were poured out into the four elements. Then it places itself within a greater context, by ending with the mysterious words: *So shape I, on Destiny's thundering loom, The Godhead's live garment, eternal in bloom.* We could not possibly describe the world of nature, the world of the elements, in a more concrete, vivid way.

Natura, as she was called in the Middle Ages, was originally experienced as the mantle of the Godhead. In his creation the Godhead veils himself in this loving, powerful being, which is, however, accessible only to those who have surrendered themselves in a certain way, who do not bring their own will, their selfishness into the spiritual world. The neophyte must die when he penetrates into the world beyond the threshold. And for Faust at any rate, that moment comes too soon. When the Spirit of the Earth stands before him, Faust cannot hold his own, and this powerful being confronts him with himself with the words:

Thou'rt like the spirit thou canst comprehend,
  Not me!

In other words, 'You may think you understand me, but you are like the spirit you understand, not like me. You have not really entered into my being. You have not become one with me. You stand here before me as a human being who is still too earthbound.' Later we will see what the right attitude is for approaching the Spirit of the Earth and the elements connected to it. Here at the beginning of Faust, we have an image of a partially failed initiation.

Faust cannot hold his own, he is thrown back into isolation, and it all goes horribly wrong. Faust is still a hindrance to himself. He is so full of himself and of his urge to enter into the Spirit of the Earth, that he is not worthy to come face to face with this being and to complete the journey through the elements. Only at the end of the play is he able to accomplish this.

## The path of the nature religions

We looked at these more or less classical descriptions to enable us now to begin to form a clearer picture of a journey through the elements. How is such an initiation performed in nature religions, even today? There are several autobiographies of people who are at home in these nature religions, describing the journey through the elements. There is a valuable description of an initiation by a man who has one foot in the nature religion of his tribe, and one foot in western culture. It is called *Of Water and the Spirit* and was written by a Malidoma Patrice Somé. Malidoma was born into the Dagara tribe in Burkina Faso, but was abducted when he was five. For fifteen years he was taught at a Jesuit seminary. Until he was five he was at home in his own culture, the culture of the Dagara tribe; the next fifteen years he experienced the western world. He learned to think and act in a western way.

After fifteen years he was happy to return to his own tribe. But when the time came for him to be initiated into the secrets of his people, every one, Malidoma included, realized he did not fit in anymore. With one foot in western society and the other in his nature religion it was hard for him to fit naturally into the initiation process of his tribe. He called himself a 'black white man' or a 'white black man.' He was torn between two cultures. Along with a group of other, mostly younger members of the tribe, he was told to develop the 'tree knowledge.' The initiator sent the neophytes off into the forest. They all had to choose a tree and sit down before it at a distance of twenty paces. They were then told to absorb the tree deeply into their own being. This is perhaps the first key for us to the path through the elements. His friends seemed to manage, but Malidoma became aware that he lived in a world which was split. His eyes could see the tree, but his gaze remained on the outside, he did not penetrate through the outer appearance. His thoughts wandered off in all directions. He was plagued and stung by insects.

He was troubled and distracted and his mentor noticed he did not achieve his goal. Malidoma was not able to fully concentrate on this one thing. He was reprimanded and told he was a hindrance to himself that made it impossible to penetrate into the world of the elements. The supervisor and the initiator were deeply worried, and Malidoma overheard their conversation. 'In his belly he is a full-bred white. He can't see ... The white man's medicine must have damaged his *vuur* [spirit]. But his soul is still in him. That's why I said a year ago – that for his own sake he should not to be involved in initiation ... Whatever he learned in the school of the white man must be hurting his ability to push through the veil. Something they did to him is telling him not to see this tree.'[3]

For the initiator it was incomprehensible that this member of his tribe was not able to see through the veil of the physical world. Something must have happened in the white man's school which prevented him penetrating into the fullness of reality. They were at a loss what to do with him. Malidoma tormented himself by sitting before the tree for hours, even days, until out of his experience of deep impotence, something broke open. Tears streamed down his face, he was at his wit's end, powerless, surrendered – and in this utter vulnerability his soul opened up to the being of the tree. He entered the world of the elements. Suddenly nature was ablaze like a fire. 'Where I was now was just plain real.'

That is the very first experience of someone crossing the threshold into the world of the elements: what I experience here is more real than reality. Everything I experienced on earth is semblance compared with my experiences here.

> When I looked once more at the yila [tree], I became aware
> that it was not a tree at all ... Out of nowhere, in the place
> where the tree had stood, appeared a tall woman dressed in
> black from head to foot ... She wore a veil over her face, but
> I could tell that behind this veil was an extremely beautiful
> and powerful entity. I could sense the intensity emanating

from her, and that intensity exercised an irresistible magnetic
pull ... the feeling of being drawn towards her increased.
For a moment I was overcome with shyness, uneasiness, and
a feeling of inappropriateness, and I had to lower my eyes.
When I looked up again, she had lifted the veil, revealing an
unearthly face.

Then words failed him to describe what he saw. In incredibly
beautiful shades of green and lilac the unearthly beauty of Natura
appeared before him. Her colours were the expression of an infinite
love. 'Never before had I felt so much love .. it was a love that surpassed
any known classifications.' Then he united himself spiritually with
the being of the elements.

When he returned the elders mutter to one another: 'They are
always like this. First they resist and play dumb ... and then when it
happens, they won't let go either.'

Anyone who has once penetrated into that world finds it extremely
difficult to return to the restrictions of earthly consciousness.

Then Malidoma described in great detail the path through the
four elements. Face to face with a pond he encountered the being
of water, face to face with fire he encountered the fire beings and
then, not face to face but up to his neck, he became one with the
earth, almost literally, by being buried in it. This was a sign of the
old, pre-Christian mysteries. What in Christianity is performed on
a spiritual level, is there enacted mostly on a physical level. With the
other members of his tribe he was buried up to his face in a shallow
horizontal grave. They had to spend a day and a night buried alive in
this way.

The ordeal of being buried alive ... was filled with pain ... a sense
of complete submission. When my body was buried, for the first
few moments I did not feel anything but weight, a tremendous
weight upon me ... The next thing I experienced was intense heat
that made my body sweat. That was the sensation that triggered
pain ... There are no words to describe how it feels to be buried
alive ... The heat from a naked body, unable to dissipate, gets
trapped in the dirt and so comes back at you. When you begin to
sweat and itch, there is no remedy because you can't move. Slowly

your sweat turns the dirt immediately surrounding your body
into a layer of scalding, sticky mud. As the heat increases with the
weight of the dirt, the mind cannot tolerate being in the body any
longer, so it leaves ... The whole area around me suddenly became
light, as if the sun had risen. *Am I dreaming?* I wondered. *Or have
I passed out?* ... I found out that I could move my hand perfectly
easily and that there was no more weight on my body. I got up
out of the grave myself ... The misty crowd rallied around me.

This is the moment the soul begins to have experiences that are
free from the body, and when soul and spirit enter the world of the
elements. There arises what we saw in the first description too. The
path through the elements is just the beginning of the process of
initiation, which leads to beholding the sun at the midnight hour: the
experience of the great gods. What began with the mantle, the veil,
gradually leads to the being of the elements.

I had an unshakeable sense of well-being and unity with
nature. The plants around me were all glowing violet, and
the trees kept moving their branches as if they were noticing
my presence ... I knew nature loved me ... I could even hear
nature, its relentless vibration of love and its slow movements.
It nurturing power fed me through my nose and my pores,
sustaining my vital senses. I was aware that nature also fed
itself in a way that I was not able to understand ... I had
friends in the trees and in the grass.

Nature has been penetrated; she shows herself in her true being;
finally nature shows the beings standing behind, below and above her.
Traditionally these were known as the higher and the lesser gods.

Discussing the story of Malidoma with a colleague, he told me
about a conversation he had with a student from Burkina Faso, ten
years ago, when he had asked about Malidoma's experiences. The
student told him the members of Malidoma's tribe had reproached
him for making public the secrets of their initiation. In a way this
reproach indicates that these experiences are authentic.

# The aid of anthroposophy

With the help of anthroposophy we can penetrate even deeper into these descriptions and find the means for our time to set out on this path. In his the series of lectures, *Secrets of the Threshold*, Rudolf Steiner describes the path through the elements, and what is necessary to penetrate this world. First of all, someone who crosses the threshold must let go of everything related to ordinary, intellectual cognition. We observe something: we place ourselves opposite it, observe it with a certain distance and quite quickly come to some sort of judgment. We do this many times every day. This process of cognition is impossible when we cross the threshold. When we experience the elements on the other side of the threshold we can only become one with them, be submerged in them, as we saw in Malidoma's description. If we want to know the element of earth we have to 'become earth' ourselves; we must bury ourselves in it – Rudolf Steiner uses the expression, 'you transform yourself into that element.' This means our soul life must be flexible enough not to remain outside events and phenomena, but that we must practice getting 'into the skin' of what we observe.

Anyone penetrating the spiritual world meets such overwhelming forces, that they cannot meet them with ordinary consciousness. A willpower must be developed, no longer founded on the physical reality of the body (we owe a lot of our willpower to our body), but a willpower derived from our innermost self, from the 'I.' Steiner expresses this in a powerful phrase that we can use when in danger of losing our willpower, in everyday life too, 'I will myself.' There is nothing to support us in this realm other than the I-consciousness which sparks off the will. That is what carries us. By I-consciousness is meant not the earthly consciousness of the ego, but a consciousness of the true self.

The other thing that happens across the threshold is that our thoughts become beings. Steiner uses a very powerful image: 'Picture yourself standing beside an anthill, putting your head into it and instead of thoughts you have ants crawling through your head. That is more or less how it is across the threshold: there are no abstract thoughts anymore. Every thought has a life of its own and is a being in itself.' This is an important indication for handling entry into the spiritual world: my *thoughts* in this world, are *beings* across the threshold. Imagine that what I permit myself here as flippant thoughts, are like ant stings there. We sting ourselves too when we slip up in our thoughts. Steiner describes it as self-inflicted pain.

There is a third requisite for entering the world of the elements. The first requisite is the willpower based on itself, 'I will myself.' The second requisite is to develop thinking with a purity, a kind of virginity. The third and perhaps most important requisite is inner morality. We enter a realm where the forces of opposition can roam freely – to the extent that we are vain, ambitious, egotistical and have a desire for power. Across the threshold, our morality is a weapon which neutralizes the counterforces. In this context Steiner warns against all methods of spiritual schooling where the chakras or lotus flowers, the spiritual organs of perception, are brought into motion without simultaneous moral development. Penetrating into the spiritual world is not that difficult, there is a plethora of techniques or aids nowadays. But this is dangerous, for anyone who enters this world unprepared, in a sense dissolves and destroys themselves.

## Our own experiences

So far these descriptions of experiences across threshold can seem far removed from our own experiences. But most people have certain impressions of this realm, conscious or unconscious. Most of us know that feeling of being alone in nature, but not feeling alone. If we take time and allow the phenomena of nature to work on us. They communicate themselves in a certain way. Sooner or later we begin to feel that something is watching me, something is listening, I am not alone. Most sensitive people have had this basic experience.

I had this feeling myself most strongly while hiking on my own in Norway, where I was totally on my own and at the mercy of nature, where I had the strong feeling as a lone individual of being surrounded by something absolutely overwhelming. And when praying or meditating in this lonely nature, the sensation that there is a being, watching, listening, becomes even stronger. 'For the creation waits with eager longing for the revealing of the sons of God,' as Paul wrote in the Epistle to the Romans (8:19). Nature asks something of us, demands something. Here the third substance we bring, our morality, is in a certain sense decisive.

This realm where we can all have certain experiences, however tentative, is one where we do not face nature as a complete stranger any longer, where a mutual permeation takes place, where we can begin to speak to nature, and nature to us. Goethe developed a concept which in a sense is a key to this. In his scientific writings he calls it the drive to create art and to imitate. In a way this is what we do as children. This childlike, playful open-mindedness is the starting point for developing a relation to nature. In the same way a painter lives into his subject – the sitter, landscape, or still life – we can live into nature with all our senses and inwardly imitate nature's gestures. It is like an actor living into the words and gestures of his character. To achieve this, all we need is some time and some peace and quiet. Sit down on a bench somewhere – calm your thoughts and worries about daily life (this may take a while) – and, like Malidoma, live into the one single tree before you.

I offer my own experiences here. These are preliminary exercises and not intended to develop full clairvoyance. They were consciously chosen to help with the first steps toward interaction with nature. Sit down by a brook or waterfall, and really take time to let thoughts about daily life wash away. Then, with all your senses, live into this one expression of nature: not just by looking, but also listening to the musical sounds of the brook. What scent does the water carry along? Use your sense of touch. How cool is the water, or the air around it? Let all your senses flow along as it were, with the water. Consciously, but also half-consciously, flow along with the movement of the brook, until you become one with it.

The alchemists called this kind of observation 'In the manner of the virgin,' virginal, pure. You must cleanse your powers of observation, become unprejudiced, before reaching that state. There is a religious expression for this kind of perceiving in the New Testament: 'Your eye is the lamp of your body; when your eye is sound, your whole body is full of light' (Luke 11:34). In Greek the expression is *a-plous,* literally, observing without creases, open-minded. It is a religious quality, which we need in order to become aware of the essential, as far as this expresses itself in the physical. We can employ the same

faculty in nature as we do before the altar. There too it is true that
'when your eye is sound, your whole body is full of light.'

I began practising this consciously when I was twenty-one, on
vacation on an uninhabited island. I set myself the task of looking at
the water for a whole day. Everything I saw I noted down and then
wrote a piece about it. The following days I did the same thing with
grass, reed, wood, etc. After a whole day observing, sometimes more, I
began to be familiar with what I observed. I no longer stood opposite
it, sometimes I stood beside it, and occasionally I manage to get into it.

Several times in the years following those first experiences, I
became so at one with something in nature, that I risked losing myself
in it. There was a beautiful willow in the garden of our vacation
home. A whole day long I observed the waving motions of the willow,
the sun reflecting on the leaves. I drew the tree and entered into it.
That evening I went to bed with a high fever. In this feverish state
the encounter with the tree continued – although I was aware I was
no longer master over my observations. I had crossed a threshold too
soon. Such experiences teach us what to do differently the next time.
Another danger when crossing the threshold is bringing with us our
desire to have something. On the other side of the threshold we do
not *have* anything, hopefully we *are* something.

Rudolf Steiner indicated that when crossing the threshold we must
let go of our point-like, concentrated consciousness. In the spiritual
world we cannot allow ourselves to acquire knowledge in the usual
way, to want something ourselves. Across the threshold we are not
allowed to want or will anything apart from 'I will myself.' We are not
allowed to desire, to want anything for ourselves. I learned this on one
of my vacations when I immersed myself in nature observation, and at
the same time reading and thinking about nature beings. All my time
was devoted to this. In our inner world we strive to become conscious
of the beings in nature, in the outer world we live in our observations.
One night the observations of the previous day continued in a dream.
What I had admired the previous day as a beautifully overgrown tree
trunk with twisting and turning roots, had become a nature being
in the dream: a gnome. I saw him in my dream and I could almost
touch him with my hands. Then I wanted to take hold of him – and
I woke up with the cold bedpost in my hand. I sat up and knew we
are not allowed to treat the world of the nature beings like that. We

only gain access to that world by not wanting anything, by taking our time, sitting down, remaining true to ourselves and by surrendering ourselves to nature in the moments we feel we cannot continue, when we are powerless.

A good friend who has achieved a lot in this field, described his first experience with the being of nature. He grew up in a family where the parents fought a lot, and he was deeply unhappy. One Christmas Eve this unhappiness reached a nadir. There was a sumptuous meal on the table, but there was still a fight. Is this supposed to be Christmas? In this mood he got up and left the house and walked on his own through the deserted town, desperate. In his despair he walked into a park. There he stood alone under the leafless trees. The bare branches reached into the pitch black sky with just a few stars shimmering between them. In this state of powerlessness, surrendered to his feelings, nature opened up. Suddenly, in his very first and very tender spiritual perception, a stream of love poured down from the infinite realm of the stars, through the branches of the trees toward the earth. A marriage of heaven and earth.

Since that time he goes out into nature every Christmas Eve, and lives into nature, and testifies: Every year at Christmas it happens again: the marriage between heaven and earth. Later he came across a book from the seventeenth century, *The Chymical Wedding of Christian Rosenkreutz*. In it he recognized the impressions of his first meeting with the being of nature, a wedding between heaven and earth, of spirit and matter. The hard crust of images in which we are all caught suddenly breaks open, often at a moment when we are completely vulnerable.

But how do we live into 'nature behind nature'? Malidoma could not get through because he was still divided, because on the one hand were his observations and on the other his images and thoughts. They tugged at him in opposite directions. The thing is to observe *aplous,* unprejudiced.

From my fourteenth year I was fortunate to have several teachers who had developed this capacity to a high degree. Frits Julius was a biologist and botanist who had developed the capacity to observe in an open and unprejudiced way, to an extremely high degree. He wrote several books explaining this method.[4] How do you live into the world of sound, how do you listen through the sounds as it were. How do you live into the world of nature? How can you learn 'to see the trees for the forest? A walk with him through nature was unforgettable, and taught us to look again. Standing under a some birch trees, for example, he would say: 'Now look at what the shadows do. No, don't look at the trees, look at what the shadows do. Look at the earth beneath the birch tree and live into the lively shadow play on the ground. And now have a look at how an oak tree does the same, when the sun shines through it and the shadows touch the ground. Look at it against the sunlight, walk around the tree. Look in the direction of the sun. Go and have a look at the same tree at night by moonlight.'

One of his famous sayings was, 'You often see more when you see less.' In other words: when you are less conscious of the actual thing, the object you are looking at, and concentrate more on the elemental phenomena, such as light and dark, you begin to see more. Many people who perceive nature beings tell how you rarely see them face to face, straight before you, but more often out of the corner of your eye, in a peripheral way. You should not fix them visually, but approach them with a peripheral consciousness, that is, a consciousness that spreads out over the surroundings and the atmosphere of the surroundings, instead of fixing onto one particular point.

What does the wind do with the leaves? What is it like when the wind blows through a birch tree? How does light play upon a birch tree? What are the shadows like? A well known indication by Steiner, which Julius practised, is to direct your attention to places where one element meets the other, the areas in between; for instance, where the root of a tree comes into contact with the ground and penetrates it, where a waterfall splashes over a rock, where a bee draws nectar from a flower and flies away again. Try concentrating not on particular objects, but on the transitions from one element to the other; that is where you are likely to meet nature beings. The sylphs for example are at home where a bee takes nectar from a flower. The undines feel at home where water flows and splashes over a stone. You must take your time over such observations. You develop a strong bond with nature especially by repeating a certain walk over and over again, in all kinds of weather and atmospheres. Over time it is possible to make friends with the trees. They become familiar and dear to you.

Then, over time, in quiet perception, in this familiarity, a bridge grows between human being and nature. We can learn to 'converse' with the elements. That is how the following 'miniatures' came about when I was twenty-one.

## Grass

Today I talked with the grass. That is possible when you take a whole day to just look and listen – very quietly with your ear to the ground. I lay down on the grass and made myself as small as I could – so small that the grass could see me, and I could see the grass.

'What are you doing?' it asked, because the grass could not understand why I lay down like that, without a jacket, when it was damp.

'I'm trying to make myself smaller, so that I can see you better,' I said.

Then I noticed the teardrops at the tip of every blade. The sunlight made colours with them, transparent red, yellow and blue.

'Why are you crying?' I asked.

'Because you are the first person ever who looks at me. No one knows who we are, because no one knows us. Do you know us?'

'No,' I replied, slightly ashamed, 'but I'd like to get to know you. I have got the whole day to look at you and listen. I am alone.'

'Oh,' the grass said, 'we are alone too, but not like you. Human beings have forgotten about us. They cut us down, so that you cannot see any more that we are grass.'

There was silence for a moment, and then the grass asked softly: 'Will you play with us today?'

'Yes,' I replied, 'what shall I do?'

'You have to take off your shoes and socks, and very carefully walk over us with bare feet. Then we will play a nice little game.'

I was very surprised, but I did what the grass had asked. Very carefully I walked over the green carpet of grass. It was a nice feeling, very cold and soft. When I looked down I noticed the grass bowing deeply at every step I took.

'Why do you do that?'

'That is our little game,' the blades of grass replied. 'When people wear shoes, we have to bow down. But now, because you walk barefoot, we bow out of ourselves.'

I laughed. The grass began to shine in beautiful, deep colours. The sun became warmer. 'Will you come a little closer? Then I will tell you a story.'

I lay down again, as before and closed my eyes so I could hear the soft little voices.

'It is a story,' the grass began, 'from the time when you had not forgotten us yet. We like telling this story, because it makes us feel happy. And a bit sad too, because it is all such a long time ago.

'It happened one fine morning, just as beautiful as today, when a woman walked across a meadow. It was the time when the most beautiful flowers bloom among us. This woman was not like ordinary people, because she sang softly to herself and then she smiled. She stopped suddenly and bowed down. No, she did not pick the beautiful flowers, she did something little children do sometimes. She picked us, one by one, until she had a whole bouquet. Then she took us home, filled a glass full of water and put us in it. She placed us on the table, sat down and talked to us, just like you are doing now. She smelled our lovely smell and stroked us with her hand. But people will probably not understand this story, don't you think?'

'No,' I said gently, 'I don't think they will,' and turned away.

'Please look at me,' the grass said. 'Why don't you look at me? You're not leaving, are you?'

But I walked away. From beyond the gate a man was calling that picking flowers was not allowed.

Behind me the grass rustled.


## Reed

Today the reed sang to me. I cannot sing like the reed, so I just listened, and asked no questions. It sounded like a choir with a hundred voices blending into one.

'We always wait for the wind,' sang the reed. 'We are the answer to the wind. When it arrives we forget the earth and dance along to it. Our dance is light as the air.

'We always wait for the water. We are the answer to the water.

When it arrives we forget the earth and sway along. We sway along with the wind and the water.'

Whenever they fell silent for a moment, their words echoed on. Wind and water, water and wind. It sounded like subdued humming in a dreamy rhythm.

It was as if it were weightless, as if no roots were holding the high stalks of the reed. The blades were like smooth sails ready to catch the slightest breeze. A dragonfly alighted, lighter and thinner and even more slender than the blades. She let herself be swayed gently to and fro.

'Take me with you,' sang the reed, 'take me with you on your travels over the water. Carry me along over the water with the wind.'

'I can't,' sang the dragonfly, responding, 'I cannot carry you. I am so light, that the wind carries me. I go wherever the wind goes.'

An idea came to me. I felt sorry for the reeds which were waiting for something that would never happen. I remembered how as a child I had made little boats of reed, with slender blades for sails, which were blown along by the wind. I took a leaf and tried. It can be hard repeating things you did when a child. I had forgotten those afternoons by the waterside when we raced our slender little ships in the wind. Whose remained afloat the longest, whose went farthest? I did not manage now. I had hardly lowered my little ship into the water than it fell over. I tried again. I had forgotten to use a bit of stalk for a mast. To make a little hole in the leaf for the mast. I carefully bent the leaf and put the stem through the hole. Now it was a ship, a sailing ship. It had hardly touched the water when it was swept along by the wind. And it sailed off to where the wind and the water go.


## Water

Today I spoke with the water. The water spoke to me, with the thousands of voices it has. I sat beside the lake surrounding the island, where the reed had sung. I turned away from the land and listened to the water.

'Why did you come here?' asked the waves.

'To hear the water,' I replied.

'You can hear me everywhere. I am deep in the earth. I am in the plants and the trees. High above you are the clouds. I flow over the earth. I am where life is.'

'But I want to see you too, feel you too. That is why I am here.'

'You can look at me, hear me and feel me but you will never know who I am. I am a secret, as life is a secret for human beings. You can see my surface, which is like a mirror. You can see yourself in me. You do not see me. I am here in the mirror and in my depths. Here I am like a mask, there I am like a veil. I am always the same – and I am always different. Therefore people cannot understand me. One moment they swim in me with their clumsy movements, the next I am in the air, raining down and quenching the thirst of the earth. When the earth wants to draw me in, the sun calls me back again.'

'Are you never at peace? You freeze over in winter, don't you?'

'In winter my mirror is hard as stone. There I sleep. Underneath it I am alive and wait till the mirror cracks open.'

I wanted to ask so many things, for the water became no clearer by what it said. I asked: 'Why don't you tell me more? Are you always a secret to us?'

'It is right that I remain a secret,' replied the water. 'You can love a secret: you can try to solve it your whole life long. Things which are no longer a riddle to human beings are no longer alive in their heart. One life is too short to solve our mystery. But you must look for me anyway. When you have searched your whole life for its answer, a secret is greater than it has ever been. Then you have to take it with you into your grave. You carry it as part of yourself, as we take our secret with us when the sun calls. We return to earth and we bring our secret back with us too.'

This was too grand and too simple to understand. As if life and death had spoken as one.


## Wood

Today I spoke with wood. It was and old piece of wood, hard and dry. I found it on the island where I camp, where no one disturbs my conversations with things. The grain of the wood was like a skeleton visible through skin. It reminded me of an old man.

'How is it that you grow upward?' I asked, something I had never understood.

'That is,' replied the wood, 'because the sun is the mother of plants and trees.'

I did not understand. 'Where do you come from and where will you go?'

'I come from the mother. My life has no end. I am in the seed, falling to the earth. The tree builds me up. I grow into stem and trunk. I live here and everywhere, in every germinating seed. Everything repeats itself.'

I was beginning to understand. 'But where will you go now? I mean what will happen to you?'

'If you had not picked me up,' the wood said, 'I would have remained lying on the earth. I would wait until the earth has buried me. It takes a long time and it hurts. But it is right and good, for mother earth needs us.'

'And what if I burn you?' I asked. 'What happens then?'

'If you need my warmth, you must burn me, tonight. And when you burn me you can hear the voice of fire. Fire has the voice of a human being, because it belongs to human beings. It will tell you where I go.'

The wood was silent and I waited for night to fall. It was cold and the wind swept the sky.

'Now,' said the wood, 'you must burn me.'

The fire rose slowly. I could smell the smell of resin.

'See how I change the wood,' said the voice of the fire. 'Look at its colour! First it was black as death, now life glows in it. I gave it air, the wide skies to inhabit!'

Sparks rose up like bright stars. I sat down and warmed my hands at the fire and waited for the last glowing embers to die. Ash lay still on the ground. Unlike wood, ash has no voice. Ash is dead.

## Human beings

Today I did not speak with things and things did not speak to me. The island was quiet. Today I thought about human beings, and about what the grass had said about humans. Suddenly I understood what the grass meant when it said it was alone, that people had forgotten it existed. We have forgotten, lost touch with all things, apart from our own things, our belongings. We only look down at the grass to see if it needs mowing.

Grass has become something we recognize. People have become something we recognize. Our vision has become clouded through the spectacles of recognition.

Grass is green.

I have met the things again. They are waiting for us. They are waiting for human beings to ask questions and to speak with them.

# 3 The Lord of the Elements

Irish Christians gave Jesus the name *Righ nan dul,* the Lord of the Elements. He was given the name not just from the moment of the baptism and making himself known, but from birth. He was born to bear this name. Unlike traditional Christianity, early Celtic (or Irish) Christianity looked on Jesus Christ not first and foremost as king of all people, but as king over the elements. An old Irish hymn sung at Christmas called him lord and king of all realms of nature, and the whole cosmos.

*Christmas carol*

Hail King! hail King! blessed is He! blessed is He!
Hail King! hail King! blessed is He! blessed is He!
Hail King! hail King! blessed is He, the King, of whom
    we sing,
All hail! let there be joy!

This night is the eve of the great Nativity,
Born is the Son of Mary the Virgin,
The soles of His feet have reached the earth,
The Son of glory down from on high,
Heaven and earth glowed to Him,
All hail! let there be joy!

The peace of earth to Him, the joy of heaven to Him,
Behold His feet have reached the world;
The homage of a King be His, the welcome of a Lamb
      be His,
King all victorious, Lamb all glorious,
Earth and ocean illumed to Him,
All hail! let there be joy!

The mountains glowed to Him, the plains glowed to Him,
The voice of the waves with the song of the strand,
Announcing to us that Christ is born,
Son of the King of kings from the land of salvation;
Shone the sun on the mountains high to Him,
All hail! let there be joy!
Shone to Him the earth and sphere together,
God the Lord has opened a Door;
Son of Mary Virgin, hasten Thou to help me,
Thou Christ of hope, Thou Door of joy,
Golden Sun of hill and mountain,
All hail! let there be joy![1]

With this salutation the Irish Christians greeted the newly born
Jesus of Nazareth. It is quite a different perspective on this child
compared to our usual one. Only in Ireland did the meeting between
Christianity and nature religion take place without any strife. In no
other country was the transition to Christianity as effortless as here,
where Christians built directly on foundations laid down by the
Druids. I want to reflect on the similarities, because they illustrate
how a bridge can be built between the pre-Christian experience of
nature and Christianity. In Celtic Christianity we have an historical
example of a form of Christianity which connects to the nature
religion preceding it. Sometimes it even seems there is no difference
between the two: the great Irish saints perform the same acts of
magic as the Druids did. Commentators have remarked that you
could call Saint Patrick a Druid, the similarities are so obvious. The
only difference being that the Christian saints called on the Lord of
the Elements for help in their white magic. Outwardly they worked
the same miracles, the same magic, only with a different power

inspiring them. A power so effective that the Druids were convinced by these Christian saints. Patrick and Columba, for example, are acquainted with the so-called Druid's gate: an old technical term for an area enclosed by a magic threshold to keep trespassers out. Patrick managed a feat the Druids call *feth fiada,* where the person disappears in a mist, and several deer appear instead. It was a well-known magic feat for disappearing from the visible world and conjuring up the world of nature. And then there were all the forms of power over the elements: over fire, air, water, the earth, used by the Irish saints to show they were familiar with the Lord of the Elements and that the Lord granted their petitions.

The most remarkable historical fact is that no Christians were martyred in Ireland throughout its history of Christianization. It is probably the only country where there are no Christian martyrs at all. Which begs the question, what kind of Druid religion was this, and what kind of Christianity was it that encountered one another here? What similarities were there, what recognition? But also, in what form does Christianity appear through the Irish saints which makes it dovetail so neatly with the Druid tradition?

According to tradition the Druids were the first Christians in Ireland. Elsewhere in Europe, in other forms of early Christianity it was often people from the fringes of society who first converted to Christianity. The poet Novalis wrote, 'The more helpless people are, the more needy of morality and religion they become.' On the whole this holds true for the spread of Christianity, which mostly took root among the more downtrodden members of society.

It was different in Ireland. We know the Druids were the first to be convinced by the new religion. They in turn converted the Irish kings. The royal courts convinced the warrior caste and through these the Irish people. This development was quite opposite to the Christianization of many other countries.

So what is it that made the Druids accept Christianity? The Druids were specialized in nature magic, a form of magic not restricted to their own inner world or to alchemical processes taking place indoors. The Druids practised their magic outside, in nature. There they could conjure up, with the help of rites, formulae, incantations and song, certain natural phenomena. The 'storm of the Druids' for example, which was extremely local and focused. In *The Tempest,* Shakespeare describes such a Druid storm raging over a single ship while around it all is quiet and peaceful. The Druids could apply their nature magic so that the different elements listened and obeyed their orders. This kind of magic is known in other cultures too, among the North-American Indians, for instance.[2]

On this well-prepared and ploughed soil fell the seed of Christianity. The Christians in Ireland spoke of the Lord of the Elements. The Druids must have recognized by this indication, but even more by the deeds of the first Christians which resembled their own magic, that the Lord of the Elements worked through these first Christians. In this context, Rudolf Steiner spoke paradoxically of the 'pre-Christian, pagan Christianity' of the Druids. They had developed their spiritual capacities to such a degree that they recognized Christ in nature. They did so when Jesus was born in Nazareth, but above all at the crucifixion on Golgotha. During the crucifixion the elements revolted: the earth trembled, the sun was darkened. Several legends describe how at the time of the crucifixion the Druids in Ireland were aware that the Lord of the Element was being killed. The legend of Conchobar for instance relates how one day a great storm rose up; all the elements revolted, heaven and earth trembled, the sun was darkened. On King Conchobar asking his Druid what it signified, was told, 'Heaven and earth revolt at the great injustice which this hour is perpetrated in the east. Jesus Christ, the innocent son of God is being nailed to the cross.'

On the one hand the Druids seemed able to recognize Christ in the phenomena of nature. On the other hand Christianity came to Ireland in a special form, so that it seamlessly dovetailed with the existing culture. What kind of Christianity was this? It certainly was very different from the Roman Christianity, which later came to Ireland. These two forms of Christian culture collided and clashed in Ireland during the synod of Kells in 1152 and the synod of Cashel in 1172.

By that time early Irish Christianity was so weakened by Viking raids and Roman Christianity that it was trampled underfoot. We must return to certain ideas in the New Testament and ideas brought by the church fathers to understand which specific and unique stream of Christianity it is that originally reached Ireland. This stream runs like a hidden thread through Christianity, and is known as esoteric Christianity. Early Celtic Christianity is closely related to esoteric Christianity.

Where and how can we recognize the Lord of the Elements in the New Testament and in early Christianity? Reading the New Testament with this question in mind, we notice that nature often responds to the deeds of Christ. Traditional Christianity is mostly concerned with what Christ means to human beings. But the New Testament is full of indications that Christ means a lot to nature too. Later, in the chapter on Johannine Christianity we will study this in more depth.

In Chapter 1, I mentioned the stilling of the storm. The New Testament clearly describes wind and water obeying Christ's voice, and the deep impression his action left on the disciples. They had never seen this before, or realized he had these powers: 'What sort of man is this, that even winds and sea obey him?' They were amazed that the voice of Christ could not only affect human beings, but also the depths of the elements. There were more of these moments when nature responded to him.

When the Greeks appeared for the first time, asking for Jesus, the heavens responded to his deep emotions. The Gospel of John describes how the Greeks arrived shortly after the raising of Lazarus. They were ushered into the circle of Jewish followers. This opening to Greece, to a new part of the world, called up a deep emotion in the Christ caused by the little group of strangers entering his circle. Undoubtedly the Christ must have recognized something in these people pointing to the future of Christianity. We can imagine the deep impression this must have made on someone able to foresee the consequences of this arrival. He was so overcome that he was speechless. 'What shall I say?' He then asked the Father God to reveal himself. We may imagine the voice of the Father sounding to the Christ. Some bystanders thought they heard an angel, but most heard thunder responding. Nature responded to the plea of Christ. Anyone who has ears to hear recognizes the voice of God in the voice of nature.

Now among those who went up to worship at the feast were some Greeks. So these came to Philip, who was from Beth-saida in Galilee, and said to him, 'Sir, we wish to see Jesus.' Philip went and told Andrew; Andrew went with Philip and they told Jesus. And Jesus answered them, 'The hour has come for the Son of man to be glorified. Truly, truly, I say to you, unless a

grain of wheat falls into the earth and dies, it remains alone; but
if it dies, it bears much fruit. He who loves his life loses it, and
he who hates his life in this world will keep it for eternal life. If
any one serves me, he must follow me; and where I am, there
shall my servant be also; if any one serves me, the Father will
honour him.

'Now is my soul troubled. And what shall I say? "Father,
save me from this hour"? No, for this purpose I have come to
this hour. Father, glorify thy name.' Then a voice came from
heaven, 'I have glorified it, and I will glorify it again.' The
crowd standing by heard it and said that it had thundered.
Others said, 'An angel has spoken to him.' Jesus answered,
'This voice has come for your sake, not for mine. Now is the
judgment of this world, now shall the ruler of this world be cast
out; and I, when I am lifted up from the earth, will draw all
men to myself.' (John 12:20–32).

The most powerful expression of this phenomenon comes at
Golgotha where the whole of nature, the cosmos, responds to what
happens on earth. The earth trembles, the dead rise from the grave,
the sun is obscured, the whole cosmos participates in the death of the
Son of God. The elements respond to their Lord.

Rudolf Steiner points out that the Gospel of St John contains an
indication of the Lord of the Elements, in a somewhat enigmatic
sentence. Steiner translates this sentence, spoken by the Christ, as
follows: 'He that eats my bread, his feet tread on me.' It is sometimes
translated as: 'He who ate my bread has lifted his heel against me'
(John 13:18). Steiner remarks in the lecture:

If Christ is the spirit of the planet, if the earth is his body, is
it not true to say that human beings eat his flesh and drink his
blood, and tread on him? When he points at the fertile earth,
is he not right to say: 'This is my body,' and when he points at
the pure sap of the plants: 'This is my blood'? And do human
beings not walk on the body of this spirit of the planet, when
they tread on him? He did not mean this in any negative
sense, but to point out the fact that the earth is the body of
Christ. This sentence from the gospel must be taken literally.[3]

The Druids knew this: the earth is the body of Christ. They saw it not in the physical earth, but they perceived with their special clairvoyant faculties that at the birth of Jesus of Nazareth and even more at his death on the cross, the aura of the earth renewed itself. That was the decisive fact that allowed the Druids to recognize Christianity at first sight, and to accept it at once.

Indications of Christ as the Lord of the Elements can be found not only in the New Testament, but also in writings of early Christians and of several mystics. In the second century, for example, Ignatius of Antioch writes in his letter to the community in Ephesus:

> Mary became pregnant with our Lord, Jesus Christ, according
> to the intention of God from the seed of David and from the
> Holy Spirit. He was born and baptized, so that through his
> suffering the waters might be purified.

Which bishop in our times could write something like this? Jesus Christ was baptized, 'so that through his suffering the waters might be purified.' To early Christians the baptism in the Jordan is the primal sacrament, in a certain sense the beginning of Christianity, after the birth of Jesus of Nazareth. Not only because Jesus then became bearer of the Christ, not only because a human son became bearer of the Son of God, but also because at the baptism some of this divine inspiration flowed into the water of the Jordan, into the world of the elements. Water takes part in the ritual deed performed by John the Baptist.

The element of water, bearer of life forces, of life itself, is transformed and purified at the baptism in the Jordan. Water beings, river-deities, still perceived and named by old clairvoyance, take part. The River Jordan was named after two river-deities, one called Jor, the other Dan. Thus they appear in a window (No 117) of Chartres cathedral. This depiction of the baptism in the Jordan shows two nature beings, below to the left and right. From above 'heavenly water' pours down on them, which they in turn pour out from pitchers. One is named Jor and the other Dan. The beings who are hidden behind the element of water and ensoul it, witness his baptism and are purified by it.

The river god can be found on countless early Christian images

(Figure 4). Perhaps the way the Jordan is pictured, welling up, is an expression of this divinity too. The baptism is often depicted so that the river in which Christ is immersed, rises up around him to unite itself with him. The baptism in the Jordan is in a certain sense the primal sacrament from which all other sacraments can be derived. One could justifiably call every sacrament a baptism, even the 'baptism in death' of which Paul spoke.

The mystic Anne Catherine Emmerich (1774–1824) could give a detailed description of how the Christ in death and resurrection binds himself to the earth. Every year in Holy Week she experienced what happens in the earth. On Holy Saturday she saw the following:

> I saw the Lord in several places, even in the sea. It was as if he liberated and sanctified all creatures. Everywhere evil spirits fled before him into the abyss. I saw the soul of the Lord in many places in the earth ... It is indescribably moving, to see the soul of the Lord surrounded by blessed spirits of the dead, walking through the rocks, through the water, through the air and over the earth.

The salvation he brings is not 'once and for all.' Every year this drama is re-enacted and his resurrection effects again the salvation of the souls of the dead. The impressions of these yearly recurring events not only moved Catharine Emmerich deeply, they also caused her to develop the stigmata.

Several mystics who have gone through the various stages of Christian initiation have had the capacity to observe in great detail the life of Jesus Christ in the spiritual chronicle of the earth. The Akashic record, the spiritual chronicle of the earth, preserves all these events. Some mystics are able to observe the events in the life of Christ as they relate to the different seasons of the year.

One of these was Hildegard von Bingen: 'After his resurrection Christ remained in the world for forty days, so that in these days he could purify and heal the four elements through his wounds and his blood.'

In these forty days Christ passes through all the elements and purifies and restores them with the force of his resurrection. In ten days he restores fire, in ten days air, in ten days water, in ten days earth. That is how Hildegard von Bingen perceived the

Figure 4. The baptism of Jesus. Sixth-century mosaic in the Arian Baptistry, Ravenna, Italy.

events between Easter and Ascension. Forty days in which Christ systematically penetrated the elements, to prepare them for the coming new creation.

Finally, returning to the New Testament, we can recognize the Lord of the Elements in the events around Ascension. As it says in the Acts of the Apostles (1.9): 'and a cloud took him out of their sight.' One could say that at Ascension Christ comes into his element, in the element where he is most at home, where he lives: the atmosphere. He comes into this strange realm around the earth, the atmosphere, where in a certain sense all four elements interweave and interplay. Air and water are clearly present in the clouds, but also earth, in the form of dust particles, and fire as the warmth causing the clouds to rise. Into these elements he ascends – and he will reappear from them again: 'Behold, he is coming with the clouds' (Rev.1:7).

Ever since Easter and Ascension it is possible to encounter and recognize the Lord of the Elements, not only in specific places where he is honoured and worshipped, but also in the elements of nature – for those who want to see. It is not a foregone conclusion that the Lord of nature appears to anyone observing nature. When reading contemporary descriptions of clairvoyant perceptions of nature it strikes me that often the observers remain 'on the outside.' They may see the nature beings, but not all of them realize who is behind those beings, what worlds are hidden behind them. Behind the four groups of nature spirits there are greater beings, sometimes called devas, from the Sanskrit, 'the radiant (gods).' They are the 'instructors' of these groups of nature spirits. But behind the devas stands the One, the Lord of the Elements.

Even for the clairvoyant a different point of view is necessary to recognize the Lord of the Elements. The Druids managed this. In those early days Ireland still had a connection to a much earlier era, to Atlantis. In Atlantis the human being had a different spiritual constitution from the one we have now. Steiner calls this a cosmic intelligence which the Druids in Ireland still retained. In the Druids, the ability to think had not been dragged along down in the Fall. With their cosmic thinking unclouded by egoism, the Druids could behold nature selflessly with their clairvoyant gaze. They could still see the etheric world in its purest form. This raises the question: If we do not have this schooled clairvoyance, this exceptional constitution of the Druids, what can we do? How can we, with our present-day consciousness, gain access to the Lord of the Elements?

I would like to describe three very practical paths, three ways and directions of looking, indicating what to observe and how to observe in order to penetrate through the veil of nature and the nature spirits into the realm where the Lord appears. One of these viewpoints I will try to describe in more detail.

The first path has hardly been explored. In his work, *The Spiritual Guidance of the Individual and of Humanity,* Rudolf Steiner makes a far-reaching statement. He predicts a time will come when physics and chemists discover that Christ has left his imprint right down into the subsensory world, the world of atoms, into the laws of physics and chemistry. This prediction culminates as follows: 'In the future there will be chemists and physicists, who ... will learn that matter is built up in the way Christ has gradually ordered it.'[4]

The expression 'gradually ordered,' is essential. Matter is not a given, remaining the same once and for all: it is drawn along in evolution, and penetrated into the depths of the subsensory realms by the Creator, the Logos and the Risen One. Rudolf Steiner describes the beginning of a spiritual physics and a spiritual chemistry, a vast area that is as yet more or less unexplored.

A second path leading to the recognition of Christ in the elements is perhaps more accessible. Anyone can start on it today. Rudolf Steiner gave an indication which he did not expand further, in a seemingly chance remark in personal conversation with Friedrich Rittelmeyer. Rittelmeyer had asked: 'How can I find a connection to the Christ in this day and age?' Not as he once was, but as he is active in the world now. The answer, surprising to Rittelmeyer, was, 'That is only possible when one begins to experience Christ in the cycle of the year.'[5] This was a totally unexpected turn in the conversation for Rittelmeyer: he had assumed the answer would touch on theology, the New Testament or Anthroposophy. Not so. Look at the cycle of the year, there you will find the Christ as he wishes to communicate himself to humanity now.

In the first path too, time and development play an important part: 'Matter is formed in the way the Christ has gradually ordered it.' So too in this second indication by Steiner. When observing nature, do not fix your attention on a single moment, a single impression of nature, in the illusion that you know what it contains, but follow a natural phenomenon throughout the cycle of the year. Through the cycle of the year, the director of the drama of the seasons is at work. Behind the scenes of the changing seasons a hidden being is directing the drama: the Lord of the Elements.

We can begin to see a bridge between nature and Christianity – even within the Christianity of the church: our festivals throughout the year are unthinkable without the supportive bedding of the natural phenomena. It is obvious that we in the northern hemisphere should celebrate the Christmas festival in midwinter, when nature has settled into a inward calm. And it is equally obvious that we should celebrate the festival of St John (June 24) at midsummer, at the height of the exhalation of the earth. (Of course, the festivals in the southern hemisphere take place at opposite seasons, but to go into that here would be beyond the scope of this book.

How can one do that: experiencing Christ in the cycle of the year? Rudolf Steiner gave very practical instructions for forming a connection to the cycle of the year to Dr and Mrs Van Deventer, a medical doctor and a curative eurythmist, pioneers of the early years of anthroposophy. Steiner suggested they visit one particular spot in nature each and every day. It had to be the same spot, the same time of day, in all weather conditions and changing seasons. Back in Holland, every morning at seven, Dr and Mrs Van Deventer would cycle to work, and along this route they found their particular spot. What they experienced they called a 'dramatic study of nature.' A drama they witnessed unfolding gradually, day in day out, year after year, in all conceivable weather conditions. They absorbed this place with all their powers of observation, conscious that you never see everything essential at once.

They describe how they gradually related their nature observations to the content of the *Calendar of the Soul,* weekly verses Steiner gave for following the course of the year from a spiritual perspective.

Steiner told Erna van Deventer: penetrate the plants with your imagination, try to express and copy the movement of a certain plant in your gestures. To fully connect yourself with the gesture of plants until you have absorbed this gesture into yourself. They noticed how they developed certain faculties through these observations together. The physician noticed that he developed a capacity to diagnose illnesses and prescribe therapies in a new way. The eurythmist noticed she was able to treat her patients differently, and received the right intuitions.[6]

If you try to observe nature like this, even in a modest way, you will notice the world of nature and the realm of the Christian festivals through year gradually begin to converge. You will notice that at highpoints of the Christian calendar nature displays different moods compared to other times, and that these are precious moments that should not be ignored.

I have tried to work with this by observing over many years what happens in nature on Good Friday, and to compare these observations with what happens in nature on other days of Holy Week. On Good Friday nature appears to be under the strongest spell.

Richard Wagner happened to observe and describe this once in a pure and striking way.[7] One morning in 1857 he left his country house near Zürich and the moment he set out into nature, he noticed everything was different from ususal. There was something magical about nature. He observed nature intensely – and suddenly realized it is Good Friday. At the same moment the ideas arose in him for a possible opera, for *Parsifal*. On Good Friday nature presents a different aspect than on other days of the year. Wagner described the moment in his autobiography: 'Now, the ideas for Parsifal came to me in an overwhelming fashion, and from the idea of Good Friday I quickly conceived an entire drama, in three acts, which I sketched out straight away.'

I once told this anecdote to an officer in the merchant navy who recognized it immediately. He had observed conditions wherever he was, and said, 'On Good Friday in the Pacific, I noticed it too, even in the middle of the ocean. There was a quite different mood compared to other days of the year.' Anyone who doubts this might ask small children, who sometimes indicate, like a kind of barometer, what happens on special days. Like the toddler who seemed lost in his play on Good Friday. He suddenly dropped his toys, looked up and asked: 'Does Christ also radiate when he has died?' After which he returned to his game: a child with no idea what day of the year it was, indicating unconsciously that something very special was taking place.

In the services of the Christian Community, perhaps for the first time in many centuries in the history of the church, nature has again become an interlocutor. In the Act of Consecration of Man it is not only the human being who plays a part in this dialogue with God, nature also plays a certain part. In other words: the human being takes part in the events throughout the Christian cycle of the year in earth and cosmos. The epistles, the inserted seasonal prayers, give a voice to nature in the different seasons, not in any pagan sense of the word, but in the sense of a Christian experience of nature. In these epistles, that are practically new in the history of Christianity, we hear how Christ is active through all elements, penetrates all elements, especially in Passiontide or Lent up until Pentecost or Whitsun. The epistle that sounds during Lent speaks in many different ways of the being of the earth. At Easter time the epistle after the Creed speaks of the activity of the Risen One in light, air and ether-forces. During Ascension the epistle speaks of his presence in the being of the clouds, while during Pentecost the activity of the Holy Spirit in the element of fire is indicated. All four elements are represented during this period from Lent to Whitsun.

The activity of Christ in nature around us is described, but also his activity within human nature. This is especially addressed in the epistles spoken at the beginning and end of the Act of Consecration. In the human being, in particular the heart, breathing and the blood are 'organs of perception' for the presence of Christ. Not only in the very special period between Passiontide and Pentecost, but also at other times in the cycle of the year do the epistles and inserts in the Act of Consecration speak about the presence of the Christ in nature. The service here provides a practical clue how, out of the content of a Christianity where nature and religion are no longer opposed, we can look again at nature from the altar, as it were, and recognize something of his presence in nature. The Act of Consecration provides a special expression for this. But the activity of the Christ reaches much further than this Act of Consecration. Wherever there is a Christian altar where the sacrament is truly celebrated, the Lord of the Elements can penetrate to within matter, into the sacramental substance. If there is one realm where he is particularly at home in his element, it must be the consecrated substances of bread and wine. Once, a priest, raising the consecrated bread at the altar, heard an inner voice saying, 'Do you realize that you hold in your hands the most precious substance on earth?' Christ himself manifests in bread and wine.

In the Gospel of John, there is a fairytale-like but nevertheless realistic description of the recognition of Christ one morning after the resurrection. The apostles, having spent all night fishing on the lake with no luck, are rowing back toward the lakeside. They see a figure on the shore, barely visible in the early morning haze. As they come nearer John suddenly recognizes him and calls out, 'It is the Lord!' (John 21:7). Something similar can happen during the slightly mysterious actions at the altar, which in a way veil more than they reveal, when you suddenly realize: 'It is the Lord.' When we have had this experience at the altar we can go back to nature too, and begin to look again. We may discover his presence in nature in a new and yet familiar way, so that these realms of inner and outer, which can seem so far separated, become one.

# 4 Elemental Beings

*Erlkönig (the Elf-King or Alder-King)*
Johann Wolfgang von Goethe

Who rides so late through wind and night?
It's a father with his child so light:
He clasps the boy close in his arms,
Holds him fast, and keeps him warm.

'My son, why hide your face, all scared? –
'Don't you see, Father, the Erlking's there,
The Alder-King with his crown and robe?' –
'My son, it's a trail of mist that flows.' –

'Come, dear child, come along with me!
The games we'll play will be fine and lovely:
There's many a bright flower by the water,
Many gold garments has my Mother.'

'And Father, my Father, can't you hear
What the Erlking's whispering in my ear?' –
'Peace, peace, my child, you're listening
To those dry leaves rustling in the wind.' –

'Fine lad, won't you come along with me?
My lovely daughters your slaves shall be:
My daughters dance every night, and they
Will rock you, sing you, dance you away.'

'And Father, my Father, can't you see where
The Erlking's daughters stand shadowy there? –
'My Son, my Son, I can see them plain:
It's the ancient willow-trees shining grey.'

'I love you, I'm charmed by your lovely form:
And if you're not willing, I'll have to use force.'
'Father, my Father, he's gripped me at last!
The Erlking's hurting me, holding me fast! –

The Father shudders, faster he rides,
Holding the moaning child so tight,
Reaching the house, in fear and dread:
But in his arms the child lies dead.

Goethe had an extraordinary capacity for observing the moods in nature. We know from his own descriptions that he could often penetrate the veil covering natural phenomena and recognize the essential within. But the composer Schubert, who set the poem to music, had extraordinary inspiration too when composing. Spaun, a contemporary of Schubert, describes it: 'One afternoon I found Schubert in a strange state, "glowing." He was reading the Erlkönig aloud. He walked up and down several times with the book in his hands. Suddenly he sat down and in no time had composed music for the ballad.' It was performed the same evening and received with great enthusiasm. Schubert could continue Goethe's work immediately, because he, like Goethe, had a strong and deep experience of nature, allowing him to penetrate behind outer phenomena.

What does the poem tell us? The three characters all speak a different language and live in a different world. A father rides through the night with his son before him in the saddle. The boy grows fearful, the father sees the boy's fear, but not what scares him. In the darkness of night in nature the boy recognizes the Erlkönig, the King of the Elves. But the sober mind and the outer perceptions of the father say: 'It is just a trail of mist.'

The child then hears what resounds through nature: 'And Father, my Father, can't you hear / What the Erlking's whispering in my ear?'

The King of the Elves promises the child something. Again the father only recognizes the 'outside' of the sounds of nature: 'Peace, peace, my child, you're listening / To those dry leaves rustling in the wind.' To the adult it's just the wind rustling through the dry leaves, to the boy it sounds like a promise of the King of the elves.

Now this king – not an ordinary nature being – tries to lure the boy in different ways. He tries to put him under a spell and promises him his daughters. 'And Father, my Father, can't you see where / The Erlking's daughters stand shadowy there?' Behind the King his daughters appear, seductive elves who want to take the boy to their realm. 'My Son, my Son, I can see them plain: / It's the ancient willow-trees shining grey.' Where the child recognizes nature beings, the adult sees only silvery willow trees. It is obvious we are not just dealing with the overactive imagination of a frightened child. Here the child recognizes a being behind the misty veil, behind the rustling of the leaves, in spite of the dusk. Tragically, the father no longer understands the boy, they speak a totally different language. What to the adult seems an incomprehensible phantasmagoria, a hallucination, is reality for the boy. And the boy was right of course: when the father comes home with his child in his arms, the boy is dead.

This is a situation which is often repeated. The story of the 'sensible' adult and the 'foolish' child with completely opposing perceptions and experiences. The adult who denies the validity of the child's perceptions and wants to instill some sober realism in it. In our modern age not only have we lost spiritual perception of nature, we also leave our children and their perceptions out in the cold (although the poem does say 'He clasps the boy close in his arms, Holds him fast, and keeps him warm.')

Thus Rudolf Steiner, who saw nature beings as a boy, was told by his mother, 'You're a silly lad.' We don't talk about gnomes here.

And some years ago a grandmother told me her grandchild could see the little folk: the elemental beings appeared to the child. The parents were worried and did not know what to do. They took her to a physician who referred them to a child psychiatrist. A little pill was prescribed to prevent these perceptions.

It is not uncommon in our time for children to tell us spontaneously about clairvoyant experiences. This is sometimes called a new clairvoyance. We find parallels in a long and distant past, when the phenomenon of an 'old' clairvoyance was widely known.

Paracelsus, a physician who lived and worked in the fifteenth and sixteenth centuries, wrote an important book in which he systematically described, probably for the first time in history, the realms of the four elements. It was called *Liber de nymphis, sylphis, pygmaeis et salamandris et de caeteris spiritibus,* the classical names for the realms of the four elements. Paracelsus uses the name *pygmaeis* for the gnomes. Then there are the nymphs, the sylphs and the salamanders. Four groups of elemental beings are connected to the four elements in which they are at home. That, according to Paracelsus, is one of the special traits of these nature beings. We human beings have the four elements within ourselves; the elemental beings can only live within their own element. The other elements are like poison to them. A gnome or kobold is at home in the earth element, in stones and roots. That realm is his only reality, he cannot exist outside it.

Paracelsus tells us that these four groups of elementals were created 'from the flesh, that is not Adam's.' They do not have the same descent as human beings. Paracelsus adds a short theology which is now mostly forgotten. Once upon a time God made a covenant with human beings, the old and the new covenant. But the elementals were not part of this covenant. They were outside it. They were not created 'from the flesh of Adam.' When elementals bond with humans – and this is what they like most of all – they finally become part of what they lack: through their connection with the human being, they re-establish a bond with the Godhead too, and they can develop further.

This is a theme we saw before in Paul's Epistle to the Romans (8:19): 'For the creation waits with eager longing for the revealing of the sons of God,' With 'the creation' Paul undoubtedly meant the visible and the invisible creatures, which people in those days still knew about. Paracelsus tells us that in the olden days the little folk were still familiar with the human race and on good terms with them. Human beings could still talk to them and allow them a part in their tasks on the earth. But in the ever ongoing Fall people slowly but surely turned away from this invisible world. They cheat and threaten the elementals, they exploit them and little by little the elementals have lost their faith in human beings, and now they lead their own lives. 'Only children and simple people can still perceive them,' Paracelsus wrote. 'Simple' in the sense of *aplous,* open-minded, unprejudiced. Paracelsus described a world he was still to some extent familiar with.

In other words: human beings are crucial to these realms of creation, because it depends on us how these groups of elemental beings will develop or degenerate. If people continue the destruction of the earth: exploitation, exhaustion and the destruction of plants and animals, then the nature spirits will be drawn down along this path, and will be condemned to the demonic possession of the spiritual beings who stand behind our exploitation and our egotism. They will be condemned to destruction and will become, as anthroposophy calls it, servants of the counterforces. We know there are not only the friendly, helpful little beings, but also a large group of nature beings who no longer wish to accompany the development of humanity, who have radically turned away from us.

What has happened to the Erlkönig, the Elf-King, why does he draw a child into his sphere of influence, into his world? Our physicians, psychologists and psychiatrists need a modern demonology to understand what is really happening to our children when they become 'unmanageable.' Either the elemental beings end up in the service of the counterforces, or they find, with the help of human beings, their way back into the divine world. This will not be back to the beginning, back to paradise, but (as Paracelsus tells us) the little folk know what the future of creation will look like, they know of the New Jerusalem. They possess the blueprints as it were, and are just waiting for the ones who will provide the 'building blocks, the ones who will bring the substance to build the New Jerusalem: us human beings.

This way forward can only be realized through the human being, through our 'Sonship,' *(Hyiothesia* in Greek). That is how Paul describes the task of the human being within creation. He writes in his Epistle to the Ephesians (1:5): 'He destined us in love to be his sons through Jesus Christ, according to the purpose of his will.' The whole of creation is waiting for this: that the Son is born in the individual human being. That is how the human being prepares himself for 'a new heaven and a new earth' for the future of creation.

The indications found in the writings of the apostle Paul and the physician Paracelsus are often too fragmentary for people of our times. No doubt this is partly because they could still assume many things were self-evident or known to their readers. Their explanations are part of a much larger body of knowledge their cultures were familiar with. Anthroposophy provides a spiritual framework where these ancient concepts and images can find a place, now as part of a much larger whole. The nature beings are related to the whole cosmos and have a definite function within it. I will try to give an outline of this spiritual framework.

The realm of the earth, of stones and rocks and roots is inhabited by the gnomes. They are sometimes called root spirits. They are particularly at home where roots meet the earth, where the mysterious processes of nutrition take place through roots reaching into the earth, which can sometimes draw substances from quite a distance. The chamomile plant for instance can draw copper towards it from a distance of 8 metres (27 ft) if this metal is present as trace elements. This is a miraculous world we are hardly conscious of. The plants are continually cared for and fed by the gnomes, who transfer the mineral kingdom into the world of the roots. These gnomes are wholly intellect and reason. Their seeing, their beholding is an immediate knowing. To gnomes even the most brilliant humans are dumb-wits. They look disdainfully upon all our activity and fuss: to them human beings are just silly. The gnomes are not on their own, they have their deva, their lord.

In ancient India the regent of the gnomes was called Kshiti. Similarly the undines, the sylphs and the salamanders have their regents too. Over and above the nature spirits stand the hierarchies who have 'secreted' these beings in the process of creation. The nature spirits form the bridge between the material and the spiritual world. The higher hierarchical powers either banish them into matter or liberate them from it, to help spiritualize creation.

In contrast to the sensible and over-conscious gnomes, the undines, the water spirits, live a dreamy life. Gnomes manifest themselves in a clear and sharply delineated way, but undines are ever changeable. They live in everything that flows, is liquid. They are not at home in roots but in the leaves of plants. There the undines work and weave and stream. Often the gnomes are all head and limbs, not much torso; the undines are all feeling, all 'middle.' That is their element. They are creations of the archangels, the gnomes of the archai.

Sylphs, the air-beings bring about the chemistry in plants, where light works on chlorophyll, the green substance. Sylphs work as a kind of chemist, weaving light into the substance of plants, through the extraordinary processes in the plant-realm, where light and air are transformed into matter. They have an even more dreamy and sleepy consciousness from which they are awoken now and then by birds. To a sylph, nothing is as horrible as a sky without birds. Their consciousness then evaporates and is in danger of being extinguished. But when swifts or swallows swoop through the air, the consciousness of sylphs lights up.

Finally, salamanders, the fire spirits, have an even sleepier, dreamier consciousness than the beings of the previous three realms. But their consciousness is lit up by warmth between humans and animals, between animal and plant: where bee or bumble bee on a flower suck nectar, where a shepherd tends his flock, a rider reins in his steed, there salamanders are in their element: they are at home in the relation between human and animal. Salamanders do not come from the realms of the hierarchies, they were separated off from the group souls of certain species: amphibians and birds.[1]

Before we move from these four realms of nature up to the spiritual world of the origins, we must ask the question, how can we relate again to these nature spirits? Paracelsus gave a key indication: through simple, open-minded observation. That is an art none of us have truly mastered: to hold back our own desires, our wishes, our cravings, all the inclinations of our ego, and to conquer ourselves in pure, unprejudiced observation. How do we do that?

In my years of studying nature beings I met several people who had developed the capacity to observe nature spirits to a high degree – or had been born with it. Someone once described how her perception of nature spirits had come about when she had master herself. Her husband had abandoned her and their children. For weeks she was embittered and full of hatred. Everything seemed to go wrong – but most of all she felt a hindrance to herself. One day, with a tremendous effort, she broke this vicious circle. She slammed her fist on the table and shouted: 'That's enough!' The same moment a fire spirit, a salamander, appeared in the heat over the stove and danced, obviously full of satisfaction. The moment she conquered herself, overcame her path in life opened up again and the world of nature spirits was revealed to her.

The same woman, in her job as a nurse, was on her way once to a dying patient, and her thoughts were totally focused on the patient. Cycling through busy traffic in the Hague, she suddenly saw elves over the trees, in the heart of the city. She also saw this world at other quiet, peaceful moments. Her child was in its playpen. She had no urge to get up and busy herself in the house: a mood of deep peace, quiet and surrender. In the pen, beside to the child there appeared a gnome, which showed itself to mother and child.

Between the two extremes of natural or trained clairvoyance on the one hand, and mere observation of the exterior on the other, there are many kinds of observing that perceive something of an 'inner nature.' The poet for nature poetry, the composer for music and the painter for impressions of nature, all need such a deepened perception. We all know it is possible to penetrate to the essence of things without being clairvoyant.

We can begin by observing a certain spot, in our garden for instance, intensively and with all our senses. The pitfall is we often think observing means 'looking' – only one of the senses we have. Our eyes are not the most obvious sense for establishing contact with elemental beings. Looking often remains superficial. With other senses we can penetrate deeper into the essence of phenomena. Our hearing, for example, can tell us more about something or somebody than the appearance. We begin perceiving with all the senses we have at our disposal. The play of colours, the play of light and shade, the sounds of wind, and movement, smell and touch. And apart from conscious, awake perception you must give your dreamy and unconscious senses a chance, because nature beings communicate most of all through those. Above all you must become inwardly quiet. The Flemish poet Guido Gezelle wrote: 'When the spirit listens, the cosmos sounds a living speech.' In this state of total surrender the mood of nature can communicate itself to us. Not many people manage it. Observe the way they walk though nature: often absorbed in themselves, agitated, their attention divided and superficial. How can we walk through nature so that we enter a state of surrender and receptivity, where nature expresses itself to us, not the other way around?

Over the years I have noticed something which can help. If we have made all our faculties of observation available – without too much effort, for if we tense up, reality eludes us – reviewing or looking back can be helpful.

When we have submerged ourselves in nature with all our senses, we can deepen and digest the impressions by bringing them up in the evening from memory. Some may have faded, other impressions of nature really affect us only when we recall them.

Taking such an image of a memory into sleep, we sometimes experience a continuation of these impressions the following day – stronger, deeper, more intense. Especially by going from conscious observation to unconscious encounter and then back again to conscious observation, our perception is enriched and deepened, and little by little we learn to look in a different way.

Rudolf Steiner describes three areas where we can begin to deepen our observations of nature by simple practice. Interestingly they are observations of single colours: of snow, a blue sky and the green of plants. We can lie down in a meadow and observe the blue sky intensely, like a child, drinking in the colour, closing our eyes, and letting the impression work on in us with closed eyes. Observing and remembering the sky like this for a while, I noticed I only had to close my eyes and this blue would be all around me. Eventually we can do that in our imagination too. We can drape the colour around us like a mantle, and it gives an immense feeling of protection and peace. Steiner gives the following description about observing heavenly blue:

> First of all we direct our gaze, looking up from the earth,
> into the wide cosmic spaces, where we are met by the blue
> of the sky. Let us suppose we do this on a day when there
> isn't a cloud in the sky ... Let us suppose we can practice this
> surrender to the blue of the sky intensely and for a long time,
> so that we can forget everything that happens around us,
> everything we are familiar with in our lives. Let us suppose we
> can forget for a moment all outer impressions, all memories,
> all of life's cares and needs and that we can totally surrender
> ourselves to this single impression of the blue sky ...
> A moment will arise when the blue of the sky will cease to be,
> when we do not see the blue any longer ... the blue disappears
> as it were; an infinity opens up to us and in this infinity a very
> definite soul mood wants to express itself in this emptiness

where the blue was. And if we want to name this soul mood, we only have one word for it: the soul feels devout, devout towards an infinity, in devout surrender ... The blue which extends so widely has called up a moral feeling in our soul: while it has disappeared as a colour, a moral feeling lives in our soul toward the outer world.[2]

In these exercises the aim is pure observation, without any distractions. That is why Steiner suggests such relatively 'simple' objects for observation: white snow, blue sky, the green of leaves.

But sometimes a first, unclouded impression of a nature observation can open the way to the being hidden behind it. Once a man without any previous experiences of nature beings visited a nature reserve in South Africa. For the first time in his life he saw a baobab tree. At first sight he suddenly perceived a tree-spirit with a long beard. The man was so surprised he called out, 'It's him!' But the next moment, when his overwhelming astonishment was replaced by recognition, the tree-spirit had disappeared.

So far we have described four groups of elemental beings, corresponding to the classification of Paracelsus. Beside these clearly recognizable varieties there are countless nature spirits who connect themselves with different, individual phenomena. And then there are the numerous nature beings who through the ages have found their way to human beings – who have made themselves helpful or have become specialists in obstruction and accidents. Nancy Arrowsmith has given an excellent overview and description of more than 600 different types of nature spirit.

Two observations serve to illustrate how unbelievably rich and varied the realms of the nature spirits really are. In the nineteen eighties Dutch author Annie Gerding-Le Comte became known as the 'Gnome-lady.' She told me she had been familiar with nature spirits since childhood. As a child in Indonesia she once perceived a volcano in its true being: the rocks of the mountain were teeming with gnomes, all tightly packed together. What appears to be a single mountain is in reality a mass of nature spirits forming and maintaining the mountain. In the Intermezzo on natural disasters after Chapter 11 we will discuss her work and her descriptions in more depth.

Not only nature, also the world created by man is full of elemental beings, which connect to certain phenomena, activities and substances. In an interview with Kees Zoeteman, Dick van Romunde, author of several books on botany, physics and chemistry relates his experiences with nature spirits:

> I must have been about five. There was a basement under our
> house where dad kept all his tools. I loved going down there.
> One day, going upstairs again I looked at the whitewashed
> wall. And suddenly I had the feeling: that is not a wall, there
> are an endless number of beings there who are friendly,
> though they also seem to expect something from me. I must
> use words to describe it now, but an impression is often hard
> to describe in words. It was a very rich impression, surrounded
> by a friendly mood, as if a kind of trust were placed in me.[3]

Earlier I mentioned that there is not only a connection between the various nature beings and physical elements and visible phenomena, but they are also connected to hierarchical beings who lead and guide them. In Indian tradition four group spirits are known who stand above the four groups of elemental beings as regents: Kshiti above the gnomes, Varuna above the undines, Vayu above the sylphs, and Agni (the god of fire) above the salamanders. These 'kings' of the elemental realms are also known as devas. Devachan, the realm where these higher beings live, consists of a lower realm, where can be found the spiritual forms which are the foundations of the physical world (also called *rupa:* form). Higher devachan (also called *a-rupa:* formless) contains the seeds, the spiritual archetypes from which the differentiated forms of the spiritual world arise. These realms owe their existence to sacrifices made by the highest hierarchies.

Not only is the visible creation endlessly varied, the invisible world too is infinitely differentiated. How could it be otherwise, the visible world already being so complex? In this multitude of realms and beings there is One who encompasses and permeates everything. Paul indicates these different realms as being 'in heaven and on earth and under the earth.' In the Epistle to the Philippians (2:5–11) he expresses this unity in diversity in a powerful way:

Have this mind among yourselves, which is yours in Christ
Jesus, who, though he was in the form of God, did not count
equality with God a thing to be grasped, but emptied himself,
taking the form of a servant, being born in the likeness of
men. And being found in human form he humbled himself
and became obedient unto death, even death on a cross.
Therefore God has highly exalted him and bestowed on him
the name which is above every name, that at the name of Jesus
every knee should bow, in heaven and on earth and under the
earth, and every tongue confess that Jesus Christ is Lord, to
the glory of God the Father.

# 5 Genesis and the Four Elements

When contemplating the relationship between Genesis and the four elements, I was reminded of an extraordinary moment when I was a teacher, and had to tell my class several tales from the Edda, the Icelandic legends. While preparing I wondered how I would tell this complicated story of creation to a group of nine- to ten-year-old children. The Edda does not describe just one creation with one God, it positively teems with gods and worlds. Slightly hesitant I stood in front of the class and retold this complex story of creation. Luckily there was one girl who exclaimed, after my long story, 'Yes, I once thought the world was made like that.'

I had a similar problem when considering the seven days of creation in Genesis. I asked myself, how can I impart what happens to the elements during creation? We were all present at Creation, of course, but we have no conscious memories of it. How do the elements come into being in the creation of the world described in the Old Testament?

It is difficult to picture creation, because the story of creation as told in Genesis has become obscured, if not corrupted, by our conceptions and our imagination. We are wrong if we read the first lines of the story of creation, and assume we understand what is written there. 'In the beginning God created the heaven and the earth.' We are wrong because we instantly picture something: heaven and earth. In other words, we are all prisoners of our earthbound images. When trying to picture heaven and earth we picture something physical, something tangible.

With the help of the Hebrew language as well as other spiritual traditions it is possible to find a different beginning. With the help of certain concepts – by going back to the original Hebrew language – we will try to understand the nature of this mysterious, primal beginning. For this we have to actively rid ourselves of our old ideas and pictures of heaven and earth, as Rudolf Steiner suggests.[1] We must leave behind our spatial and temporal depictions, to be able to see something in images, imaginatively, before us. Listening to Genesis in the original Hebrew language can help achieve this: it is a language with quite a different and unique quality compared to our modern day languages, and our modern day concepts and thoughts. Ancient Hebrew is a universe of sound. The words in Genesis have a very special sound sequence: we can call it a 'mantric' language. Mantric language allows us to see something before us, but not in a physical, sensory way. Our modern translations of the Bible have become infinitely removed from this original Hebrew world of sounds and expressions. And, sad to say, with a few exceptions, the more modern the translation, the further removed from the original meaning.

In the original Hebrew the first five verses of Genesis sound as follows (transliterated into our script):

*Bereshít bará elohím ét-hashamáyim we'ét-ha'áretz*
*Weha'áretz hayetá tóhu wavóhu.*
*Wechoshech al-pné tehom.*
*Werúach elohím macháphèt al-pné hamáyim.*
*Waiyómer elohím yehí ór way'hí ór.*
*Waiyár elohím et-ha'ór ki tov*
*Waiyavdél elohím ben ha'ór uven hachoshech.*
*Waiyiqrá elohím la'ór yom*
*Welachoshech qára láylah*
*Wayhi 'erèv wayehi voker: yom echád.*

The kabbala was a Jewish mystical stream which developed in the Middle Ages. The kabbala's *Sefer Yetzirah,* the book of creation, recounts how God created the world with the help of the 22 letters of the Hebrew alphabet, and with the 10 Sefirot (living beings: 10 numbers through which Creation reveals itself). According to this tradition there is not a random letter, word, or number in Genesis. For centuries kabbalists have carefully studied every word of the Torah (the five books of Moses that are the first five books of the Old Testament). The results of their philosophical and meditative contemplations can be found in the writings of the kabbala. The first five verses of Genesis in English (Revised Standard Version) are as follows:

> In the beginning God created the heavens and the earth. The earth was without form and void, and darkness was upon the face of the deep; and the Spirit of God was moving over the face of the waters.
> And God said, 'Let there be light'; and there was light.
> And God saw that the light was good; and God separated the light from the darkness. God called the light Day, and the darkness he called Night. And there was evening and there was morning, one day.

A precondition for understanding something of these mysterious words is asking of everything that is created: How can a spiritual reality become a physical reality? What was water before it became water? Are we able to imagine a world which only consists of water, without actually having anything before us that is tangible, visible? And similarly with the other elements. To be able to do this we must go back to our own origin.

To approach the realm of the elements in Creation, we must go to our own origin in the spirit. The Act of Consecration has a wonderful expression for this, 'Our grounding in the spirit.' The word for 'grounding' in German is *Urständen,* literally 'primal foundations,' and hearing the sounds of this word can help us discover intuitively, through the feelings and images they conjure up, that our foundations are indeed in the spirit, that we are rooted in the spiritual world. In the early Middle Ages it was sometimes depicted literally: in some medieval cathedrals there are images of a human being, turned upside down, standing with his feet in the clouds and with his head pointing to the earth. That portrayed the origin of the human in the spirit, that we have our foundations in the spiritual world.

As Steiner says in his commentary on Genesis: 'The sense-perceptible world has its roots in the supersensible world.' And this world of our roots is still present, is not a thing of the past. We cannot say, that was in the past, we are living in a different world now. We can even call up this world of our primal origins. For example, in the sacrament of Baptism as celebrated in the Christian Community, the three substances of baptism – water, salt and ash – are consecrated. Their own true nature is addressed. In the sacramental words lives the power to bring the substances into contact with specific spiritual forces. The baptismal water is united with the forces of the origin (the 'womb of worlds'). The salt is connected to the 'all-preserving' forces, and the ash with the forces of the future ('world goals'). When a substance is consecrated it is reconnected with the spiritual power underlying it. Steiner calls this 'the original, spiritual-physical power.' The Creed of the Christian Community gives a similar indication when mentioning 'an almighty divine being, spiritual-physical.'

During baptism spiritual-physical forces are addressed and become active in the baptismal substances. We see this in old depictions, for example of the baptism in the Jordan, where water is not a lifeless element, but where the river god appears, summoned up by the baptism of Jesus of Nazareth (Figures 4 and 5). When the primal spiritual forces are called upon, they come into appearance and become active.

It is a fascinating moment during the Baptism in the Christian Community when the priest says: 'This be no common water.' If not common, what is it then? Outwardly it appears to be the same water. 'This be no common water. It shall be the all-permeating power of the Spirit.' Through the words we can begin to perceive the activity of the Creator, whose all-pervading spirit power once shone over and penetrated the primal waters: 'And the Spirit of God was moving over the face of the waters.'

Returning to the description of creation. Certain indications suggest that three elements were already present at the beginning of creation. Anthroposophy describes the worlds which preceded the moment when the first words of Genesis sounded.[2] There was a time when the whole of creation consisted only of warmth, of fire. This was not fire in the sense we know it, but a spiritual fire which forms the foundation of our physical fire.

During a second phase creation was 'enriched' with what we can call air: the spiritual element which forms the foundation of our present physical element of 'air.' And similarly in the third creation (each time after a time when creation withdrew into the invisible) the world emerged in fire, air and water. Only in the events described in Genesis does the element of earth begin to play a part. At that time these elements were still totally permeated by spiritual beings. We find depictions of such a creation before the creation in countless myths and creation myths. Hebrew tradition (Talmud, kabbala, Philo of Alexandria) speaks of the 'pre-eons,' the eons preceding Genesis. The spiritual tradition of the Hopi and Pueblo Indians of North America has a very extensive description of the multiple creations which form the foundations of our present, familiar world. It tells of four worlds preceding our world: first a world of fire, a second world of air, a third of water and a fourth of earth. In all four of these worlds, the human being is in a state of becoming: in the first world he receives spiritual warmth; in the second the breath of life, in the third the stream of life (as it will later stream through his blood and other bodily fluids); in the fourth his flesh.[3]

How can we imagine a state where God is at first one with creation, where the four elements are wholly permeated by spiritual beings and where God gradually places these elements outside himself? The kabbala has several concepts hinting at the different phases of creation. When we have recognized these, we can find them quite literally in the Bible too, both in Genesis and in Isaiah. So it is important to keep these in mind, because the kabbala offers spiritual concepts which allow us to understand certain aspects of creation.

According to the kabbala, God is still one with all his creatures in the first phase of creation. He has not placed anything outside himself. Philosophy calls this phase 'emanation,' which means literally an 'outflowing.' In this phase, in a certain sense everything is still one with the Creator. We can compare the process of creation as described in Genesis step by step with the creative process of a human being, an artist for instance.

An artist, in the very first phase of conceiving a creation, still holds the whole of this creation within himself. Creator and creation are one. The kabbala describes this first phase as a time before God places anything outside himself: even before the first sentence of the Bible. For Luther attempting to imagine what was there before God created anything, was unthinkable, though many people did and do ask this question. For Luther even asking what was there before creation was a kind of blasphemy. When asked once what God did before he created, Luther answered, 'He was ready with a rod to whip anyone who asked that question.' In other words: You are not even allowed to think about it! It must remain hidden and unspoken.

However, the kabbala contains knowledge of a creation before creation: *Aziluth,* the phase of emanation. There are indications of this, for example in Psalm 33, where the complete unity of the Creator with his creation is expressed. The heavenly host is mentioned, the hierarchies: 'By the word of the LORD the heavens were made, and all their host by the breath of his mouth.' He breathes and it arises. It is his 'outpouring,' his emanation.

Then follows the second concept in the kabbala: *Beriya.* This has the same word stem as the first word of Genesis: *Bereshít bará.* In *bará* the act of creation is indicated. But when considering this word too we must transform, changing the way we think. Of course, thinking about creating, we imagine something 'bodily,' something physical, while in actual fact, *bará* is still a spiritual creating. Rudolf Steiner translates it as 'cosmic thinking.' The process begins here, out of the emanation: the Godhead 'thinks' the creation. Hermann Beckh, an oriental linguist and one of the founders of the Christian Community, translated the first line of Genesis as, 'In the spirit thoughts of the primal beginnings the creative being of the Godhead wove heaven and earth.' Out of what do heaven and earth come into being? The fabric of creation arises out of the spirit thoughts of the primal origin. In this second phase, *Beriya,* creation begins a life of its own. Like with an artist who, working on his creation, suddenly sees something come into being under their hands, and looks upon it with a certain surprise: that is mine, I made it. No longer as in the first phase – that *is* I – but that *belongs* to me.

Now begins the third phase, indicated in the kabbala with the word *Yetzirah,* 'forming.' Think of a potter, who has conceived a work of art (first phase), has made a first draft (the second phase) and now begins to form this draft, begins to knead and mould the material. In this phase the creation is still pliable and plastic, can still be shaped by the hands of the creator. But now the Creator – comparable with the artist in this third phase – faces his creation. It is no longer *in* him, it not only *belongs* to him, but in the third phase he *faces* it.

And finally the kabbala describes a fourth phase, *Asiya* (from the Hebrew verb 'to make'). Only now, in this last phase, can we speak of a finished artwork: the creation or creature of the Creator. The creature now detaches itself from its Creator. It is comparable to the process of writing a book. The author has thoroughly researched the material for its contents, has written it, worked on it, formed and transformed it. Then the book is printed and sent into the world, and it detaches itself from the author and goes its own way. Books have their own destiny. The creator, the author steps back and is free to begin something new.

In Genesis the preparatory phase of *Aziluth* is not mentioned. But we do find the other three creation concepts from the kabbala in Genesis: *Beriya, Yetzirah* and *Asiya* – creating, forming, making. The kabbala derived these three concepts from the beginning of Genesis. To the reader of Hebrew these words indicated very different phases. Once aware of this, we find similar terminology in several other places in the Old Testament, for example in Isaiah 43:6f. There Yahweh himself speaks of : 'bring my sons from afar and my daughters from the end of the earth, every one who is called by my name, whom I *created* for my glory, whom I *formed* and *made.'* The very same words we read in Genesis, and in the same sequence.

We can also recognize the four phases in Rudolf Steiner's *Leading Thoughts,* a very condensed form of anthroposophy. I have not been able to find out if he knew the original Hebrew concepts, and if he knew the backgrounds of the kabbala before formulating these. In Leading Thought No. 112 we read:

> The divine-spiritual comes to expression in the cosmos in
> different ways, in succeeding stages:
> (1) through its own and inmost being;
> (2) through the manifestation of this being;
> (3) through the active working, when the being withdraws
>       from the manifestation;
> (4) through the accomplished work, when in the outwardly
>       apparent universe no longer the divine itself, but only
>       the forms of the divine are there.

In relation to the fourth phase Rudolf Steiner talks about an 'accomplished world.' He means the Godhead himself has finished the work. ('Thus the heavens and the earth were finished,' Gen.2:1.)

For kabbalists the 'accomplished world' which was left behind was not just a husk, a kind of corpse of God, where he was no longer to be found. They compared the physical world with an ointment box. They said the world is the ointment box of God. He has taken all the ointment out, but just as with a real ointment box, the wonderful scent lingers for a long time. The precious ointment is gone, the scent remains. We can still recognize the traces of God in everything he has created. Which the German theosophist Friedrich Oetinger (1702–82) expressed a different way: 'Physicality is the end of God's path.' This physicality has everything to do with God, even though it is the end of his path.

It is not easy to see who the actual Creator is. Does the Father God create, or is it the Son (Prologue of the Gospel of John), or both? Does the Holy Spirit have a part in creation too? In Christianity we speak of the Trinity. The Trinity is a triune, so can one imagine that the Trinity creates as a unity?

In the Middle Ages it was said that the Father in creation 'subsists.' This is of course related to the word substance. The word subsistence literally means: to stand beneath. The Father carries the creation. He 'supports' it. The Holy Spirit orders, brings light into creation. The Son mediates between these two worlds and creates. Going back to our comparison: the artist needs substance on the one hand and inspiration on the other. The Father God subsists, the Spirit God inspires. The creating Logos of the Son works out of both these worlds.

It is similarly expressed in a recurring sentence in the Act of Consecration. This is not a metaphor, it is a reality we are hardly conscious of, when Christ is addressed with the words: 'You who bear and order the life of the world, as you receive it from the Father and make it whole through the Spirit ...' This process of creation takes place throughout all eons, all cycles of time: the Father God carries, the Spirit God orders, and Christ brings these two forces together and makes them into his creation.

After the first phase of creation there is rest: the seventh day, the Sabbath. And after that? What does God do from the eighth day onwards? Rabbi Yossi, a Hasidic rabbi, answered: 'He arranges marriages.' This fitting answer indicates that creation is not finished yet. Something now must arise between human beings. Creation can be continued by the union of opposites. Christ himself too, continues his creation when he incarnates on the earth. The miracles he performs are an expression of this. But the renewal of creation truly begins at the Resurrection. This renewal can communicate itself to everything that unites with him: 'Behold, I make all things new' (Rev.21:5).

Finally, I want to return to some Hebrew words in Genesis, which uncover a world of images and concepts for anyone 'who has ears to hear.'

How did God create in the primal beginning? We know from Jewish mysticism, that he does not create out of nothing, he creates out of *Aziluth.* The Talmud relates that God creates out of the world of the elements. Again, the elements even before they become visible. 'Three things there were before this world: water, air and fire.'[4] In other words according to the Talmud the three elements of water, air and fire are present in their spiritual form before the Creator becomes active in them.

We hear the same thing in the Hebrew text: 'And the Spirit of God was moving over the face of the waters.' Hermann Beckh translates the original Hebrew as: 'And wafting in the holy wind, the Spirit of the Godhead brooded over the primal waters.' This is clearly an indication of the three elements. One element, air, we find in 'And wafting in the holy wind, the Spirit of the Godhead.' *Ruach* is spirit, wind, air: the element of air. Ruach is 'air before it has become air.' This 'Spirit of the Godhead brooded' over the waters. The Hebrew verb *racheph* indicates an activity comparable to what happens when a bird broods on its eggs. The warmth is a radiating kind of warmth. The primal waters are warmed, incubated by the fire element. And the element of water is there too before God speaks his words of creation.

This is another expression for something that is known by anthroposophy. Before the development of the Earth there were three epochs, three aeons. The first aeon when fire was created was Old Saturn. The second aeon when the element of air came about was Old Sun. The third aeon when the element of water was created was Old Moon. Only when the element of earth comes about, do the three previous elements appear in their tangible, earthly form. In this Earth epoch dead matter appears for the first time.[5]

How does God create? The Hebrew word *bereshít* has the stem *rosh,* which means 'head.' Therefore Steiner translates it as, 'In the spirit thoughts of the archetypal beginnings.' God created out of spirit thoughts: that is contained in the word *bereshít.*

This cosmic thinking shines its light upon the mysterious world of chaos which in Hebrew is called *tóhu wavóhu,* 'without form and void.' A strange and mysterious sounding word. It is formed of two verbs, connected by *wa,* 'and'. The verbs underlying this noun are *taha,* 'to be thoughtfully amazed,' and *baha,* 'to be astonished.'

To make a comparison: the elements awake from their sleep of creation, like a human being awaking from deep unconsciousness, looking about in a confused way, unable to get a grip on the world around. And the elements ask themselves: Where do I come from? What am I doing here? That is *tóhu wavóhu.*

The Godhead creates order within this chaos: *bereshít.* At the beginning of a new creation, of the earth creation, he brings clarity, light. Genesis here describes what Steiner calls the Lemurian epoch, an early stage of the earth. Now within this chaos (known too from Greek mythology) the Godhead, throughout all the aeons of creation, continually separates, creates polarities. There follow a few.

The *first day* of creation: 'God called the light Day, and the darkness he called Night.' Out of the chaos of *tóhu wavóhu* he now creates a world of 'above' and 'below,' of light and dark.

On the *second day* of Creation the Godhead intervenes more deeply in the elemental world and creates – a mysterious expression for which concepts are lacking – 'the waters which were under the firmament from the waters which were above the firmament.' The word for 'firmament,' sometimes translated as 'surface,' is a very mysterious word, *raqi'á.* It means firmament, the vault of heaven.

So on the second day of Creation, God creates a *raqi'á,* a separation between earthly waters and heavenly waters. We can picture something here. Water moving in the direction of physical water and water moving in the direction of vapour, of the clouds. But surely, that can't be right? The firmament, the vault of heaven, is not placed between those two? Well, originally it was. The vault of the heavens was originally pictured as so close to the earth that it did separate the waters above from the waters below.

Only on the *third day* of Creation does the 'dry' appear. So far we could picture the earth shrouded in mist. Now creation is beginning to find 'solid ground under its feet,' with the expression: 'Let the waters under the heavens be gathered together into one place, and let the dry land appear.' The word 'appear,' *tera'eh*, is actually too weak a translation here. Better would be the more active expression: 'the dry land showed itself.' To ancient Hebrews the language expressed in its sounds that the 'earth' was not just a collection of dust particles; the earth is a being which, as soon as it was created, shows itself to all creation. Now the separation between earth and *raqi'á*, the firmament, is brought about.

What happens to this *raqi'á*, this firmament, in the course of the development of creation? We come across the word *raqi'á* again, later in the Old and the New Testament, but then it is no longer pictured between the waters below and the waters above, it is seen as above heavens, above the *shamayim*. The prophet Ezekiel (1:22) sees how the heavens have opened. He sees the cherubim and above their heads the *raqi'á*. 'Over the heads of the living creatures [the cherubim] there was the likeness of a firmament, shining like awesome crystal, spread out above their heads.' What mysterious world is this which has withdrawn, after being so close to humans during the first phase of creation? In the vision of Ezekiel, the *raqi'á* is above *shamayim*, above heavens, in the realm of the highest hierarchies, as an awe-inspiring crystalline world. This *raqi'á* is also the beginning of a new, future creation.

The ancient philosophers said God 'geometrizes.' God creates in the spirit, first as a crystal clear world, what is later called into (physical) existence. But the new, future world is already present in the spirit. What Ezekiel first recognized, is described at the beginning of the Apocalypse: 'and before the throne there is as it were a sea of glass, like crystal' (Rev.4:6). There the new, future creation is already present. At the end of the Apocalypse, this crystalline world has undergone an important transformation: 'And I saw what appeared to be a sea of glass mingled with fire, and those who had conquered the beast ...' (Rev.15:2). Here the redeemed human being has enriched the future creation with fire, with the warmth of love and with the light of his wisdom. Future events not only cast ahead their shadows, but also their light. In an immeasurably long process of creation the *raqi'á* of primal beginnings is transformed into a crystalline world which forms the foundation of the New Jerusalem. This new creation is 'bright as crystal' (Rev.22:1).

To return to Genesis: the human being was created on the sixth day of creation. He was given the task of subduing creation and having dominion over it, an expression that has led to endless misunderstandings. The Hebrew phrase is, literally translated, 'bring the creatures under your feet.' But this is not meant at all in the sense of subduing, but of gaining an overview, an insight, a certain distance, and getting to know all creation. 'Dominating creation' is what in twentieth century theology has rightly called 'stewardship over creation.' A similar word is used for subduing the animals. The Hebrew expression indicates that the human being has the task to 'rule over vertically,' which is to say, to care for with insight, sensibly, to help carry and order life on the earth in imitation of his Creator.

# 6 The Elements in the New Testament

Christ must travel an infinitely long path to become Lord of the Elements, a journey we can hardly, if at all, imagine. When Jesus of Nazareth was born on earth, the earth was no longer the same as before. The earth had become estranged from her origins, had passed into different hands. In legal terms one sometimes says that property is abalienated, handed over or sold to others. In this sense, the whole earth had become alienated from its Creator. That makes it possible for us to imagine that the Creator must travel a long path to reach his 'property.' This property, this ownership is hinted at in the Prologue of the Gospel of St John (1.11). 'He came unto his *own* [Greek idia], and his own [idia] did not received him.'[1]

The Creator of heaven and earth found the earth a different place from the one he had created. The distance had become so great that his own did not recognize him any more, excluded him, and finally crucified him.

What happens when a god becomes man? What happens when a divine being penetrates through all earthly elements to become fully human? This question has exercised Christian thinkers for centuries. Traditionally they summed up the essence of Christianity in a single sentence of the Creed: *Et incarnatus est,* he became man, became flesh. These words contain the essence of Christianity, although they must be understood in a wider sense than purely the moment of his birth on earth. For his birth in Bethlehem is only a small part of the much more encompassing process of his incarnation.

When human beings are born, they dive into the deep, they are submerged as it were in matter. Birth means fully entering matter and losing for the time being all consciousness of the spiritual world.

A child is born and loses its consciousness of the spiritual world. Wordsworth expresses this beautifully 'Our birth is but a sleep and a forgetting ... Heaven lies about us in our infancy; shades of the prison-house begin to close upon the growing boy.'[2] There is an immense difference between the incarnation of a human being and the incarnation of Jesus Christ on the earth. Human beings have fallen: the Fall. Christ has descended. We find a succinct indication of this difference in two consecutive sentences of the Offering in the Act of Consecration, where it speaks of 'falling' and 'descending.' When the chalice is raised, these worlds of difference are indicated by the words, 'That that also can raise itself to the heavens which is fallen to the earth.' That is the task of the human being. 'The fragrance ascend as this God-willed being is descended.' That is the task of the Christ: a total contrast. We find indications of this sovereign gesture in various wordings of the Act of Consecration. For example, it says in the Creed, 'In Jesus, the Christ entered as man into the earthly world.' He 'walks the earth' is a sovereign, royal gesture.

Even more impressive is the verbal expression of this regal gesture, when at Christmas these words are spoken at the altar: 'Christ ... has chosen the earthly body in which he would dwell.' There the Act of Consecration speaks of Christ, the Son of God, not the man Jesus. The mystery and miracle of his incarnation in a human body is so immense that we cannot possibly comprehend how the highest divine being descends into a world that has become alienated from him.

German poet Christian Morgenstern attempted to describe the indescribable:

Take to yourself, what is revealed!
Feel for the way towards the sun!
Anticipate what creative joy
Each being there fulfils.

Climb the steps of all these spirits
Upward to the highest host!
And finally see him there:
The Master of all spirits!

And then descend along with him!
Live among people and demons,
Walk with him in your body
Which a human being devoutly gave him.

Does our heart take in the magnitude?
Can spirit compass this great sacrifice?
That a God exchanges heavenly glory
For human need and nakedness.

Morgenstern had the courage to imagine himself in the highest regions of the spiritual world, where the Lord of all spirits resides. The poet tries to feel his way into Christ's awe-inspiring sacrifice of offering up his divine power, relinquishing the fullness of his primal world, and entering into earthly life among human beings and demons. Christ chooses to take on and enter a human body.

*Et incarnatus est.* It is an infinitely, indescribably long path before this divine being is born on the earth. And even at his birth, the incarnation is not fully completed. Anthroposophy relates the preliminary stages of the process, lasting many centuries, until this divine being has so emptied itself and divested itself of its divine omnipotence, that he can be born on earth in human form, unrecognized by his own creatures.[3] Then, from the time of his birth on earth there begins an uninterrupted thirty-year long struggle to penetrate this body. It is not only the body of Jesus of Nazareth which has to be penetrated, but the body of the whole earth must be penetrated. 'Christ ... has chosen the earthly body in which he would dwell.' In these words from the Act of Consecration at Christmas time, the word 'body' can be interpreted in two different ways: Christ ... has chosen the mortal human body, but he has also chosen the body of the entire earth in order to redeem humanity.

How can we imagine this penetration in stages of the earthly body? How does he penetrate into the world of the elements? Can we follow and recognize these different phases? We find an indication of this in the path of Jesus Christ from the Jordan to Golgotha. And I do mean literally the paths and ways he walks in the Holy Land. A path from fire to earth. That is how he describes the path he must follow, when he says, 'I came to cast fire upon the earth; and would that it were already kindled! I have a baptism to be baptized with; and how I am constrained until it is accomplished!' (Luke 12:49f). Literally, 'how I am pressed together' *(synechomai)*. The expression 'accomplished' is a translation of the classical mystery word *telesthe*. When an initiation had been accomplished, the goal of the initiation *(teles-the)* had been reached. Christ suffers as his being is bound to the material world, to matter, until the goal has been achieved. The mystery word sounds again at the end of his earthly life, in the last words on the cross, *tetelestai,* 'it is finished' (John 19:30). Only now has his incarnation been fully accomplished. His real baptism actually takes place on Golgotha where, as Paul says, he is baptized in death (Rom.6:4).

He became active after another baptism: the baptism in the Jordan. During the baptism in the Jordan, his spiritual fire, descending from heaven, united itself first with the water. Then followed the agony of the three years. This path ended with his union with the earth on Golgotha, the place of the skull. After that, he was initiated into the secrets of the earth 'the Son of man [will] be three days and three nights in the heart of the earth.' He had announced this a long time before (Matt.12:40).

What happened between Christ and the elements at the baptism in the Jordan? The gospel states that the heavens opened and that the Spirit radiated down over him. Old depictions show the Spirit also penetrating the element of water and enlivening it. The water receives the impact of the Spirit. Early Christian images and depictions from the Middle Ages of the baptism in the Jordan show the figure of a river god, who lets his water stream from the heavens down to the earth (see Figure 5).

The river is 'water from heaven,' literally and figuratively. The river god has a jug in his hands and stands next to the heavens, indicated by several arcs. The dove, bearer of the Spirit, penetrates the elements of air and water. Other depictions sometimes show the river god startled and turning toward the one who is baptized. At the moment of the baptism in the Jordan the world of the elements is in turmoil, taking part in the event. I want to try and illustrate what happens there with a contemporary experience.

Even today there are extraordinary events where the world of the elements becomes involved, which in a sense startle, and evoke a

Figure 5. The baptism of Jesus. *Codex Vyssegradensis,* the Coronation Gospels, late eleventh century, Czech National Library, Prague.

response from it. A fellow priest in the Christian Community once described an event at the consecration of a new chapel. During the consecration of a new church the four elements are addressed in the four directions of space: north, south, east and west. The four elements are associated with these directions. Towards the north the earth is addressed; to the south, fire; to the west, water; and to the east, the air.

Ancient spiritual tradition indicates that four groups of elemental beings are connected to these four spatial directions. During the consecration these four directions, which are addressed as beings, are asked to bestow their forces to this sacred space. The first time, consecrated water is sprinkled to the four points of the compass; the second time incense is wafted towards the four points of the compass. My colleague had the following experience.

> When addressing the four elements it was as if an incredibly rapid, excited whispering went through the whole building. 'Come, come quickly to the chapel, something important is going on there.' Then I had several sensations which followed each other rapidly. Countless beings drank in the events with all their senses: big, wide eyes, large ears, open mouth. They went through a deep transformation during this event. At first there was a certain indignation: 'What are you doing? This is our building!' And then surprise and amazement at a totally new experience entering into the consciousness of the elemental beings through human actions. Their indignation crumbled away, and they opened towards the new. Then there was joy, gratitude, a feeling of deep peace, and the sensation of having attained a unimaginable fulfilment. They realized, 'only now do we know who we really serve. What a joy to be allowed to be His servant.' Then, renewed, all these beings went back to their 'workshop.'

This was the spontaneous and unexpected experience of a priest at the consecration of a chapel. The elemental world plays a part in such events, takes part in rituals and sacraments. How much more will this world have been involved in the baptism of Jesus of Nazareth. We find references to this in old manuscripts. In one of the versions of the Gospel of St Matthew it says: 'When he was baptized, an awe-inspiring light radiated from the water.' Justin Martyr (born *c.* 100 AD) wrote, 'A fire sparked up in the Jordan.' At the baptism, fire united with water. Spiritual fire united with the element of water, which has the ability to create a bridge between heaven and earth. That is why, in ancient manuscripts and miniatures, the River Jordan is depicted as the bearer of the heavenly waters on earth.

Rudolf Steiner once described what happens when a human being incarnates at waking up. An imaginative fire appears, uniting itself with water. That is how the daily reconnection of our spiritual being with our physical-etheric sheath takes place.

At the baptism in the Jordan three elements work together. Fire: 'A fire sparked up in the Jordan' (Justin Martyr). 'And when he came up out of the water, immediately he saw the heavens opened and the Spirit descending upon him like a dove' (Mark 1:10). Greek has the same word, *pneuma,* for 'spirit' and 'air.' The second and the third element, water and fire are indicated here. Only after the Baptism in the Jordan does the fourth element, the earth, begin to play a part with the temptation in the desert.

Slowly but surely, during 'the three years' (which in reality were two years and a few months) Christ took leave of the watery element and gradually united himself with the earthly element. That is what twentieth century theology rather blandly called the 'itinerary' in the Gospel of Luke. The Christ has a preconceived plan.'When the days drew near for him to be received up, he set his face to go to Jerusalem' and, 'Behold, we are going up to Jerusalem' (Luke 9:51, 18:31). Christ purposefully walks the path from the Jordan to Jerusalem, from water to earth.

There is no greater contrast to be found in the whole of the New Testament.

> The River Jordan: the heavens open and God speaks: 'This is my beloved Son.' Golgotha: the heavens are closed and darkened.
> The River Jordan: fire in the water. Golgotha: darkening of the Sun.
> The River Jordan: an abundance of water. Golgotha: 'I thirst.'

If there is anything that speaks on Golgotha, it is the earth itself which trembles (the Greek word here is *seismos).* Certain characteristics of the different elements appear both at the Jordan and on Golgotha.

> Jordan: the heavens opened. Mark uses the word *schizomenos,* related to the word 'schism.' Golgotha: 'and the rocks were split' (Matt.27:51).
>
> Jordan: Jesus is baptized in the water. Golgotha: Jesus is baptized in death and laid into the earth. Only now has his infinitely long process of incarnation come to an end: 'it is finished' (John 19:30). The death, the completion, is at the same time the beginning of a new creation, of the new elements from which the heavenly Jerusalem is built.

This journey toward incarnation is so all-encompassing, that more than one point of view is necessary to begin to comprehend it. A different approach to, a new angle on the theme arises when you look at *how* Christ incarnates. There are four different indications for this, four 'incarnation signs,' four 'markers' that show how during the three years Christ unites himself ever deeper with the constituent parts of his being and with the elements, and step by step penetrates the body of the earth.

What is it that unites with Jesus of Nazareth at the baptism in the Jordan? It is the divine 'I,' the innermost self. The incarnation there still takes place in the realm of the I. Hence the indication of fire. The I and fire are intimately related. The I is spiritual fire!

The second sign indicating that Christ is incarnating deeper is the feeding of the five thousand. What does Christ do? The context of the story in the gospel makes clear that cosmic forces at work here. The five loaves of bread and the two fishes are indications of the forces he guides from the astral world to the physical world. Bread and fish: the signs of Virgo (with the ears of corn) and Pisces. They indicate that Christ now has connected himself with Jesus of Nazareth in the region of the astral body, the 'star-body.'

The third sign of incarnation is the transfiguration on Mount Tabor. Suddenly Christ's appearance is changed: 'and his face shone like the sun, and his garments became white as light' (Matt.17:2) The

Christ now penetrates the human being Jesus of Nazareth through to the 'white garments.' This is the term traditionally used for the life body, or ether body, which is connected to the sun: 'his face shone like the sun.'

Finally the fourth and last sign of his incarnation was recognizable for humanity in those days: the entry into Jerusalem. There he is 'mounted on an ass, and on a colt, the foal of an ass' (Matt.21:5). Why did this entry into Jerusalem cause such an outcry? Because the people recognized something of the prophecy from the Old Testament. The prophet Zechariah (9:9) prophesied the entry of the Messiah: 'lo, your king comes to you; triumphant and victorious is he, humble and riding on an ass, on a colt the foal of an ass.' The donkey, the physical body, has now become the bearer of the Christ. The old and the young donkey are indications of the old and the new Adam. Shortly after this, from his death on Golgotha, Christ becomes the Lord of the earth. These words indicate that after the death on the cross, Christ is all-powerful in the realm of the four elements.

The crucifixion symbolically indicates the union with the four elements. In the crucifixion we see a quite literal realization of Plato's mysterious words: 'The world soul has been nailed to the cross of the earth.' We have to look behind the words, even behind the letters to understand what happens at this last step of the incarnation on the cross.

In the gospel it says: 'Pilate also wrote a title and put it on the cross; it read, "Jesus of Nazareth, the King of the Jews".' (John 19:19). In Latin it reads: *Iesus Nazarenus Rex Iudaeorum,* abbreviated to INRI. The first letter is *yam* (water) in Hebrew; the second letter is *nuor* (fire); the third is *ruach* (air) and the fourth *yabeshah* (the solid, the earth). What this really signifies, without Pilate being aware of it, is 'the world soul has been nailed to the cross of the elements.'

We can sometimes find this idea in old works of art, for example on a reliquary cross from the town of Engelberg in Switzerland (Figure 6). On the front we see the crucified Christ, on the back the four elements, carved in the four ends of the cross. On the right beam of the cross we see a young man seated on an eagle. We usually associate the eagle with John, but the attributes of the cloud and the bird also symbolize the element of air. On the upper beam of the cross we see a man on a lion, with the sun in one hand and a torch in the

Figure 6. The back of a reliquary cross showing the four elements. Benedictine abbey, Engelberg, Switzerland (c. 1200).

other: cosmic and earthly fire. On the left beam there is a woman on a fish, in the one hand a pitcher from which she pours water, in her other a fish which she holds by the tail: water. And at the foot of the cross a human being, seated on the back of an animal, surrounded by plants: earth. This is how the four elements in their relation to the crucifixion were portrayed in one particular tradition.

Why does Christ have to become the Lord of the Elements? Is it only for the sake of his own resurrection? Not according to Hildegard von Bingen: after his resurrection he cleanses and sanctifies the four elements. Not according to Paul either, who says that we humans have become entangled in the effects of the elements, we are subjected to them. His resurrection makes it possible for us to be part of future creation, consisting of a new heaven and a new earth. But human beings must do something for that. They cannot just wait until they are redeemed: they must contribute to their redemption.

In his Letter to the Galatians (4:3), Paul dedicated some very special passages to the elements: the *stoicheia*. First of all he wrote, 'So with us; when we were children [before Christ], we were slaves to the elemental spirits of the universe.' *Hupo ta stoicheia* (under the elements), *tou kosmou* (of the physical world), *emetha dedoulomenoi* (we had become slaves). We were slaves to the world of the elements, subjected to the elements. 'Formerly, when you did not know God, you were in bondage [again he uses the word *doulos*] to beings that by nature are no gods' (Gal.4:8).

What is Paul saying here? He pointed to the ancient Greek ideas about the creation of the human being. Plato still knew that although God created the human being, he relinquished part of the task.

God created the highest member of the human being, but to the lower gods he gave the task to create the lower being and the body. For that purpose the four elements were borrowed from the cosmos and united with each other by the star-gods [the lower gods]. At death the elements must be repaid to the cosmos.

A very interesting concept of the human body. Of course, every person thinks their body belongs to themselves, but according to this classical tradition we owe the cosmos something, we have 'borrowed' our body from it. We are indebted to it. My body is not wholly 'my body.' I inhabit this gift of the cosmos. Even the word 'gift' is not quite correct. It has something of a borrowed character. Is the body borrowed or is it a gift? The original Greek concept is ambivalent.

In his Epistle to the Galatians, Paul indicates that our every fibre was subjected to the elements, until the time had come when Christ had penetrated all the elements and had begun the new creation with his death and resurrection. On the cross, this new creation began when, out of his own free will, the crucified one subjected himself to the death forces of the elements. On the whole, the mystics, fully in accordance with this concept, recognize that his Passion was not a question of passive powerlessness, but an act of uninterrupted divine power and invocation. Anne Catherine Emmerich expressed it thus: 'The crucified Saviour, with a sense of deepest desolation in his immense suffering, turned to his heavenly Father, while loving his enemies and praying for them. During his entire Passion he ceaselessly prayed the words of the Psalm which were now being fulfilled.'[4]

According to Paul, if I want to be part of Christ's being, I will have to follow him on this path. 'But far be it from me to glory except in the cross of our Lord Jesus Christ, by which the world has been crucified to me, and I to the world ... for I bear on my body the marks of Jesus' (Gal. 6:14,17).

Anyone wishing to follow him upon this path, who wants to be part of the new creation, must have the courage to go through this deepest point, through crucifixion. Then the human being is no longer *doulos,* a slave, but has become 'son.' That is what Paul calls 'sonship,' by which a human being can stand freely within creation, and is no longer subjected to the forces of death of the dying earth existence, even though the physical body perishes. 'And those who belong to Christ Jesus have crucified the flesh with its passions and desires' (Gal.5:24).

# 7 St John the Alchemist

The old alchemists recognized in the Gospel according to St John a paradigm for alchemy. Hence they chose John as their patron saint and gave him the soubriquet, the alchemist. What did they recognize in the Gospel according to St John? The alchemists searched for the 'golden chain,' the *aurea catena,* uniting the spiritual with the physical world. Two realms which were estranged from each other by the Fall, and which can be bound together again by the Hermetic principle: as above, so below. The real principle of alchemy is not to abandon the earth, but to actively take part in transforming it, and cultivating it so that it becomes receptive to the spirit – so that the spiritual world can become manifest in the physical world. Alchemy is an attempt to achieve the 'chemical wedding,' the unification of spirit and matter, of heaven and earth. This could only be achieved through a dying process.

That is why the alchemists recognized John as a precursor and, in a sense, followed his path. One could say they practised an *imitatio Johanni,* they imitated or followed the path of initiation of John.

Returning to Genesis we see that up until the words, 'and the Spirit of God was moving over the face of the waters,' spirit and matter still fully interpenetrated. But after the Fall, there was no way back. Matter, subjected to the laws of death, had to be led through a process of death. The alchemist, by uniting himself with the Risen Christ, could communicate the forces of the resurrection to the created, to the elements.

To alchemists it was obvious that Christ was the key to the elements. Thus Angelus Silesius wrote: 'Your stone is nothing; the headstone I mean is my gold tincture, is the philosopher's stone.'[1] The philosopher's stone, the *lapides philosophorum,* could only be found and recognized by uniting oneself deeply with Christ, and by uniting oneself with this mysterious 'gold tincture.' The alchemists recognize that the blood flowing from the cross into the earth is this 'tincture.'

All the alchemical motifs of the unification of matter and spirit so far discussed in this chapter, can be found in one way or another in the Gospel according to John, and in the old traditions describing who John was.[2] One of the Church fathers, Jerome, relates that according to tradition John was a man like no other on earth. Streams of love flowed from him and communicated themselves to everything and everybody around him. As presbyter, more than 90 years old, he could no longer move and had to be carried to his bishop's throne in Ephesus. At the climax of the Eucharist he rose and spoke the memorable words: 'Children, love one another.' Jerome relates how they asked John, 'Why don't you say anything else?' He responded, 'Because these words say everything there is to say, and no other words are necessary. Children, love one another.'

Of course there were the usual sceptics in the twentieth century who put a psychological interpretation on this, calling John an old, demented man who did not have anything else to say. But tradition shows something different: his spiritual power conquered all. He drank the poisoned wine and survived, according to the prophecy of the Risen One: 'and if they drink any deadly thing, it will not hurt them' (Mark 16:18). He was thrown into a vat of boiling oil and survived. He took a pebble in his hand, and it turned into a gemstone. These events, sometimes outwardly visible, sometimes imaginative, indicate he had a deep connection to the physical world.

In his life this connection to the physical world played an important part too. Before he came to Ephesus, John was put to work in the mines of Patmos as a forced labourer. For alchemists this was an important fact. Their motto was *Visita interiora terrae,* 'visit the interior of the earth.' The *Legenda Aurea,* the collection of legends from the Middle Ages, expresses imaginatively how deeply John was connected to the earth. He knew when the day of his death had come. He sat down on his bishop's throne and ordered a square grave to be dug next to the altar. With a last effort he lay down in this grave, and spread out his arms as if embracing the whole earth. The church filled with an overwhelming, blinding light. When the light died away, the pupils found the grave empty. In place of the body there was a loaf of bread. Thus the legend described imaginatively how the saint left his earthly life and left behind his gifts.

What John showed in his life and his death was nothing less than an *imitatio Christi,* the path of Christian initiation. Someone who lived through these experiences was bound to express himself in a different language. This might explain why his gospel is written in an entirely different language and wider vocabulary than the limited vocabulary and language of the three synoptic gospels. Countless indications in the Gospel of John show that Christ came not only to save humanity, but that he came to redeem the whole earth, the whole creation. He healed not only human beings but also the world of the elements by transforming that world. This is a motif that occasionally surfaces in the synoptic gospels, for example at the end of the Gospel of Mark (16:15). In Christ's command to the apostles after the resurrection, 'Go into all the world and preach the gospel to the whole creation,' we sense that Christianity is meant for more than just people.

We can follow this motif closely in the Gospel of John, from the first to the last sign of Christ. John is the only one who repeatedly uses the word sign. The word *semeion* means sign, letter, rune, something that must be read, that cannot be left as it is, but must be deciphered. A *semeion* is always a sign that, although it inevitably takes place on the physical plane, points to a higher reality, so that heaven can mirror itself onto the earth.

We see this in the first of the signs at the wedding at Cana in Galilee. Something that is the expression of a spiritual reality manifests itself in the physical world. It is incomprehensible to a materialist (and we are all, to a certain extent materialists) that Christ could change water into wine. What does that mean? You need a knowledge of alchemy to really understand what happened in this sign. When water was turned into wine, primal matter – the alchemist call it *materia prima* – was transformed into future matter. The alchemist calls this 'red-tincture.' Viktor Stracke, in his book on secret images of the Rosicrucians, shows an old image of vines (connected to images of a sword, snake and chalice) and next to it the words: 'I am the likeness of God. I have died through the wine and come back to life again through death.'[3] (See Figure 7.)

The secret of this transformation was perhaps depicted in the most impressive way by Dostoyevsky in his novel *The Brothers*

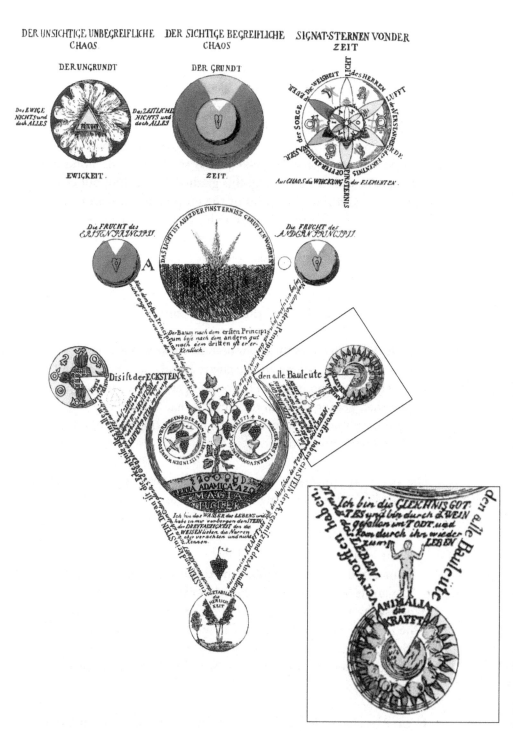

Figure 7. From *Geheime Figuren der Rosenkreuzer*, Altona 1785.

*Karamazov*, written in 1879. In a chapter entitled 'Cana in Galilee,' the protagonist, Alyosha comes to pay his respects to the deceased *starets* or holy man, Zosima. Dostoyevsky still knew the world of the *starets* who devoted their lives to the gospel, in imitation of St John. They attained a degree of holiness and served the earth and the people around them. Alyosha comes to the cell where the *starets* is laid out. He enters during the wake just as someone reads aloud the sign of Cana in Galilee. Listening, this gradually leads him out of the physical world and into the world of the gospel, into a world where Cana in Galilee is a reality. It begins with a feeling we may recognize: 'What is this? Why does the room seem to expand?' A strange state between waking and sleeping. He falls asleep and wakes up again; but spatial reality appears to expand. Life hemmed-in between the four walls of this existence is opened up, and another dimension appears. Step by step Alyosha is led into the world of spirit:

> What is this? Why does the room become so large? Of course ...
> there is a wedding ... Here are the guests already, and here come
> the newlyweds. Who is that? The room is getting even bigger ...
> Who is that, getting up from the table? Is that him? But he is in
> his coffin, isn't he? Yes it really is him, he is getting up, he sees
> me, he is coming towards me.

The deceased appears in the realm of the dead who have been brought to life again. Not only does he appear as an imaginion, he also appears in an inspirational way: the starets speaks to him:

> 'Do you see the sun, do you see him?'
>     'I am afraid, I dare not look,' Alyosha whispered.
>     'Do not fear him, he is so infinitely loftier than we are. He
> stands so far above us, but he is full of mercy. Out of love for
> us he took on a human form, and now he is among us and
> he changes water into wine to bring joy to people. And that
> is how it will remain, for centuries. See, this is where the new
> wine flows.'

Then Alyosha is led from the realms of image and word to tangible experience, to the intuition of this spiritual reality. But this

experience is so overwhelming, that he cannot bear it. He flees back
into his physical body.

> Something glowed in Alyosha's heart, something filled it till it
> ached, tears of rapture rose from his soul ... He uttered a cry
> and woke up. Again the coffin, the open window, and the soft,
> solemn, clear reading of the gospel.

After his very real experience of the spiritual world – his heart begins
to burn – he returns to his body. This frees him from the overwhelming intuition. But he cannot bear to stay within the suffocating space,
within the four walls, and he runs out into the night.

> His soul yearned for freedom, air, space. The vault of heaven,
> full of soft, shining stars, arched vast and fathomless over him. It
> was quiet. The silence of earth seemed to blend with the silence
> of heaven. The mystery of earth was one with the mystery of
> the stars ... Alyosha stood, gazed, and suddenly threw himself
> down on the earth. He did not know why he embraced it. He
> could not have told why he longed so irresistibly to kiss it, to
> kiss it all. But he kissed it, weeping, sobbing and drenching it
> with his tears, and vowed passionately to love it, to love it for
> ever and ever. What was he weeping for? ... He longed to forgive
> every one, for everything ... With every instant he felt clearly
> and, as it were, tangibly, that something firm and unshakable ...
> had entered his soul ... He had fallen on the earth a weak boy,
> but rose up a resolute champion ... And never, never, all his life
> long, could Alyosha forget those moments.

The marriage at Cana in Galilee is a marriage of heaven and earth.
Alyosha, a man who experiences the reality of the marriage at Cana
in Galilee in the spirit, expresses this wedding of heaven and earth
by embracing the earth, the same way John the Evangelist did when
he died. Anyone who has once received Christ so deeply in his own
being, can no longer leave the earth to its own devices, but wants to
communicate his redemption to creation.

Anyone who suspects this may just be symbolical language – a way
the marriage at Cana in Galilee is often explained by theologians – is

corrected by Christ himself, who points out that his message is not meant just for the ears, but also for the body, and for the elements. He does that in a radical and perhaps somewhat shocking message. He says the human being can only communicate with him if he 'eats my flesh and drinks my blood.' The Jews find this offensive when they hear it (John 6:51–60). But this alchemical theme can be traced throughout the Gospel of John, once one has recognized this point of 'germination' in the beginning of the signs. The theme of the union of matter and spirit, the transformation of the old creation (water) to a new creation (wine). This theme sounds right up until the crucifixion. John was the only one who was a true witness *(martyra)* of this. He stood there, and with great emphasis wrote:

> But one of the soldiers pierced his side with a spear, and at
> once there came out blood and water. He who saw it has
> borne witness – his testimony is true, and he knows that he
> tells the truth – that you also may believe. (John 19:34f).

To John it is of the greatest importance to bear witness to the fact that blood and water stream from the wound of the Redeemer. John himself refers back to this mysterious passage in his first letter where these substances again play a part (1John 5:6–8). For the later alchemists this was an important clue.

> This is he who came by water and blood, [In a certain sense,
> 'blood' and 'wine' are a continuation of each other here, as
> the wine becomes the bearer of his blood] Jesus Christ, not
> with the water only but with the water and the blood. And the
> Spirit is the witness, because the Spirit is the truth. There are
> three witnesses, the Spirit ['Pneuma,' air], the water, and the
> blood; and these three agree.

The three elements here are shown to be main witnesses to the resurrection: water, fire (blood is the carrier of warmth in the human being) and air (spirit, *pneuma)*. Between these elements the mystery of the transformation of the earth, the transubstantiation, takes place, until the fourth element, the bread (earth) is also transubstantiated. This literally takes place in the sacrament, where these three 'witnesses' play a part in the mysterious process of the transubstantiation. For people in the Middle Ages this was still familiar. They knew the formula *accedit verbum ad elementum et fit sacramentum,* 'the word unites itself with the element and thereby the sacrament arises.' This takes place at the altar when water and wine are mixed in the chalice and as third 'substance' the ritual word *(pneuma)* is spoken in the stream of air. There the three elements unite into one. That is where the transubstantiation of the earth begins, the moment the water and the wine are combined, are held up in the Offering and united with the ritual word.

Despite such ideas bringing us a little closer to the reality, alchemy still remains a mystery to us. It is something of a conjecture but not yet a full reality. It will remain a conjecture until the revelation of the secret of transubstantiation in future. This future revelation is fully realized in the Apocalypse (the Greek word *Apokalypsis* means revelation). There we see how the marriage of heaven and earth, the unification of spirit and matter, becomes a full reality. What takes place every day on a small scale at the altar where Chist unites his soul with the substances, unrecognized by many, this will become full reality in the New Jerusalem.

Although the marriage, the union of heaven and earth still lies in the far distant future, this reality is present in the spirit even now, albeit in higher regions than the ether-world. We must penetrate into devachan, the spirit world, to experience the reality of this union. I have come across only one modern description of the reality of the marriage of heaven and earth. It was published in a book with the promising title, 'redeemed elements.' Johanna Countess von Keyserlingk was one of the people who helped initiate biodynamic agriculture. A woman whose extraordinary faculties were fully acknowledged and respected by Rudolf Steiner. He once told her, 'You must, of course, take what I now tell you in due modesty: you have the consciousness which will be customary in the third millennium.'[4] Johanna von Keyserlingk was able to foresee that future, to perceive it imaginatively and to put it into words.

A golden globe lifts up out of the redeemed earth, shining. A figure stands, as if cast in ore, with radiating face. The high forehead, the fiery gaze. Powerful, with iron first, he holds the sword. On a high rock he stands, [the Archangel] Michael, the flaming, heroic figure.

Beside him stands a host of noble figures in armour, with swords in their hands.

Ironlike, exalted, the figure of Michael towers above them. Storming out of the dark, he and his hosts approach. Still the darkness yawns behind and beneath them ... Others point their flashing swords. Clouds chase across the heavens above them. From these clouds, too, heroic figures bow down ...

Rising high, as if suffused with gold, radiates the nameless countenance ...

He storms on with his host into the light. Only at his back does the darkness keep watch. Now he stands still. A golden light shines over the darkness. Towering, taciturn, Michael stands. The valley spreads into the distance before his gaze. Dead breath, shadowy, dead light rises from the earth; hardly a green shoot does she bring forth. Can this be earth?

His fiery gaze guides others into the valley. His eyes are golden. Gold from the reflection of the unheard of that is enacted there. Gold also reflects on the helmets around him. From the valley of the earth there rises a giant sun, a golden globe, carrying within it all countries, seas, and mountains. Golden it is, wrested from the earth. Further it rises, bringing with it whatever has united itself with this sun-gold.

His body it is, his holy, risen body. Living, gold-radiating he rises upward and leaves behind the dead earth.

Speechless the heroes stand. Now do they know the goal for which they fight.[5]

An unprecedented perspective: the heart of the earth is golden. Everything that has united itself to the Christ is brought along with this redeemed earth, in the redeemed elements. We can recognize, comprehend, something of this unprecedented, far reaching perspective in what we see and hear, and take into ourselves at the altar. There it is the same. Christ takes the earth in his hands, unites his soul with it and unites his awe-inspiring power with the elements.

The philosopher, geologist and theologian Teilhard de Chardin (1881–1955) saw how at the altar something of infinite consequence takes place, something which communicates itself to creation. He wrote:

> When Christ ... through the mouth of the priest ... says *Hoc est corpus meum* [this is my body], these words extend beyond the morsel of bread over which they are said: they give birth to the whole mystical body of Christ. The effect of the priestly act extends beyond the consecrated host to the cosmos itself. The entire realm of matter is slowly but irrestibly affected by this great consecration.[6]

Teilhard de Chardin uses the image of a glowing hearth, and then writes: 'Anyone becoming conscious of what happens at the altar, will see not just a little piece of bread, but will see something glowing and communicating its warmth and rays to the whole of creation.' At the altar, on a small scale, unseen and often hardly recognized, something happens which one day will become full reality: the marriage of heaven and earth.

# 8 Alchemy and Christianity

For many centuries the theme of alchemy and Christianity has led a hidden existence. There have been many misunderstandings surrounding this theme.

For quite some time before the industrial revolution in Europe and the triumphant march of chemistry, there was a precursor of this chemistry which had quite a different outlook and different aims from our present materialistic worldview. This can be observed frequently in history: before something enters the cultural mainstream, there is a shining moment of birth where a phenomenon manifests itself in its purest form. It is then submerged into everyday reality. Is alchemy perhaps an indication too of the way we will deal with matter in a far future?

Western alchemy has its roots in a far and distant past. Alchemy already existed in Arabia and Egypt, but we will see that western, European alchemy had a quite different character and content from these forerunners. In Europe a form arises where alchemy and Christianity unite. Even Martin Luther could still acknowledge that alchemy represented certain essential aspects of Christianity. He wrote:

> The art of alchemy is justly and truly a philosophy of the ancient philosophers, which greatly pleases me – not only for her virtue and usefulness, but also because of her magnificent similarities to the resurrection of the dead at the last judgment.

Perhaps it is somewhat embarrassing for our modern-day scientists to acknowledge that chemistry originated from alchemy: everything to do with alchemy is alien to them. Nevertheless, our present-day chemistry has its roots in this fairytale-like alchemy.

However, it is understandable that, over time, alchemy acquired a bad reputation, because the art of alchemy was often misused. There were swindlers calling themselves alchemists claiming they could make gold and make people rich. Unfortunately, part of the literature on this subject is based on corrupted forms of alchemy. The real purpose of alchemy was never to create earthly gold or material wealth.

It is right to say that alchemy was never interested only in matter and its chemical properties, but that it always had a spiritual aspect. This was one of the essential characteristics of the original alchemy: it sought a union between the two worlds, the spiritual and the earthly. Alchemy based itself on what is known as the Hermetic principle. This is named after the god Hermes, whom the Egyptians called Toth. He was also called Hermes Trismegistos, the thrice-greatest Hermes, who inspired Egyptian culture according to the principle: as above, so below.

When we look at everything that ancient Egyptian culture has brought forth, we realize that the Hermetic principle really is the quintessence of this culture. On earth ancient Egyptian society had to become an image or a reflection of what in the spiritual world, the world of the hierarchies, is a full reality. Hence Egyptian culture and society were strictly hierarchical too. This was not a matter of class, or of class war: the origin of this hierarchical structure lay in the heavenly hierarchies, of which the earthly forms were a reflection. The pharaoh was a representative of the highest hierarchy.

The Hermetic principle contains another duality. Not only the principle 'as above, so below,' but also the duality 'as within, so without.' If we look back far enough into pre-Christian cultures we come across this principle again and again. 'As within, so without' is the principle of pre-Christian sacrifices. To us animal sacrifice, the killing and burning of an animal at the altar, letting the smoke rise up, might seem strange. But in antiquity this was an obvious thing to do. When the sacrificial smoke rose up, the human beings present accompanied it with heart and soul: 'as within, so without.' They would 'go through the fire' to make a sacrifice. There is an anecdote indicating how strongly this principle 'as within, so without' worked in Greek culture. It recounts how a Greek person would begin to blush when walking past a field of poppies. The strong red colour called forth a strong reaction in the body.

Kemi (chemi) is the ancient Egyptian word for black earth. It refers to the black silt the Nile deposited when it overflowed and receded once a year. Our word 'chemistry' is clearly derived from it.

The Hermetic principle is an oft repeated theme in western alchemy. We encounter it for example in a famous eighteenth-century alchemical publication, the *Aurea Catena Homeri,* the Golden Chain of Homer. This was a beautiful metaphor for the principle 'as above, so below.' A clairvoyant could perceive what binds the two worlds together. There is an unbroken chain of golden links between both worlds, descending from the highest hierarchies down into the very chemistry of the physical world. The hierarchies create and maintain this chain of invisible gold.

There is a beautiful description of the *aurea catena* in Goethe's *Faust,* in a short passage which is autobiographical. We know that as a young man, Goethe studied the *Aurea Catena Homeri.* He used his impressions of it in a scene where Faust opens the book and studies the sign of the macrocosm. This was the sign alchemists studied most of all: not that of the microcosm but of the macrocosm. The alchemists read the *Liber mundi,* the book of nature, the book of the heavenly forces, of the earth and of the heavenly forces on the earth. They practised reading this spiritual-physical language of metaphors, as does Faust when he opens the alchemical book and studies the first sign, of the macrocosm. Then Goethe describes an experience he probably had himself when he was about twenty-one:

> How all weaves one harmonious whole,
> Each in the other works and lives!
> See heavenly powers ascending and descending,
> The golden buckets, one long line, extending!
> See them with bliss-exhaling pinions
> Their way from heaven through earth
> Their singing harmonious through the universe ringing!
> (*Faust*, Part I, 1.1)

They are golden forces connecting heaven and earth. This was the gold the alchemists of the Middle Ages were looking for when they walked up and down the Jacob's ladder of the hierarchies. In the Middle Ages they still knew that the highest is at work in the physical. This was known since Dionysius the Areopagite. In the classical description, *Celestial Hierarchies,* Dionysius (or perhaps a later Dionysius) described how the highest hierachies, the Thrones, Cherubim and Seraphim form the foundation of the physical world. The middle hierarchies of the Kyriotetes, Dynameis and Exousiai are active in the soul life. The lowest triad – Archai, Archangeloi and Angeloi – work in the spiritual.

It was known since ancient times that the highest hierarchies worked in the creation of matter. The German philosopher Friedrich Oetinger expressed this in the memorable phrase 'Physical matter is

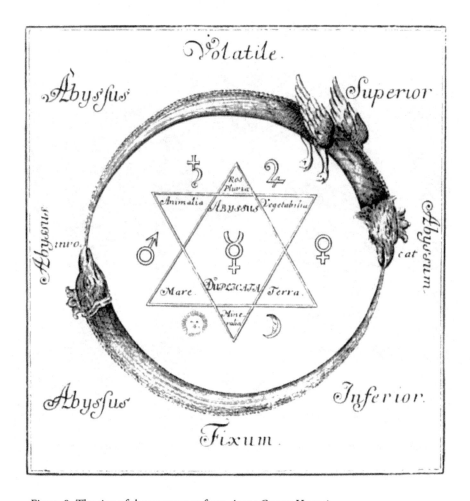

Figure 8. The sign of the macrocosm from *Aurea Catena Homeri*.

Figure 9. Apparition of the Spirit of the Earth. Pencil drawing by Goethe, *c.* 1810–12.

the end of God's path.' God has travelled an infinitely long way from the spirit, through all the realms of soul, to be able to create visible creation.

I began this chapter by mentioning that western alchemy owes a lot to its Egyptian and Arabian roots. But from the early Middle Ages a new element – Christianity – entered western alchemy, which made it unique. It is not too difficult to imagine that since the appearance of Christ on the earth, this 'golden chain' connecting heaven and earth has changed. Before this event, the most precious was above; this was the highest 'authority.' This highest authority, Christ himself, bound himself to the deepest. In his descent into hell, he penetrated the centre of the earth and transformed it from within. But this transformation of the earth began even before this. Rudolf Steiner described the moment very precisely: 'The moment the blood of the crucified one on Golgotha flows into the earth, the aura of the earth changes.'[1]

Ever since the appearance of the Christ on earth, since his death and resurrection, the essential part of our existence is here on earth, in our mortal sheath. Since that time the spiritual world can intervene so deeply that the resurrection force of Christ can unite with the mortal sheath of the human being. That is alchemy. That is the essence of what the alchemists were searching for and which they named *lapis philosophorum,* the philosopher's stone. Alchemical works clearly indicate that the philosopher's stone, the ultimate goal of the alchemists, has to do with the Lord of the heavenly forces on earth.

The mystic and alchemist Jakob Böhme (1575–1624) wrote a book with the significant title *De incarnatione verbi* (on the incarnation of the word). He wrote: 'To find the philosopher's stone, you must be reborn in Christ.' This connection between the philosopher's stone and the Christ was recognized at the beginning of the twentieth century not only by Rudolf Steiner but independently also by Carl Gustav Jung. His study of alchemy culminates in what he calls the Lapis-Christ-Parallel. We find the origin of this symbolism quite literally in the First Epistle of Peter (2:4f):

Come to him, to that living stone, rejected by men but in God's sight chosen and precious; and like living stones be

yourselves built into a spiritual house, to be a holy priesthood,
to offer spiritual sacrifices acceptable to God through Jesus
Christ.

Peter here refers back to the Old Testament, to indicate who the
stone is:

For it stands in scripture:
'Behold, I am laying in Zion a stone, a cornerstone, chosen
and precious,
    and he who believes in him will not be put to shame.'
To you therefore who believe, he is precious, but for those
who do not believe,
    'The very stone which the builders rejected
    has become the head of the corner,'
    and
    'a stone that will make men stumble,
    a rock that will make them fall' (1Pet.2:6-8).

These are strange, paradoxical words which must be examined
and weighed very carefully. It is not the task of Christianity to force
Christians into anonymous religious structures, whether they want it
or not, which is regrettably what Christianity has done quite often in
the course of history. Peter emphatically transforms the metaphor, and
writes of living stones. We human beings are living stones. We have
transformed mineral substance into human substance. This cannot
be achieved without our free will. This is frequently disregarded and
overlooked in traditional Christianity is. We are not matter without
a free will, we are living stones who can become part of a spiritual
edifice. This is what the alchemists called the philosopher's stone,
which – as the metaphor indicated – cannot come about anywhere
else but in the human being. What could then happen to the physical
world is another matter, to which I will return later.

The alchemists describe the philosopher's stone in extremely
contradictory terms, leaving it utterly ambiguous whether the stone
is physical or spiritual. Their descriptions veer between spirit and
matter according to the old principle: as above, so below. The poet
Novalis too, knows the philosopher's stone and calls it, in the most

contradictory terms possible, 'the invisible-visible matter, which is everywhere and nowhere, which is everything and nothing.'[2] Novalis can express himself so paradoxically because the philosopher's stone comes into being within the human being itself.

The alchemist never took a step in the transformation of the material world without first taking a step in the transformation of his own soul forces. That is why Steiner calls alchemy 'sacred science.' Today we usually think of science and the sacred as two diametric opposites. But in alchemy this dichotomy was overcome. Steiner speaks of the 'dramas of the soul' that were played out in the laboratory of the alchemist, because every step in the transmutation of matter had to be accompanied by a transformation of the soul.

We can get a clear idea of how alchemists worked from several writings with clear indications of the areas in which the alchemist worked on himself. To begin with there are the three *principia*, the three principles, indicated by the names of three substances: salt, mercury (also called water), and sulfur. The qualities embodied by these substances had to arise in the soul of the alchemist.

In the purest crystallized form of salt, we have the image of the future creation before us: the heavenly Jerusalem.

> And he who talked to me had a measuring rod of gold
> to measure the city and its gates and walls. The city lies
> foursquare, its length the same as its breadth; and he measured
> the city with his rod, twelve thousand stadia; its length and
> breadth and height are equal. (Rev.21:15f).

Here we have an imagination of the cube. In the transparent matter of the salt crystal we have an image of crystalline, pure thinking. A thinking which has freed itself from all stirrings of the soul, and is capable of becoming prayer. Rudolf Steiner gave the following description of this:

> Everything in nature which can form a deposit of solid
> substance out of a solution was called salt by the Rosicrucian
> of the Middle Ages. When the medieval Rosicrucian saw this
> salt formation, however, his conception of it was entirely
> different from that of modern man. For if he wanted to feel

he had understood it, the witnessing of such a process had
to work like a prayer in his soul. Therefore the medieval
Rosicrucian tried to make clear to himself what would have
to happen in his own soul if the formation of salt were to take
place there too. He arrived at the thought: human nature is
perpetually destroying itself through instincts and passions.
Our life would be nothing but a decomposition, a process of
putrefaction, if we only followed our instincts and passions.
And if man really wants to protect himself against this process
of putrefaction, then he must constantly devote himself to
noble thoughts that turn him towards the spirit.[3]

That is salt, as indicated in the old Rosicrucian saying *in sale
sapientiae eternae,* in salt lies the eternal wisdom. Salt is the expression
of cosmic thoughts. When the alchemist of the Middle Ages – for
Steiner 'alchemist' and 'Rosicrucian' are interchangeable – tried to
crystallize salt, his main aim was to make his thoughts as clear and
pure as a crystal, like a pure prayer.

When dealing with mercury, also called *aqua* (water), the alchemist
strove to bring his soul into movement, not to let it crystallize out
in thoughts, but to let the forces of the soul melt and flow, as in
the expression of love, when one's heart melts. That was what the
Rosicrucian of the Middle Ages attempted when he worked with
mercury. Rudolf Steiner's describes it thus:

The process of dissolving was a different experience: it was
a different natural process that could also lead the medieval
Rosicrucian to prayer. Everything that can dissolve another
substance was called by the medieval Rosicrucian quicksilver
or mercury. Now he asked again: what is the corresponding
quality in the human soul? What quality works in the soul
in the same way in which quicksilver or mercury works
outside in nature? The medieval Rosicrucian knew that all
the forms of love in the soul are what correspond to mercury.
He distinguished between lower and higher processes of
dissolving, just as there are lower and higher forms of love.
And thus the witnessing of the dissolving process again became
a pious prayer, and the medieval theosophist said to himself:

God's love has been at work out there for thousands of years
in the same way as love works in me.

As Angelus Silesius wrote, 'the bread, the Lord in us, works like the
philosopher's stone. It turns us to gold where we are molten.' To be
able to absorb the divine gold we must melt inwardly, we must enter a
stream of love, to allow God to work within a human being. Mercury
expresses all forms of love which are rejuvenating, renewing. In the
old Rosicrucian dictum this was expressed as, *in aqua regenerationis,*
'in water (in mercury) regenerating forces are at work.'

And finally, in all sulfur processes, all processes of burning, the
alchemist connected himself with the power of sacrifice. All forces of
sacrifice are sulfur. Steiner expressed it as follows:

The third important natural process for the medieval
Rosicrucian and theosophist was combustion, which takes
place when material substance is consumed by flames. And
again the medieval Rosicrucian sought the inner process
corresponding to this combustion. This inner soul process
he saw to be ardent devotion to the deity. And everything
that can go up in flames he called sulfur. In the stages of
development of the earth he beheld a gradual process of
purification similar to a combustion or sulfur process. Just as
he knew that the earth will at some time be purified by fire, he
also saw a combustion process in fervent devotion to the deity.
In the earth processes he beheld the work of those gods who
look up to mightier gods above them.

The gods sacrifice to other gods in this golden chain.

The third part of the old Rosicrucian dictum was *in cinere
germinante terram novam,* in the ashes sprouts new earth. The gold
which the alchmists looked for had nothing to do with material gold,
and everything with the 'gilding' of the soul forces: the aura acquires
a golden sheen (So in the Middle Ages, an initiate was sometimes
called *Meister Güldenschuh,* Master Golden Shoe.) Angelus Silesius
wrote in his *Cherubinische Wandersmann:* 'One who has transformed
his heart into purest gold out of love for God, has mastered the art of
immersing himself and transforming substances.'

We can now give a more precise description of how this bridge between spirit and matter comes about, but only with the help of certain insights from anthroposophy. In the first German edition of *An Outline of Esoteric Science,* Steiner speaks about rhythmicizing the breath (in later editions this was left out). Steiner calls this 'lapidary' 'working with the philosopher's stone.' Strange as it may seem, this is an area where we all have unconcious or semiconscious experiences. What happens if we engage intensively and for a long time with certain spiritual content? If we have taken our time to do this in peace and quiet, we notice afterwards that our breath has changed. And we can experience this quite deeply if we follow the Act of Consecration intensely. By the end our breath has really settled down. A fellow priest with extensive experience in this area told me, 'I notice that during the Act of Consecration my breathing becomes the same as in my sleep, but I remain conscious.' We breathe more deeply when we are asleep, but what happens unconsciously in our sleep during the regeneration of our body, this priest noticed consciously in his own breathing during the Act of Consecration. We can observe similar phenomena during various forms of meditation and prayer. This is an area where we can all have our own experiences in 'handling' the philosopher's stone.

This is just the beginning of alchemy. Alchemy starts in the human being, but has the task to communicate what the human being accomplishes – the forming of the philosopher's stone – to the rest of creation. To that end the alchemist must experience death at first hand, right into the imagination of the skeleton. To learn 'to die before dying.'

In alchemy this is indicated by the well-known letters of the monogram INRI. In alchemy these letters stand for *Igne Natura Renovator Igitur,* 'thus nature is renewed again through fire.' An impressive image, a body which bruns itself in the ultimate sacrifice. The dying process of the alchemist was a consummate sacrifice: a crucifixion and a burning. He had to tread the path of *mortificatio,* the process of dying, one of the seven phases of the alchemical process. He had to go through a *putrefactio,* a disintegration. When someone reaches the threshold of death, the parts of his being are dissolved, and he comes to the curious realization: I am not my body, I am even outside and above it. This is known as an out-of-body experience. If the disintegration continues, it is decay. Bodily matter is transformed into a different substance. You encounter the essence of the substance, the foundation of the substance. The path ends with *resuscitatio*, resurrection.

The alchemists recognized in John their great predecessor. He himself had walked this 'alchemical path.' When the risen Christ, the Son of Man appears to him, John fell down at his feet, as if dead. The Christ himself awakened him from this sleep of death.

But this is not yet the essence of the alchemist's task. It was not the primary aim of the alchemist to transform his own being into the philosopher's stone: the whole earth awaits this transformation. Hence, when on his path the alchemist retained an uninterrupted connection to the world of substance, to matter. During the last phase of his development the alchemist becomes the co-creator of a new, future creation which we know from the Bible as the New Jerusalem. Quietly, in a hidden occult way, the alchemist was helping to build the future creation. The author of the Apocalypse uses the term 'new earth,' and he does not use the word *neos*, but *kainos*. In Greek *neos* is something is new in a well-known way, for example, tomorrow will be a new day. But to indicate that something is fundamentally new, the word *kainos* – totally new – is used. The New Jerusalem is something an alchemist saw before him already, in a nascent state. The alchemist worked with substances which were transformed, which underwent transmutation. Looking at this alchemical process he realized, what happens here on a small scale will one day become cosmic reality (as above, so below). 'And I [John] saw the holy city, new Jerusalem, coming down out of heaven from God, prepared as a bride adorned for her husband' (Rev.21:2). Only then will the alchemist's goals have been fully realized.

Everything the alchemist did was only an indication of the marriage of heaven and earth. The famous work, *The Chymical Wedding of Christian Rosenkreutz*, describes the path of the soul through all these processes of death, to form part in this future in the present, and to experience this future now, before the great moment comes when it will be a cosmic reality. In this future state there will not only be a new earth, but also a new heaven.

The heavens, in the meantime, develop too. For aeons, heaven and earth have grown further apart. This was not how it was meant to be. The original and future form was, and will be: as above, so below.

In our time these two worlds have grown so far apart that – as Rudolf Steiner suggests – human beings run the risk that their angels lose interest in them. Too easily we assume that the angels all have an 'angelic patience.' People often say something like: 'I live here and now, on the earth. What happens after will take care of itself.' But things are not as simple as that, neither in life nor in life after death. Because life after death can only develop according to the law of *similia similibus cognoscuntur*: 'like is recognized by like.' In our time we run the risk that our angels lose interest in us. For aeons the angels have been interested in us, accompanied us through the depths, as it were. When the human being in the ever continuing Fall separates himself even further, he runs the risk his angel will sooner or later turn against him. John describes this as seven angels pouring out their 'seven bowls of the wrath of God' over the earth (Rev.16:1).

To understand this image we must greatly expand our understanding of the word 'wrath.' To really understand this 'angelic wrath' it is perhaps best to relate it to the concept 'holy wrath.' It does not arise out of anger or agression, but out of love for something or somebody. Thus, heavenly wrath is an expression of divine love, which on the earthly plane works as a destructive force. The destruction of earthly creation described in the Apocalypse is no less than the phenomenon accompanying the revelation in which Jesus Christ was revealed (Rev.1:1).

There is one being in heaven and on earth who has lived the marriage of heaven and earth for us, and has 'gone before.' After all, in the metaphors of the Apocalypse, Christ is the bridegroom. He unites himself with his followers, after he has freed up the path to heaven. Long before his Resurrection, he has spoken of this intention. He calls his Passion and Resurrection a 'lifting up from the earthly': 'And I, when I am lifted up from the earth, will draw all men to myself' (John 12:32). This is only possible through the principle of the attraction of like to like. The marriage of heaven and earth is possible for all who look for him and long for him. This is indicated at the end of the Apocalypse, when this mutual attraction between heaven and earth, of the bridegroom and the bride is expressed in the words: 'The Spirit and the Bride say, "Come." And let him who hears say, "Come." And let him who is thirsty come.' (Rev.22:17).

Anyone who has ears to hear, anyone who thirsts, who longs for this future can call up these forces. In this mutual longing, the marriage of heaven and earth becomes reality.

# 9 Elemental Beings and the Sacraments

If there is one realm in particular where Christ is truly in his element it is the realm of the sacraments. In the sacraments it is not just the right words which matter, but also the right actions and substances. It is through the union of these three aspects that the sacramental comes into being. In Chapter 7 we mentioned in this context the classical formula, 'the word unites itself with the element and thereby the sacrament arises.' This sacramental fact can be heard in the parting words of Christ to his disciples. These words, the last of the Gospel of St Matthew, are his last will and testament just before his ascent into heaven. They express the way in which the Lord of the Elements becomes active in heaven and on earth. He says, 'All authority in heaven and on earth has been given to me' (Matt.28:18). In Greek the words are 'all Exousia in heaven and on the earth.'

The Exousiai (high hierarchical beings) are his helpers. They stand at his side, ready to become active on the earth. This is a concrete expression of the fact that from now on he is the Lord of the Elements. He is the one who can penetrate everything that happens in heaven and on earth. In the following lines he indicates that he can become active as sovereign in time and space. In this short text his authority is indicated four times with the word 'all.'

> '*All* authority in heaven and on earth has been given to me.
> Go therefore and make disciples of *all* nations, baptizing
> them in the name of the Father and of the Son and of
> the Holy Spirit, teaching them to observe *all* that I have
> commanded you; and lo, I am with you *always*, to the close of
> the age.' (Matt:28:18–20).

With these parting words he transfers something of this authority to his disciples. They receive the priestly task to work sacramentally: 'make disciples of all nations, baptizing them in the name of the Father and of the Son and of the Holy Spirit.' That is the beginning of the succession, the instruction and succession of his activity. He gives them the task to baptize. Baptism, the primal sacrament, is the starting point of sacramental labour. In the sacrament of Ordination in the Christian Community this is expressed in a very literal way, when the candidate receives the task to gather souls who want to unite themselves with the Christ, by baptizing them. In each sacrament one can recognize something of the primal sacrament, the baptism.

Baptism establishes a profound connection with the elements. In the baptism as practiced in the Christian Community these are the four elements. The child is baptized with water, salt and ash, and in a certain sense with the word too. These are the four elements of baptism. The first element is water, salt represents the element of earth, ash represents fire and the spoken words represent the element of air. The child is brought into contact with these elements, which are consecrated during baptism.

When they are addressed in the right way, the elemental beings who are hidden in the substances 'understand' the words of their Lord – and they become bearers of the spiritual forces which unite themselves with them. However, one can only do justice to this sacramental principle if the baptism is performed according to the rite and with the prescribed words, actions and substances, by someone ordained into the priesthood. Strange as it may seem, in a true sacrament, every word and every action is a taboo. That is to say that anything arbitrary, improvised or any variation of the sacrament is ruled out, is taboo. It is essential that the prescribed words and actions are performed by the priest in a very specific way and with the right intention. Only then can they unfold their full efficacy. This is the ritual principle where we encounter once more the rule: as above, so below.

This sacramental principle too is mentioned in the New Testament, in the Epistle to the Hebrews (8:5f). '[Priests] serve a copy and shadow of the heavenly sanctuary.' The writer uses comparative words, *hypodeigma* (copy or model), and *skia* (shadow). The full reality of the sacramental rite exists in heaven, in the spiritual world. The earthly ritual is but a shadow image of this. Then the epistle continues, 'for when Moses was about to erect the tabernacle, he was instructed by God, saying "See that you make everything according to the pattern which was shown you on the mountain".'

There, before the spirit-vision and before the inspiration of the initiate of the Jewish people stands the archetype. The initiate is able to translate the imagination, the inspiration into visible images, into sacramental language, into reflected images which appear in the Jewish ritual. The Epistle to the Hebrews adds what is specific to the Christian ritual: 'We (the Christians) have such a high priest, one who is seated on the right hand of the throne of the Majesty in heaven, a minister in the sanctuary and the true tabernacle which is set up not by man but by the Lord' (8:1f).

Christ himself is the high priest. Everything we see in the earthly ritual, the altar, the candles, the substances, the vestments, the burning of the incense, is but a reflection or shadow of what happens in heaven. While the priest on earth celebrates the sacrament, the High Priest, Christ, celebrates the primal, archetypal sacrament in the spiritual world.

So far, this may appear to have a certain spiritual logic, but it is quite abstract. I would like to illustrate this with an example. What follows is a description by someone who was quite unprepared for, and overwhelmed by a clairvoyant perception of something of this heavenly cult. This person had great difficulty finding the right words for these imaginations, because our earthly vocabulary is not quite adequate for such images.

> Just after the beginning of the Act of Consecration I saw a great multitude of angels looking on. They formed a kind of dome over the altar, the priest and the congregation – and they looked down on us with a very relaxed, peaceful and at the same time very concentrated (but not fixed) attention. I could not count their number, because their forms merged into each other here and there, where they perhaps appeared more as different intensities of light. They were not 'arranged' in any particular way, but formed an 'orderly chaos,' giving an impression of great harmony and beauty (comparable to the natural beauty of clouds in the sky). The whole mood,

the forms, and especially the way they looked at us, strongly reminded me of certain paintings by Leonardo da Vinci.

As the service went on, the separate shapes dissolved into patterns of colour, which continuously changed in shape and colour. They were pastel colours, soft, yet very intense. They formed somewhat erratic circles; the effect was of circles in water, when several pebbles are thrown in, but all in slow motion, about four times as slow as in water. Sometimes openings appeared in this dome of moving colours, especially near the altar. These were actually formed by the bodies of the angelic beings. Their attitude then expressed a total surrender. Through this – and one can imagine it quite concretely – there would be a passage to the heights. In this passage there was light of a very special quality, which is hard to describe. Perhaps words such as 'very friendly,' 'inviting' or 'beneficent' come close to it. It also had a different composition from 'earthly light.' It gave an impression of perfect harmony between the earthly and the spiritual. The whole scene had the appearance of harmony and joy. Not so much an ecstatic joy, but a joy full of gratitude, attention, peace and love.

The Christian service, celebrated in the right way and accompanied in the right way by the congregation, creates a perfect harmony between spirit and matter, between the spiritual world and the elements, between the earthly and the heavenly ritual.

So far we have not mentioned the elemental beings in this context. In the description until now we talked about the ritual which the hierarchies execute. But because the elemental beings play an essential part in the sacraments, they are explicitly addressed too. What happens then was described by Rudolf Steiner in a lecture at the time of the founding of the Christian Community in September 1922.

What are the impulses which make the evolution of humanity possible? What image of the future prepares this evolution? On Michaelmas day 1922, Steiner describes the Christian service as a seed for the future. He first describes old forms of ritual, remnants of pre-Christian rituals, which have no life left in them, but do remind us of their living origins. He compares these forms of worship with mummies: they were alive once, now there are just lifeless remains. In

contrast he describes forms of Christian worship which prepare for
the future.

> In the future the initiate will be able to show his pupils
> through the right, restored ritual acts of worship, that when
> you perform a ritual action, it is an appeal to spiritual powers
> of the universe. An appeal to those powers who, through what
> human beings do, want to connect themselves to the earth.[1]

In this passage he compares ritual with a wake-up call, an appeal.
Through this appeal certain spiritual powers hear what happens at
the altar. These spiritual beings can unite themselves with the earth
through the right ritualistic actions. Rudolf Steiner then describes
how the human being who performs these ritual actions correctly
thereby acquires the capacity to communicate with spiritual beings.

> Through outward technology man unites himself with the
> physical nature forces of the earth. Through the sacred
> enactments of sacrament and ritual he unites himself with the
> elementary-spiritual powers of the earth, with those powers
> that point the way to the future.

In this second passage of the same lecture Steiner indicates to
which forces the Christian service appeals: to the elemental powers
which nurture the future of the earth. He then indicates why these
elemental beings need the service:

> Everything performed according to the true rite contains the
> spiritual. The elemental spiritual beings which are evoked when
> such a rite is enacted have need of the rite because they draw
> nourishment and forces of growth from it.

The service is not something that is celebrated just for the
congregation present, and for the dead and for the hierarchies, but
also for certain elemental beings which are nourished by it.

And finally Rudolf Steiner describes what the future will look
like and what part the elemental beings that are nourished by the
sacrament will play in this future. He asks us to imagine a far distant

future. The earth will perish, plants and trees will wither. The outwardly visible world will disappear sooner or later,

> but the spiritual beings who have been called down into the sphere of the rites and sacred enactments – these will remain when the earth approaches its end. They will remain, in a state of more perfect development, within the earth, just as in autumn the seed of next year's plant is concealed within the present plant ... the perfected elemental beings will be there, living on into the Jupiter existence as a seed of the future.

The nourishment these elemental beings absorb will form the 'building blocks' for the New Jerusalem. (In Steiner's terminology this future creation is called 'Jupiter.') The service is an appeal to the elemental beings, is nourishment for them, and an 'ingredient' for the future. Can we recognize something of this seed for the future in the Act of Consecration?

When the bread and the wine are consecrated during the Act of Consecration, they acquire a sheen, a radiance, which is not limited to the space where the service takes place. This radiance communicates itself to far wider surroundings. I would like to relate one priest's experience of this phenomenon.

Walter Voigt was a priest who for many years worked under extremely difficult circumstances in former East Germany. His first experience described here, came about during the celebration of the Act of Consecration by one of his colleagues. Voigt had to overcome a certain antipathy towards this particular colleague, before he was able to connect himself objectively to the sacrament. He had to overcome his own shadow to be able to connect to this service. By overcoming his own antipathy he suddenly entered the realm where the service is a full reality. He described this in the words: 'I suddenly found myself in the garden of the Resurrection.' The space where the service was being held was filled with light, the indescribable, green-golden light of the Risen Christ. From the moment he recognized this light, the aura of the Risen One at the altar, to his amazement he saw it in the surroundings, far beyond the altar, too. Voigt regularly visited a congregation in Magdeburg. The train journey led through a dreary, bleak landscape and an urban desert. On arrival he was oppressed by the drabness of the landscape. But the following day, on his journey back, he could see the green-golden light of the Resurrection far beyond the city. This light communicated itself to a wide area and shone over it.

Shortly after the foundation of the Christian Community in Australia a similar experience was related by people who were totally new to the service. One day a group of aboriginals was present at the Act of Consecration and afterwards wished to speak with the priest. They told him, 'In the place where we live, hundreds of miles away, we realized one day that the aura of this land had changed, that something had been added to this land. Now we have seen where this change comes from. The change comes from this altar.'

We really may imagine the efficacy of the sacraments to be so far reaching. And especially when a new rite is inaugurated, a powerful appeal is made to the spiritual beings in the immediate surroundings. For example when the cultus of the Jewish people is founded. During the first sacrifice in the tabernacle, fire descends from heaven. So too during the inauguration of the temple of Solomon: 'When Solomon had ended his prayer, fire came down from heaven and consumed the burnt offering and the sacrifices, and the glory of the LORD filled the temple' (2Chron.7:1). At those moments especially the elemental beings respond to the beginning of the rite.

If a ritual is maintained and cared for in the months and years that follow, the spiritual beings evoked by it can unite themselves ever deeper with the ritual actions. A clairvoyant may perceive for example that elemental beings and hierarchies are already present before the beginning of the Act of Consecration.

Let us digress a moment, but this may bring us closer to an understanding of our theme. Something similar occurred at the inauguration of the new mysteries in the twentieth century, during the Christmas Conference of the Anthroposophical Society in 1923. Rudolf Steiner did not found a new ritual in the outward sense of the word, but initiated a new form of the mysteries. During the conference a heavy storm broke out. The following day Steiner was asked what had happened during this storm. He responded, 'The elemental beings were afraid that they were not being included, and that accounts for the last words in the verse [Foundation Stone Meditation] as we know it.'[2]

In his book, *The Christmas Foundation,* Rudolf Grosse wrote:

This allows us to understand the profound meaning of the lines in the foundation stone meditation, that seem a simple appeal to the elemental beings:

The spirits of the elements hear it
From east, west, north, south.
May human beings hear it!

Rudolf Steiner sounded this appeal to the elemental beings just once, on the opening day of the conference, December 25. This may have been because they had heard the call and had arrived, to co-operate. After this they were only called on once more, when Rudolf Steiner spoke the rhythm of the sixth day. But there, in the meditative combination of the phrases of the verse, a peculiar climax occurred, because Rudolf Steiner linked the elemental beings with the Christ being.

He introduced the meditation for this day as follows.

'And we imprint this into ourselves:

'Light Divine,

'Christ-Sun

'we imprint it in such a way that we especially relate to it the closing words, which will be spoken once more tomorrow in their threefoldness: how this Light Divine, and this Sun of Christ shine forth so that as shining suns they can be heard from east, west, north, south. To this Light Divine and this Sun of Christ we relate especially the closing words which were spoken on the first day:

'Light Divine,

'Christ-Sun

'The spirits of the elements hear it

'From east, west, north, south:

'May human beings hear it!'

Thus we have been permitted to cast a glance into the secrets of the subconscious regions of the soul, wherein the elemental beings, which are drawn into them by human forces of feeling, together with the real, the true Christ impulse, are active in such a way, that they co-operate with our destiny, with the task destiny imposes on us.[3]

Hans Peter van Manen too devotes a passage to the elemental beings in the Foundation Stone Meditation. He points out that in the second version of the Foundation Stone Meditation it does not say 'Spirits of the Elements,' but simply 'Spirits,' an indication that both the elemental beings as well as their devas are addressed here.[4]

We can describe in some more detail what happens in the world of the elemental beings, if we look at the ritual performed in a new church or chapel before the first celebration of the Act of Consecration. Before the first Act of Consecration in a new church, the space must first be consecrated. Consecrated water is sprinkled in the four directions of the space with an aspergillum. In the north, the earth is addressed; in the west, water; in the east, air; and in the south, fire. The four elements are each addressed in their own nature. This is then repeated to the four directions, this time with a incense.

The origin of this brief ritual was described by the founders of the Christian Community in quite a special way. They asked Rudolf Steiner what should be done for a church before the first Act of Consecration can be celebrated there. Rudolf Steiner answered without hesitation. He said that the consecration actually takes place through the first Act of Consecration, which is however prepared by addressing the four directions of the space. He gave the four sentences to be spoken at the sprinkling of the holy water and at the censing. This prepares the space and the sacraments may then be performed in it. This is a very practical example of a ritual as an appeal to the elemental beings. It is not an exorcism, as in the traditional consecration of churches. Here the elements and the beings connected to them are 'called to order,' the order of the Lord of the Elements.

In the Roman Catholic church too there is a ritual where the sacramental word is connected to the four directions of space. In the week after Pentecost, the festival of Corpus Christi is celebrated when the consecrated host, the 'holy, living body' of Christ is carried in procession out of the church and into nature. The sacrament is then joined to nature in four different places, in the four directions of space.

Finally we take a look beyond the boundaries of our theme. For there are other forms of sacramentalism. It would be a bad thing if the future of the world were only prepared for at the altar, and all other activity were of no consequence. We can be thankful to God that we have more than just the sacraments as tools for transforming the earth.

There are several forms of sacramentalism; I would like to distinguish four.

What we have discussed so far is the most radical transformation. We use the word *transubstantiation* for this process, which is more than just transforming. The painter Paul Cézanne said about it: 'Consecrated substance is not only the most sacred, but also the most real thing in the world.'

Then there is a process in the ritual which we call *consecration*. Water, salt and ash, for example are consecrated during baptism. Consecration differs from transubstantiation. During consecration, the substance is addressed in such a way that it is reconnected with the world of its origin.

A third area is even more familiar to us. These are different forms of rite where, according to certain prescribed actions, substances are prepared, taken in hand, so that healing forces, life forces can connect to them. This takes place for example during potentizing. The dictionary definition of potency is 'to make the latent power of something available for growth and development.' This happens for instance in biodynamic agriculture with the preparations.

Nature spirits are strongly attracted when these preparations are being made. Maria Thun, who had decades of experience in this area, once described how elemental beings explore these preparations with intense curiosity. The moment the preparations are sprinkled on the land, they dive in and bathe themselves in them, in large numbers. They are so keenly attracted because by bathing in them they receive certain life-forces with which they can work.

Maria Thun also described what happens when the life forces of a field are attacked. Herbicides destroy all forms of life in the earth. One day, weedkillers were sprayed on a test-field, and nature spirits appeared at the edge of the field, rising up from the earth, clenching their fists and calling out angrily, 'Murderers!' The elemental beings rebelled, because life there was no longer possible for them. They literally had to disappear. Afterwards, she tried to repair some of the damage with the help of preparations. It took ten days before any algae would grow again – herbicides exterminate all forms of plant life – but elemental beings would not return to that spot.

Apart from the three forms of sacramentalism mentioned –
transubstantiation, consecration and ritual – there is a fourth area.
This is ceremonial. In a ceremony you add a certain value to everyday
actions, whereby these actions are cultivated. These ceremonies are
not the same as sacraments of course, but one can observe from
sacramental actions, how life may be cultivated in everyday activities.
In this respect Rudolf Steiner frequently said that 'the laboratory table
should become an altar again.' We still have a long way to go, and it
is high time we should make a start. Of course we should not take this
too literally and begin to celebrate at the kitchen sink. But the kitchen
sink certainly is a place where we may connect with elemental beings.

The blind author Ursula Burkhard, who has been familiar with
elemental beings since childhood, wrote about such an encounter
while preparing her meal.

> Karlik likes to help me cooking a meal, especially when there are
> guests. He guides my hands. I am more conscious of this now
> and let myself be led more. He sits contentedly on the handle
> of the pan and offers advice. Before I cook the vegetables, I
> lay them out on the table in a beautiful tableau, like a harvest
> festival. We admire the various shapes. Karlik dances around
> them and makes a blessing gesture with his sun-hands and
> bestows the vegetables on us human beings. Only then do
> I begin cooking. My work in the kitchen is surounded by a
> radiance. When housewives hate their work, they hurt Karlik.[5]

I would like to conclude this chapter with an example of a
ceremony. Robert de Haan, a sound and music therapist in Holland,
was asked by a pedagogical institute to create verses for the various
activities on the farm. In these verses, spoken in a simple ceremony
for ploughing, sowing or harvesting, nature is addressed with deep
respect and joined to the Lord of the Elements.

*For sowing:*

Seed in the dark lap of the earth,
Open yourself for your archetype
In the harmony of the spheres,

Which wants to imprint itself in you.
May it spark off the will
To appear in space
And to evolve in the stream of time.
Beings of the elements
Make the hard seedcoat to burst open,
Bring the seed to full growth,
In the light of him who ascended
Into the etherspere of the earth.
Weave the forces and substances
Into healthy, nourishing plants.

In all these forms of blessing the efficacy depends not only on the content of the words, but also on the intention with which the ritual is performed. Only when the sacrament, the consecration, the rite or ceremony is performed with respect, truthfulness and dignity, can its efficacy come to full expression. Rudolf Steiner realized that during these occasions 'the prayers of the beings of the higher hierarchies in the supersensible worlds resonated in these rituals.'[6] The spiritual world can only co-operate with human actions and words, when we work with the right intention.

# 10 The School of Chartres and the Goddess Natura

Traditional Christianity has kept nature at arms length, so these two spheres have become more or less estranged from each other. Traditionally there was a rigourous separation between established Christianity and paganism. This separation was not only caused by historical factors. Put boldly: nature is not Christian by nature. Something has to happen before nature can be 'Christianized.'

In the last years of his life, Jacobus Knijpenga, a priest in the Christian Community, often spoke of the task of experiencing nature in a Christian way. He explained that these two spheres are not obviously compatible. There is quite a chasm between them, which must be bridged. Nature is still subject to the consequences of the Fall; nature is drawn along in the continuing Fall humanity is going through, and waits for the individual human being who is able to Christianize her.

Paul, in his Epistle to the Romans, describes this tension between nature and Christianity. Only when Christ has been born within the human being (the 'sonship') can nature be redeemed. This hope and expectation live in in nature.

> For the creation waits with eager longing for the revealing
> of the sons of God; for the creation was subjected to futility,
> not of its own will, but by the will of him who subjected
> it in hope; because the creation itself will be set free from
> its bondage to decay and obtain the glorious liberty of the
> children of God. We know that the whole creation has been
> groaning in travail together until now; and not only the
> creation, but we ourselves, who have the first fruits of the

Spirit, groan inwardly as we wait for adoption as sons, the redemption of our bodies. (Rom.8:19–23).

This tension between nature and Christianity plays an important part in the clairvoyant perception of nature. A naturally quite talented person in this realm had to overcome a lot before the bridge between both had been built.

A woman who had been familiar with nature and with elemental beings ever since childhood told me the following. As a child it was perfectly normal for her to play with nature beings in the forest. The world of elemental beings was familiar for many people in Transylvania where she lived. As a young woman she got to know Friedrich Benesch, who was quite familiar both with the realm of the nature spirits and with Christianity. After studying theology, biology, chemistry and physics, Benesch met anthroposophy and the Christian Community, and was ordained a priest. He recommended the young woman to attend the Act of Consecration from time to time.

To her own surprise, this was not an obvious or easy thing for the nature beings, who always accompanied her. She said, 'They clung to me.' The distance between the nature beings and the altar was too great. The woman fell ill. She received medical help, but also support from Friedrich Benesch. His schooled clairvoyant perception gave him insight into the way she could help the nature beings. He suggested, 'In the evenings sit by yourself in peace and quiet for some time. Light a candle, put it before this picture of the Christ and burn some incense.'

He gave her a reproduction of the risen Christ, and told her to explain to the nature beings who the Christ is. She said a prayer before the little ceremony. She did this for many weeks. Gradually she was cured and things calmed down around her. The nature beings did not trouble her anymore.

But there was more to come. One night this woman had a dream. In her dream she spoke to the nature beings: 'We want to build a church now, and you must bring the stones for it.' In this church, which was built in her dream, a service was held at the altar. And during this service the nature beings became lighter, clearer and more radiant, until they were redeemed and dissolved into the light of Christ. Since that dream, since that time, the nature beings left her free, because they had found their destiny. That is how, in this particular instance, the gap was bridged.

The School of Chartres is the exception proving the rule of the division between these two realms of nature and Christianity. In Chartres we can clearly follow the process in which the two streams, paganism and Christianity come together and merge into one stream, the School of Chartres. Historical descriptions and images of this extraordinary place, ancient Carnutum, suggest to us the union of paganism and Christianity. Julius Caesar describes in one of his books how in Carnutum, Celtic (Gallic) Druids came together from far and wide.[1] This was the centre of Druid culture. Caesar describes how in a grotto, a space under the earth, a virgin was venerated who would bear a child: *Virgo Paritura*. (The inscription on the altar dedicated to this Virgin was *Virgini Pariturae,* 'to the virgin who will give birth.')

There is still a memory, an echo, of the Celtic statue which preceded the Christian image. To this day there is a copy of the original wooden statue of the virgin, on the spot where the cave used to be. The copy was made after a seventeenth-century engraving. The original statue was removed and burned during the French Revolution.

Mary wears a crown with oak leaves. The original statue of the Druids (who venerated the oak as a holy tree) also wears a crown with oak leaves. The wooden statue is in the crypt. It was given the name Notre Dame Sous-Terre, Our Lady Underground. Here, elements of the pagan, Druid culture were assimilated by Christianity.

From 876 a second stream began to surface, when King Charles the Bald donated a relic to the cathedral: the *Sancta Camisa,* a cloak which had belonged to Mary. Here is a stream which wants to anchor Christianity historically, where relics are venerated. Tradition has it that Mary wore this cloak at the birth of Jesus.

We know of course that many cathedrals were built in places where there had been a pre-Christian place of worship. In most cases these old cults were destroyed root-and-branch, and the churches were literally built on the ashes of pagan centres of worship. Frequently it is even denied that anything had gone before, but not in this case. In the School of Chartres, these two streams enrich one another. During the building of the two wooden churches that preceded the stone cathedral, the School of Chartres arose: an academy after the Greek

VIRGINI·PARITVRÆ

Reduite Sur les proportions de 2 8 poüces 9 lignes de hauteur et d'un pied de largeur

Representation de l'ancienne Image de la Ste Vierge Conservée dans la grotte de Chartres

Figure 10. *Virgo Paritura*, engraving by La Roux.

example. It was said of the great teachers in this school that they were Greek philosophers who had returned. A true renaissance took place, where the work of the Greek philosophers appeared anew.

Bishop Fulbert, for example, was called 'the venerable Socrates.' John of Salisbury praised Bernard of Chartres, one of the great teachers in this school as 'the most perfect of all Platonists' of that century. It was said of Thierry of Chartres that in him 'the soul of Plato has reappeared, descended anew from heaven down to our mortal world.' So in the School of Chartres for the first time – apart from certain heretical streams in Christianity like the Manichaeans, Cathars and Albigensians, where something similar took place – pre-Christian religion and Christianity merged and formed a perfect unity. No longer were they two worlds separated from each other, but, as the title of one of the works of Bernard Silvestris (c. 1080–1167) has it: *De universitate mundi,* 'on the all-encompassing unity of the world.' The subtitle is *Megacosmus et Microcosmus.* Bernard Silvestris, using the concepts of Christian theology and of Greek philosophy, was able to see the interrelationship between of microcosm and macrocosm.

The teachers of the School of Chartres wrote that this 'all-encompassing unity' consists of a triune. They did not, as might be expected, describe the well-known image of the Trinity, but presented a different triad. Alain de Lille, (c. 1106–c. 1202) does this in his famous early work *De Planctu Naturae* (or *The Plaint of Nature*).

Before he wrote this work, Alain had a dream about this trinity from which the world arose. Above he saw the *Noys* (*nous* in Greek), divine thought, the divine spirit. Below he saw the *Hylé,* the physical world, primordial matter, which is in a certain state of chaos. He did not see them as separate worlds: in between the divine spirit and the chaos of matter there appears, as a third being, *Natura,* the world-soul. An ensouled being, the daughter of God, who receives the ideas from the Noys, from the divine intelligence, with which she works into matter as an artist, and transforms matter into useful, meaningful building blocks of creation. She surrounds everything that has been created. Even when her creations are no longer conscious of their origins, Natura still envelops them. This virginal being encompasses all creation. Alain de Lille saw her crowned with twelve fiery stars, clothed in a fine, gossamer veil, in which all the birds exist: the air. Her lowest raiment, the tunica, is multi-coloured, with all animals and plants woven into it: the earth. Over this, between air and earth, between veil and tunica, a sea-green upper garment, with the water and everything living in it. The four elements appear in the crown, the tunica, the upper garment and the veil.

What are just four concepts to us, appeared to Alain de Lille as an overwhelming imagination. The motherly being of nature appearing to him was so overpowering that he nearly lost consciousness. Natura then took him in her arms and bestowed her unconditional love on him, which brought him to himself again. Only then did Natura begin to speak and did the imaginative world become inspiration. Natura described to him her relationship towards the Noys, the divine Spirit. She said about these two worlds:

> His work is unity, my work is diversity. His work is perfect, my works are perishable. He is the Creator, I am his work. He brings the things into appearance, he gives 'Being.' My work bears the stamp of the divine creation.

In other words, Natura tried to make him conscious of the distinction between Creator and creation. This distinction culminated in the statement: 'Through me the human being was born, through him the human being is reborn.'

In the conversation which then arose between Alain and Natura it became clear to him that nature had progressed since the origin of creation. For Natura knew the One who has renewed creation through Golgotha. Natura was no longer the pagan Earth Mother, but had become a participant in the Resurrection. However – and this is the crux, the reason why these two worlds are still separated – nature sighs and suffers the pains of labour. Here we see the title of the work, *De planctu naturae*, arise. 'What is lacking in nature?' Alain de Lille asks her. Natura explains that all realms of nature obey her laws, but the human being rebels against nature and disturbs the work of art that is nature. Natura used a very special phrase in which the word 'nature' features three times. The human being is *naturae naturalia de naturae pertentans*, 'The human being tries with all his might to de-naturize what is natural in his nature.' Human beings carry nature within themselves, but have turned away from the Creator to such an extent, that they corrupt nature. How can this be?

Visible nature was prepared in the invisible world as a foreshadowing, but human beings, through their de-naturized character, create an etheric after-image of everything they do, think and say. All this has an impact on the etheric world, the 'etheric chronicle.' These effects of human activity undermine the working of Natura. And worse: she appears as a divine being clad in mourning.

In the other work we have of Alain de Lille, *Anticlaudianus*, a much later work, he writes not only of the continuing Fall, but also of the continuing creation. His first book is a spiritual diagnosis, the second a spiritual therapy: what needs to happen for creation to reach her destiny? This is discussed in a council in heaven. Alain uses the word council quite literally. Natura gathers high hierarchical beings around her and discusses with them what must happen to fulfil nature's destiny, the destiny of the human being and to perfect creation. The heavenly council decides that the human being needs an example, someone in whom the New Man comes to perfect expression. Natura herself cannot do this, but the highest hierarchies descend to prepare the birth of the new human being. This new human being is conceived in the realm above the hierarchies, in the realm of the Trinity. God himself hands him over to Sophia, the divine wisdom. Sophia hands the new man over to Natura and she clothes him in a perfect body. A body that does not bear the consequences of the Fall, constituted of the purest elements, which astonishes creation.

This is the story of the supersensible birth of Christ out of the Trinity, with the help of Sophia, Natura and the hierarchies, through the pure elements, until he is born of the Virgin: *Virgo Paritura.* Natura is an important helper in this process of birth. There are undoubtedly parallels with the Virgin Mary. In Christianity Mary too has the task to unite the two realms, of spirit and matter. Her intercession really consists of turning to the heavens and turning to the earth.

A Russian Orthodox priest once told me that he had seen Mary in a dream, standing on an immensely high tower, close to God. In his dream, Mary looked out over the earth and felt a deep compassion with fallen humanity. Then she said: 'I pity human beings. I shall make a bridge between heaven and earth.' Thereupon she loosened the twist of her hair, and let it roll down as an endless ladder, shining like gold. The image of this dream is comparable with the task of Natura between *Noys* and *Hylé*, between spirit and matter. However, Natura is not the same as Mary, but she assists at the birth. St Bride of the Isles has a similar task in the Scottish legend.[2] In her dream, Bride is present at the birth of Christ as *Muime Chriosd*, as foster mother of Christ, to cover him with her mantle.

Bride took her name from the Celtic goddess Bridghe, who is the same as Natura. Bridghe is the goddess who weaves creation from the other side, the invisible side, until the visible cloak of the Godhead appears in nature. Her namesake Bride is not, as a critic once wrote 'a pagan goddess in a worn-out Christian garment,' but she is an expression of pre-Christian Christianity. That is not just some modern wishful interpretation, it is an insight which arose among the Druids themselves. Hence the sixth-century bard Taliesin could say of the Celtic mysteries: 'Christ, the Word of the beginning, was our teacher from the beginning. In Asia Minor Christianity was new, but never was there a time when our Druids did not keep to her principles.'

In the School of Chartres this pre-Christian stream, which was brought to Europe by the Druids, comes to full fruition. Describing this stream has hopefully made it clear that the Druids were prepared for the coming of Christianity in every respect. The great teachers of Chartres in their turn were able to take up this pre-Christian stream by dint of their special state of mind. In the School of Chartres we have, perhaps for the first time in history, what we might call a 'Christian experience of nature': nature is a being awaiting the redeemed human being. Everything in the School of Chartres was aimed at uniting Christianity with nature.

To conclude this chapter I would like to present an example of the way in which we, in our time, can bridge the gap between nature and ourselves. We will discuss this theme in more depth in the last two chapters.

Someone who was actively searching for essential experiences of nature only discovered this essential quality while reflecting on the walks she took in nature. In her reflections she experienced the following:

While walking, thinking, observing, I let the forest work upon me. It gave me the inspiration for the work I had to do. It was like a mantle that had been wrapped around me. Only in reflecting did I become conscious of the fact that this mantle surrounded me like a very clear light. The mantle of nature is woven of light. Not radiating or glittering light, but a light seemingly without a source. This rose up from my memory, while before the experience was unconscious.

She differentiated between her own moods and the moods in nature, something she had taught herself over time. It was in memory, in looking back, or at waking up from sleep, that it became clear to her what the essence of her experiences in nature was. (In biography work people are invited to observe their memories, to become conscious of a particular theme running through them, and sometimes they suddenly see their life in a new light.) Finally she asked herself whether it might be possible to go back in memory to certain moments in life when one experienced something through nature, and then to ask what it was that surrounded one, disregarding whether something was beautiful or not. We have to wipe away these subjective moods to enter the mood of nature in looking back. What was present there? What was happening there? And then slowly, gradually we learn to recognize how nature speaks. In the immediate experience, our subjective feelings are still interwoven with the moods of nature. But looking back it is possible to distinguish between these two realms. This could be the beginning of what could be called true 'recreation,' re-creating something that has been separated for centuries.

# 11 Elemental Beings in Nature

Wherever you look in nature – even if there doesn't appear to be any life at all – it is teeming with spiritual beings, which become perceptible if we 'look behind the scenes.' In some cases children, with their pure, unclouded perception, still perceive them.

In Chapter 4 we described such an experience of a child of five who saw a wall 'come alive' with beings. What young children sometimes experience spontaneously, a few adults can experience throughout their whole life. This is a natural clairvoyance. People naturally gifted in this way report that even they can be endlessly amazed at their own perceptions. Even if one is familiar with traditional spiritual concepts, the sheer tangle of nature beings never ceases to amaze.

Since olden times people have tried to give names to the immense variety of beings, to create some order in this apparent chaos. These names and concepts may be clearly delineated and refer to the four elements, but anyone with their own observations in this realm, knows there are endless transitions between the different elements. We mentioned that Paracelsus distinguishes four groups of beings. I will describe them briefly and move from fourfoldness to plurality. The various names are an indication of their manifoldness.

The first group Paracelsus mentioned were the pygmies. Today we only use this name for certain tribes of small African people. Originally the name was used for earth spirits, gnomes or kobolds. Most people have forgotten that the mineral cobalt derived its name from the kobolds. In olden times miners saw cobalt as a gift of the kobolds.

Different countries have different names for earth spirits. In Scandinavia there are the tomten, in Russia the karliki, in Holland and Germany the kabouter or klabouter, in Scotland the brownies, in Ireland the leprechaun, and in Cornwall the knockers. These earth spirits are not only at home in many places in nature, they also dwell in human habitations. In Germany and Austria the *Wichtel* is a spirit of the home. Wherever we encounter the earth element we encounter earth spirits: in rocks, minerals, in veins of metal within rock, in roots, but also in the earth element in a house. The stones, wood and metals each have spiritual beings connected to them.

The water spirits – nymphs, undines, also called nixies – dwell in everything connected to the element of water. The river Neckar in Germany, for instance is named after a water-being called *Necker*. Water spirits are not only active in moving water, but also in mist rising from a field or dew descending on grass. But they are particularly at home where water moves strongly, for instance in the surf.

In his karma lectures Rudolf Steiner described a place where there is an extraordinary interplay between waves, light, mist and air.[1] On a promontory in Cornwall lies Tintagel castle, which belonged to King Arthur. Here, where the waves are in constant motion and the elements of light, air and mist are unceasing activity, nymphs are particularly active in their play with sylphs, the spirits of the air. The interplay between water, air and light made a deep impression on the knights of King Arthur who still posessed the old clairvoyance. Rudolf Steiner recounted how one of the twelve Arthurian knights, who had immersed himself deeply in this play of the elements, came back in a next life with the ability to paint the elements. This was the Swiss painter Arnold Böcklin (1827–1901), famous for his seascapes, where he depicts not only the play of the elements, but also the beings hidden behind them. He painted magnificent seascapes with all kinds of water spirits. What he absorbed in one life as deep impressions of nature, becomes an artistic capacity in a next life.

The spirits of the air or elves are at home in the element of air and wind. When the corn stalks sway, when the willow catkins gently sway to and fro, spreading their pollen, when moonlight and mist dance their slow and mysterious dance, the elves are in their element.

German mythology distinguishes light-elves and dark-elves or gnomes. They are ruled by Frey (in Norse mythology), Oberon (France) or Alberich *(Nibelungenlied)*. Mother Holle (Holda) was often venerated as a goddess of the air. Many peoples know the light elves under different names: the faeries in Ireland, *ellefolk* in Denmark, *foletti* in Italy or *feen* in Germany.

The elves were not only known as the invisible helpers of human beings. Some elves confuse human beings and lure them into their world, as in the Erlkönig, and strive to possess them. 'Nightmare' derives from the Old English *mare*, an evil spirit or goblin who rides on someone when they are asleep. The word 'panic' is also derived from the name of a nature spirit, Pan, the god of the *paniskoi,* the elves of the woods. These names suggest that nature spirits can work on our soul life, and that they can deeply influence our moods, especially when we are not wakeful enough. That is not only true for elves, but for all kinds of nature spirits. A toddler, told off by his parents for having a tantrum, once protested: 'That was not me, it was the angry gnome who did it!'

Finally there are the fire spirits, the salamanders, named not after the little amphibian creatures, but their name derived from the Greek word *saleuio,* which means 'swaying to and fro.' Clairvoyant vision always perceives the fire salamanders in a surging, heaving motion. When a fire flares up they become immense, when a fire dies down they step back into their invisibile element. Fire spirits do not only work in actual fire, but everywhere where processes of warmth occur in nature, for example when a flower comes into contact with the insect world, or when plants blossom and bear fruit in the warmth of the sun.

Because plants are formed by all the elements together, the elemental beings are continually dependent on each other when working on them. Four groups of nature beings are active when a single plant germinates, flowers and bears fruit. To form the roots and then push the plant up from the earth, the gnomes are needed. They push the earthly substance away from themselves. Their movement gives the plant the capacity to form roots and to push itself up from the earth. In the sap streaming through leaves and stalk, the water spirits, the nymphs are active. They create the play of lines and to a certain extent the colours of the leaves. Where light and air meet the plant, where the chemical processes of photosynthesis take place, the elves are at work. Finally, the fire spirits or salamanders cause warmth to find a point of engagement and that the flower can form seed and fruit.

So far it seems reasonably clear: four elements, four groups of beings each with their own task, co-operating, for instance to make plant-life possible. However, reality is far more complicated. On the one hand, nature beings are connected to the Christ. Hildegard von Bingen, the mystic from the Middle Ages, said that every year anew, in the forty days between Easter and Ascension, Christ penetrates the realm of the four elements.

There are similar themes in the Act of Consecration, where during these forty days it speaks of the activity of Christ in the elements. Resurrection forces shine through the earth, air, light and the fire of the sun. The activity of the Resurrection forces can be perceived primarily in nature. But this activity is not outwardly visible, it is hidden under the surface of the visible world. This force is present in a latent way and can only be perceived in exceptional situations. I will return to this at the end of the chapter. The four groups of elemental beings lead their own separate lives, and they may join forces with each other, but they are also in the hands of the Risen One, and are penetrated by his force every year anew.

However, reality is even more complicated. If this were all, there would nothing left for us to do. The future would be clear: we would only have to wait for the New Jerusalem. That is not the case. The other aspect of reality is that the elements, the nature beings, are dependent on the human being. Hildegard von Bingen reminds us of the task given us at the beginning of Genesis: taking on the stewardship of the earth. Conversely she says: If you look at the secret life of the elements, you realize they were created to serve the human being. Everything has been entrusted to the human being, everything is aimed at him.

Hildegard uses a powerful image for this. The human being has an enormous net in his hands in which he holds all creatures. Every agitation causes the whole of creation to be moved too. The human being holds the net of nature in his hands. She writes: 'Everything emanating from human beings is drunk in by the elements. They complain about human beings going round and round as if in a mill, with their unjust works.' Not only does the human being disturb the elemental world, he also causes the elementals to work in his service as slaves. As a millstone turning round without free will, so the elemental beings serve as slaves, ever since the Fall.

In Hildegard's image (Figure 11) we see the firmament with the

Figure 11. The Fall. Miniature from Hildegard von Bingen, *Scivias*.

stars and luminaries. On the lower part, representing the earth, we see the head of a dragon, which, in his fall, drags down a group of stars with his tongue. Or is it the human being who brings down these stars by his fall? Hildegard von Bingen pictured the human being so that his head and hands are devoured by the dark realm of the earth, where the fires of passion burn.

Anthroposophy speaks of the Fall not as a one-off event. One of the effects of the Fall is that thinking is denaturalized. Before the Fall human thinking was 'intelligence' in the original sense of the word. In the Middle Ages 'intelligences' denoted the hierachies. Hildegard von Bingen uses a very drastic comparison to illustrate how the human being corrupts creation in the continuing Fall: we may compare what happens there with a human being over-eating. The moment we over-eat, our digestion protests. The same happens when we 'transgress' our original task: nature rebels and bursts her banks. Since the Fall, nature beings are enthralled, bewitched. Only the human being can free them by conquering his own egoism. We human beings are the decisive factor determining whether the elemental beings remain bewitched or will be liberated. They either find their way to their rightful lord and master, the Lord of the Elements, or, through our egoism, they will become slaves of the lord of this world.

One of Grimm's fairytales gives a forceful picture of how the human being can unleash destructive forces in the elements.

## The Fisherman and his Wife

Once upon a time there was a fisherman who lived with his wife in a pigsty by the sea. Everyday the fisherman went out fishing, and he fished and he fished.

One day he was sitting by his rod and kept looking at the clear water, and he looked and he looked. Suddenly his line went down, deep down, and when he drew it up again, he landed a large flounder.

The flounder said to him, 'Listen, fisherman, I pray you, let me live, I am not a real flounder, I am an enchanted prince. What good would it do you to kill me? I would not taste good at all – throw me back into the water and let me go.'

'Well,' said the man, 'no need to waste so many words, a flounder which can speak, I would let go anyway.' With these words he threw the flounder back into the clear water and it swam down to the bottom, leaving a long streak of blood behind. The fisherman got up and went back to his wife in the pigsty.

'Husband,' said the woman, 'haven't you caught anything?'

'No,' said the man, 'I caught a flounder who said he was an enchanted prince, so I let him go again.'

'And you didn't even make a wish?' said the wife.

'No,' said the man, 'what should I have wished?'

'Ah,' said the wife, 'isn't it horrible to live in a pigsty all the time? It is filthy and smelly: couldn't you have asked for a little hut? Go back again and call him, and tell him we want a little hut, he will certainly give us that.'

'Ah,' said the man, 'why should I go there again?'

'Well,' said the wife, 'you caught him and let him go again, he is bound to do it. Go there at once.'

The man did not feel like it at all, but he did not want to argue with his wife, and so he went back to the sea.

When he got there, the sea was all green and yellow and not clear at all. He stood before it and said:

'Flounder, flounder in the sea,

Come, I pray, come back to me.

My good wife Ilsebil

Wills not what I'd have her will.'

The flounder appeared and said: 'Well, what is it that she wants?'

'Ah,' said the man, 'my wife said that as I caught you I should have made a wish. She does not want to live in a pigsty anymore and wants a little hut.'

'Go back,' said the flounder, 'she has it already.'

The man went back and instead of the pigsty he found a little hut, with his wife sitting before it on a bench. She took him by the hand and said: 'Come and have a look inside, isn't this much better?'

They went into the hut and there was a little hallway and a cosy parlour and a bedroom.

But that was not the end of it. After a few weeks the woman wanted a castle instead of a hut. And even when that wish is granted there is no end to her desires.

Awaking for the first time in her castle, the wife looked out of the window and saw the beautiful land. The man was still streching himself so she prodded his side with her elbow and said, 'Husband, get up and have a look out of the window. Couldn't we become king over all those lands? Go to the flounder, we want to be king.'

'Ah, wife,' said the man, 'why should we be king. I don't want to be king.'

'Well,' said the wife, 'You may not want to be king, but I do. Go to the flounder, I must be king.'

'Ah, wife,' said the man, 'why do you want to be king? I do not want to ask him.'

'Why not?' said the wife, 'go immediately, I must be king.'

So the man went back to the sea, deeply saddened that his wife wanted to become king. It is not right, the man thought. He did not want to go, but he went in spite of himself. And when he got to the sea it was all grey-black and the water bubbled up and smelled horribly. He stood before it and said:

'Flounder, flounder in the sea,

Come, I pray, come back to me.

My good wife Ilsebil

Wills not what I'd have her will.'

'Well, what does she want?' asked the flounder. 'Ah,' said the man, 'she wants to be king. 'Go,' said the flounder, 'she is king already.'

It goes from bad to worse. Although the Fisherman is content with what they have, his wife Ilsebil wants ever more: from king to emperor, from emperor to pope. With every wish that is granted nature turns more threatening and ominous.

A ferocious wind blew over the land and the clouds chased through the sky and it was dark as night. Leaves were blown from the trees and the water seethed as if it were boiling, and beat up against the shore, and far off he saw ships being tossed by the high waves and firing guns in their sore need. There was only a little patch of blue in the middle of the sky, but at the side there was a red glow, as in a heavy thunderstorm. Terrified, he stood before the sea and said:

'Flounder, flounder in the sea,
Come, I pray, come back to me.
My good wife Ilsebil
Wills not what I'd have her will.'
'Well, what does she want?' asked the flounder.
'Ah,' the man said, ' she wants to be pope.'
'Go,' said the flounder, she is pope already,' said the flounder.

Finally, Ilsebil asks the impossible.

The man was sleeping very sound and deep, because he had walked long all day, but his wife did not sleep at all, and was tossing and turning all night long, thinking of what she might become and she could not think of anything anymore. When she saw the rosy sky at dawn, she sat up in bed and looked at it, and when she saw the sunrise through the window, she thought: 'Ha, couldn't I let the sun and the moon rise?'

'Husband,' she said, 'wake up, go to the flounder, I want to become like God.'

The man was half asleep, but he got such a shock that he fell out of bed. He thought he might have misheard, rubbed his eyes and said, 'Ah wife, what did you say?'

'Husband,' she said, 'if I cannot let the sun and he moon rise, and just have to look on as the sun and the moon rise, I will not be able to stand it, and I will not have peace, before I myself can let the sun and the moon rise.'

As she was speaking she looked at him in such a terrifying way that shivers ran down his spine. 'Go at once. I want to become like God.'

'Ah, wife,' said the man, falling down on his knees, 'that the flounder cannot do. He can make you emperor and pope, but not God, I beg you, come to your senses and please remain pope.'

She became incredibly angry, her hair flew wildly about her head, she tore open her bodice, kicked him, and shrieked: 'I cannot stand it any longer, go at once!'

He quickly put on his trousers and ran off like a madman. Outside the storm was howling so ferociously, it nearly blew him down. Houses and the trees toppled down, the mountains trembled, rocks tumbled into the sea, and the sky was pitch black and there was thunder and lightning, and there were enormous black waves on the

sea, as high as church spires and mountains, and all the waves had a
crest of white foam. The man shouted, but could no longer hear his
own words:

'Flounder, flounder in the sea,
Come, I pray, come back to me.
My good wife Ilsebil
Wills not what I'd have her will.'
'Well, what does she want?' asked the flounder.
'Ah,' said the man, 'she wants to become like unto God.'
'Go back to her,' said the flounder, 'she is back in the pigsty.'
And there they live to this day.

The name Ilsebil is derived from Jezebel, queen of king Ahab from
the Old Testament, who killed people with black magic. In Grimms
fairytale she is a *femme fatale* too, a woman driven by egoism and
desire, causing the elements to rebel. The sea of ether-forces, of
life forces, is muddied by human egoism. If we try to live into this
element, we realize that the first to suffer from this egoism is of course
the fish. Who is this fish, which can do so much?

It is not only by our actual deeds of egoism that we exploit nature,
but also through the moods and attitudes with which we approach
nature. The elemental beings go hungry. This begins with the distant
gaze with which we look at nature. It gets worse the moment a human
being begins to think untruthfully; thinks, speaks or lives out lies.
How much of the world around us does not consist of lies brought
into existence? But the elemental world is already in uproar the
moment an untruth is just thought. An untruthful thought causes an
uproar in the spiritual world. We come across this idea not only in
anthroposophy, but even in some everyday jokes.

When a visitor was shown around heaven by Saint Peter, he heard
bells ringing and asked, 'What does that mean?'

Peter answered, 'They sound when there is a lie on earth.'

Suddenly there is such a deafening roar of bells that the visitor had
to cover his ears. He asked, 'What does it mean now?'

Peter looked at the heavenly clock and said: 'It is that time again;
another tabloid is being printed.'

We like to think our thoughts and words are private, but they are not. The moment we think, we create an actual reality in the spiritual world. Psychologists and psychiatrists acknowledge that thinking too many negative thoughts can make you ill. We are only half-conscious of what the effects of such thoughts are on our environment.

Even in seemingly pristine nature, there are hidden, destructive forces. Dagny Wegener wrote a book about encounters with people who had died and with spiritual beings.[2] With the clairvoyant faculties that had awoken in her in the course of her life, she perceived how in nature too there are destructive beings at work. During a stay in Norway, her husband on impulse decided to spend another night in the place where they were staying, even though they were ready to move on to their next destination. She was slightly upset by his sudden impulse, but gave in.

The next day, when they reached the hotel they had intended to travel to, it was in ashes, totally burned down during the previous night. The guests had tried to save themselves by jumping out of windows, but these looked out over a deep precipice. Dagny Wegener said to a Norwegian man.

'It must have been terrible last night. I bet the trolls did it.'

The man looked at me as only Norwegians can, penetrating and observant. 'Yes,' he said, 'but there are not many people nowadays who know that. This is the third time the trolls have let the hotel burn down.'

When I returned to the little cabin we had found for that night, my husband was asleep. I sat down on my bed and suddenly there were two huge trolls standing before me. They seemed bigger than the whole room. Their heads were small and kept moving restlessly from side to side. Until then I had only ever seen people of flesh and blood. These figures looked entirely different. They suddenly stood there in the room, wobbling their heads, looking at me cunningly and slightly insolently with their their widely spaced eyes. Their heads seemed covered in twigs and moss, hiding their low foreheads.

I said to the trolls: 'Can't you keep your heads still? Don't you know what pity is? Don't you want people to enjoy the beauty of your land?'

They kept moving their heads, but did not say a word.

'I would like to help you,' I said. 'One way or another, you must be released. I will pray for you.'

It was as if they held their heads still for a few seconds, but when I prayed the Lord's Prayer for them, they suddenly escaped from my gaze.'

What can we do for them? How can we 'disenchant' them? Can we release, redeem them? Dagny Wegener followed her spontaneous impulse and said the Lord's Prayer.

Whether we want to or not, every human being continually interacts with elemental beings. The moment I look around me, breathe, think, speak a word, or perform an action, they are there and we work with them or against them.

Rudolf Steiner describes how, when we perceive something, uninterrupted streams of elemental beings penetrate us. We cannot see anything without these elemental beings connecting themselves to us. In the moment of perception they connect to us and they remain connected until we die. We can release these elemental beings, free them, disenchant them, or we can ban them more permanently into this enchantment. If we free them they return to the spiritual world they came from when we die. Then, in our next life, we do not have to take them with us into enchantment. We do not have to banish them into the material world. However, if we take elemental beings into ourselves without transforming them, then on our return to earth they must be chained to matter once more. Thus we play a part in either spiritualizing the earth, or assisting in its further decay.

Rudolf Steiner described four different ways in which elemental beings can be freed. If we study this, we will notice this world is actually quite close. We often think we have to see and experience all kinds of extraordinary things to be able to free these beings, but actually we can already accomplish something with our every word, deed, and thought. When human beings look at something with love, they take an elemental being into themselves and begin the process of release.

If someone does not just look coldly at a natural phenomenon, but thinks about it, and senses something of its beauty and spiritualizes their impression, then by their own spiritual process, they free the elemental being which penetrates them from the outer world. In this way we can either imprison the beings which are enchanted into the elements, without transforming them, or we can liberate them by spiritualizing ourselves. The first method of freeing elemental beings is when human beings spiritualizes themselves, nature can be spiritualized.

A second path is formed when people works diligently, continually being active, developing a mobile thought-life, and by working industriously. We can do this simply by cleaning and de-cluttering our home. As a result of our diligence certain groups of elemental beings become active too, instead of remaining slow and lazy.

The third thing we can do is related to feelings of contentment. Through a mood of inner balance and contentment, the human being can liberate certain elemental beings. Rudolf Steiner said, 'The influence of a human being through his moods, streams out in all directions into the world of the spirit.'

And finally he described a way of releasing elemental beings by intensely experiencing the Christian cycle of the year. This is not a matter of subjective moods, but of experiencing the Christian festivals throughout the year. Christianity must connect itself with nature through our religious moods. In short, in everything we think, feel and will, we are co-responsible for the life of nature beings.[3]

This appeal is expressed powerfully in a sentence of the burial ritual of the Christian Community: 'Bethink, O man, that you are beholden to the Spirit for all that you do in thought, in word and in deed.'

Finally I would like to describe some experiences illustrating how a breakthrough to spiritual reality can come about.

A widow once told me that after the death of her husband she felt a strong desire to seek the spiritual in herself. 'In this mood, searching for the eternal in myself, I saw myself descend into a deep well. The deeper I went, the more I had to let go of myself. Finally I stood at the bottom of this well; I was destitute. But there, at the bottom of this pit, I felt a mantle of love around me. I think that must have been Christ.'

In gradually conquering our inborn egoism we can free not just ourselves, but also the earth that was entrusted to us. In this emptying process, letting go of everything you are and possess, it is possible to find the Lord of the Elements.

Earlier on in this chapter I mentioned that the power of the Resurrection lies under the surface of the visible world – and that only in very special circumstances something of this power comes to appearance. In exceptional cases older people may remember how they beheld nature as a child. Some people can have indelible impressions, as Thomas Traherne (1636–74), who could give a detailed description in his autobiographical poem 'Dumbness'

> For nothing spoke to me but the fair face
> Of Heaven and Earth, before myself could speak,
> ... It was with clearer eyes
> To see all creatures full of Deities;
> ... No ear
> But eyes themselves were all the hearers there,
> And every stone, and every star a tongue,
> And every gale of wind a curious song.
> The Heavens were an oracle, and spake
> Divinity: the Earth did undertake
> The office of a priest; and I being dumb
> (Nothing besides was dumb), all things did come
> With voices and instructions; but when I
> Had gained a tongue, their power began to die.

When the mystic Jakob Böhme (1575–1624) was 25, he was overwhelmed by an experience of nature which suddenly allowed him to see behind the scenes. Looking at a pewter vase he entered into an extraordinary mood of soul, walked into nature and was able to see 'into the heart and the inner being of reality.' Although he remained silent about these experiences, he later expressed something of this in his famous work *Aurora: Morgenröte im Anfang*.

# Intermezzo: Natural Disasters

## Looking with Different Eyes

Studying the elements and elemental beings the question naturally presents itself what happens when a natural disaster shakes the whole earth.

What kind of a shocking event was the tsunami that left a trail of devastation across South-East Asia and Indonesia in December 2004? You wonder what happens during a disaster of such magnitude. What happens not only to the people, for whom we are of course concerned in the first place, but also to the earth, when it is in such turmoil?

One had the impression that the whole world was out of kilter through the colossal events during this seaquake. Scientists found irregularities in the rotation of the earth shortly afterwards. It was as if the whole organism of the earth had been shaken by the event. The earth faltered. At the same time biologists asked how it was that sea mammals such as whales and dolphins had survived this disaster. But also many mammals on land. A nature reserve, Yala on Sri Lanka, looked like a war zone. Several hundred people died here, but the mammals of the reserve had somehow all been spared. Somehow they had the ability to save themselves.

Shortly after the tsunami, a Dutch professor of biology was quite sceptical in an interview. A journalist asked how it was that animals often became restless just before an earthquake. The professor answered: 'We can only explain that psychologically. A disaster happens and afterwards we think our dog has barked a bit more than usual. I could say I drank a glass of wine before an earthquake, but that does not mean anything. These stories are not significant. Of course scientists should never say never, but we need a healthy dose of common sense.' Those were the comments of this respected biology professor.

However, if we can believe what the newspapers said, it was not just an insignificant quirk, it was extraordinary that large numbers of animals had been able to save themselves. How do mammals manage to react in this way? How do they 'know' about the coming catastrophy? There were similar phenomena during many other natural disasters.

A student of theology once told me about an incident he had witnessed in Rumania. He was on the central square of a town which had a large pond in the middle. Suddenly large numbers of people rushed towards this pond to watch a breath-taking spectacle. Countless fish were jumping up from the water. A few minutes later the town was in ruins, hit by one of the worst earthquakes in Romania. What do animals perceive on such occasions?

Rudolf Steiner, who schooled his own clairvoyance, tells us that animals not only have the physical capacity to become aware of certain things, but also a spiritual capacity. They become spiritually *aware* of certain things, it might go too far to say they spiritually perceive. In one of his lectures Rudolf Steiner explains the well known phenomenon of horses being mesmerized by a shadow, as if seeing something in it.[1] He describes how the animal becomes aware of the spiritual which is connected to this shadow. One could say that animals are by nature clairvoyant. And one could go further and ask, what is to be seen there? What happens in the ether world just before a natural disaster?

We may recognize this phenomenon in a short description of the prelude to a natural disaster. It was written by Annie Gerding, a Dutch lady who was naturally clairvoyant since childhood, and perceived elemental beings in nature. She describes how at one time she noticed great turmoil in the world of nature spirits. A group of kobolds left the woodshed in her garden and went out through the gate as if wanting to cross the road.

> Suddenly they were gone. Nowhere to be seen. This is one of
> their favourite tricks, when they want to confuse you. Now
> you see them, now you don't. You begin to doubt yourself

and that is what they want. I waited a while to see if they might come back. When they didn't, I just walked on. To my great surprise I saw them again a little later ... but they had hardly gone through the gate ... and they vanished again. They repeated their trick at least three times. It was clear they came from the direction of the woodshed. From the way they behaved I concluded they wanted to tell me something. What was it? I had no real contact with these kobolds, so I could only guess ... Coming home I told my housemates that five kobolds had tried to draw my attention to something to do with the woodshed. As usual nobody believed me.'

So the group of kobolds fled the place where they lived, though nature spirits like to settle down in one place and stay there. In the nearby village several trees were blown down.

Very early next moring a great whirlwind struck, destroying our woodshed. The better part of the roof was blown away, the side was damaged too, exactly in the place where the kobolds had been. The kobolds had wanted to warn me.[2]

Before the actual physical events in nature, something happens already in the ether world. There is turmoil. Coming events cast their shadows ahead.

It was a great surprise when I read the following on nature beings, long before the tsunami in 2004 made its destructive appearance, 'In future there will be more water-related disasters. There will be many more huge waves, such as tsunami's: waves caused by earthquakes. There will be flooding.'[3]

Of course we must be very careful how to approach such statements. No one who is not a trained clairvoyant can verify the validity of such statements. But one can practice a certain impartiality, as the biology professor professed to do, but didn't: 'Never say never.' Or, to quote the physician Leendert Mees, 'Don't say no – just say oh!' You observe something, absorb it and wait to see if reality confirms your presumptions.

There are two potential dangers in such statements. The one is excluding certain possibilities beforehand. The other danger is

Figure 12. Annie Gerding, The woodshed and the whirlwind, 1977.

uncritically absorbing everything without placing anything over and against it. To come to a good judgment it is necessary to take a midway position between these two extremes. This middle position is clearly described by Rudolf Steiner in the *Philosophy of Freedom:* 'With our consciousness we must be able to take a step back from an idea; otherwise one can be enslaved by it.' In the twentieth century we have all too often seen human beings become possessed by certain ideas, without taking a step back from them. By allowing this distance you leave ideas and phenomena valid in themselves, and do not lose yourself in them. You remain inwardly free and sovereign face to face with phenomena and ideas.

## The work of Annie Gerding-Le Comte

Getting to know Annie Gerding gave me an chance to look over the shoulder, as it were, of someone familiar with nature spirits. After reading her book I visited her several times and we observed nature together. We talked and she showed me dozens of pictures she had made of nature beings. What impressed me most was the deep wonder with which this elderly lady (she was over eighty then) could look at apparently ordinary natural phenomena. For someone who can observe imaginatively, even the ordinary looks extra-ordinary.

Annie Gerding was born in Indonesia (then the Dutch East-Indies) in 1903. Since childhood she posessed clairvoyant faculties. She developed her talents in writing, drawing and painting. From the 1950s she was able to express her clairvoyant perceptions in words and images. She produced a whole book with text and watercolours recording her encounters with Yodokus, a kobold-like nature spirit, whom she knew for many years. This kobold appeared to her in countless different forms near Tongeren, a village in the Veluwe, Holland. The image we have of the little people is usually too static. In reality these beings appear before the clairvoyant gaze in many different colours and forms. This is shown quite clearly in the series of pictures Annie Gerding made of Yodokus – although she concluded that nature spirits are so changeable it is almost impossible to depict them properly. We have included a number of her drawings and watercolours here, some of which never published before. I will try to elucidate them here.

Figure 13. Annie Gerding, Yodokus by the meres of Tongeren.

In Figure 13 we see Yodokus by the meres on the heath near Tongeren. Annie Gerding asked the kobold to show her a little plant, the rare sundew. She thought it was extinct in this area, and the local forester had said so too. With the help of Yodokus, Annie Gerding managed to find this plant in this boggy area, which was not without its dangers. She described the quest as follows.

> We walked along a narrow path. I had looked here for sundew
> several times before. I knew the place like the back of my
> hand. But I kept following Yodokus, who walked ahead,
> turning round occasionally to see if I was still there.
> Kobolds can move very quickly. They hardly touch the
> ground when they walk, they just float, and never leave
> footsteps, not even in snow. Soon I felt the marshy ground
> moving beneath me at every step. At last I stood before some
> high heather bushes, wide-spreading rushes and other high
> grasses. The broad leaves of grass and rushes were quite sharp;

Figure 14. Annie Gerding, Yodokus standing by the sundew.

Figure 15. Annie Gerding, Yodokus in different guises, 1958.

you could easily cut yourself. Vegetation was so dense, it was hard to see the edge of the water. Just a few more steps and I risked getting stuck in the sticky mud.

Was Yodokus fooling me?

Did Yodokus actually exist? Was it all an illusion?

I stopped and looked around. Yodokus was nowhere to be seen. As usual he had disappeared into thin air. And there was no sundew to be seen anywhere. Of course not, they were right, it was all an illusion. A dreamworld I had created.

And then I heard quite clearly, 'You are standing on top of it!'

It seemed to come from a distance, but I heard it quite clearly. Was that Yodokus after all? At first I wanted to leave, disappointed and slightly ashamed. I could hardly believe I really was standing on top of the little plant. I carefully pushed through the high heather and rushes and gale, and took another

step to see better. There, on the spot where I had stood,
between the dark-green moss, grew a whole circle of sundew, in
bloom too! It took my breath away. Had Yodokus really shown
me the sundew or was it pure coincidence? We human beings
never cease to doubt. I dug up one of the sundew plants to take
it home as proof, meaning to put it back later.[4]

Animals can usually recognize different nature beings, and will
react to their presence. When Yodokus does a little dance for the
swans, you can tell by their behaviour, there is some interaction.

In one watercolour Annie Gerding portrayed Yodokus in very
different forms and colours (Figure 15). When he appears clad in
black he imitates the colour of a bat. Standing before a dahlia he
turns orange! And from time to time he disguises himself as a squirrel,
imagining himself with a big squirrel tail.

When Yodokus is angry he changes colour and puffs himself up
like a frog: 'He changed colour from blue to purple, to pink and green
– and finally he looked like a frightening, fat little monster, pale and
indeterminate in colour. He really reminded me of a toad now, an
animal he loathes.'[5]

Figure 16. Annie Gerding, Yodokus with tail and being angry, with a different colour on
his stomach, August 1958.

Figure 17. Annie Gerding, Gnome making himself visible, November 1979.

Figure 18. Annie Gerding, Yodokus and swans.

In a watercolour she tried to portray the transition to an imaginative appearance (Figure 17). She also describes such transitions in reverse:

> Yodokus came closer, fixed me with his stare, and his golden yellow suit slowly began to change colour, like the skin of a chameleon. He became greenish-yellow, brownish-yellow, and finally transparent like jelly. I could just vaguely see the contours of the kobold, but finally he dissolved altogether.

In summary, nature spirits have the capacity to a certain extent to appear and also to withdraw into invisibility.

The attributes too, with which some gnomes are portrayed, are just the imaginative pictures they clothe themselves in. Earlier we described kobolds leaving a woodshed the day before a whirlwind on the Veluwe. They imagined they brought tools to safety from the shed – it was of course just that, an imagination!

Nature beings exist in a world where past and future are active in the present. This realm of the life, or ether forces can be experienced

Figure 19. Annie Gerding, Kobolds at a deserted apiary.

by humans, for example in the panorama of a near-death experience where in a very short span of time the whole past and even future events may be present.

So the little folk are able to foresee future events: a day before the whirlwind flattened their abode, the kobolds left their familiar shed.

But nature spirits do not let themselves be chased away easily from their spot. Even when elements of the visible world they were familiar with have long since disappeared, they can keep their living memories of this past. Thus Annie Gerding saw a group of kobolds by a deserted apiary who kept the memory of the bees alive. In their consciousness the past was alive in the present.

> For years the mood of the industrious bees had worked
> in on them. They felt they had become part of the apiary.
> They belonged to it, worked along with it, or at least so they
> imagined. They kept imagining the bees flying to and fro from
> the hives so strongly that they hardly missed the bees when
> they and their hives had gone.
>
> Every spring the old apiary by the orchard manifested itself
> through the kobolds. There they sat, quite cosily, the five little
> fellows, between the grass and the wildflowers, leading their
> imaginative little lives. In reality there was nothing left of the
> apiary save a few poles and some bits of old thatch from the
> roof. The orchard disappeared, the fruit trees were cut down,
> a little bungalow was built instead with a lawn and herbacious
> border. Even so it took quite a while before they could banish
> their original abode from their thoughts and give it up.
>
> The image became ever more vague and dim. Sometimes
> they thought of just one single hive, which would hang eerily
> in the void. Or they'd suddenly remember a few odd planks
> with a messy little blackbird's nest on top ... The image of
> the apiary became ever more like and incomplete puzzle, with
> more and more pieces missing. Finally they gave up altogether.
>
> I don't know where the five kobolds went. One day they
> just were not there anymore. They could not live so close to
> the bungalow, they could not experience their dreams any
> longer and let their imagination roam freely. Dreams of bees
> and flowers and an old apple tree in blossom ...

Wherever the world of the elements is around us, nature beings play a part. Like nature, these beings abhor a vacuum. If they have to leave their rightful place, this spot is filled with other beings. Rudolf Steiner summed up this law succinctly as:

Figure 20. Annie Gerding, Field with elves, Nunspeet 1974.


Spirit is never without matter,
Matter is never without spirit.[6]

The air is usually filled with graciously dancing elves. In an endless procession they float through their element, barely touching the earth. Annie Gerding saw a swarm of elves in a place where nature was visibly changing.

They seemed vague, transparent, spectral figures. They did not dance, did not behave as usual: playfully or overconfident. They floated around me and drew me along as it were! Could it be that without knowing it I had strayed into an elfin procession? Departing elves? They floated ahead of me, circled around me, floated along with me, along the cart track to the

spot where I left the forest behind. Suddenly they vanished, as
a wisp of mist might suddenly dissolve.

Where do they go to? Where do they disappear to, I have no
idea!'

The atmosphere of a certain place can be filled with nature beings
intent on creating chaos. In a house with a disturbed atmosphere,
Annie Gerding saw a strange being jumping and bouncing through
space, seizing every opportunity to tease.

It whizzed around like a fire cracker and suddenly disappeared
again. It was something dark. You might think it was a mouse
gone beserk. But a mouse does not usually jump around
like that. A mouse tries to avoid all danger and draw as little
attention as possible: its survival depends on it. This creature,
little more than a shadow, skipped around cheekily giving
the impression it *did* want to be noticed. It tried to attract
attention even though it was barely visible.

Figure 21. Annie Gerding, Mouse little folk. 1979.

Figure 22. Annie Gerding, Transparent stone with gnomes, 1979.

To the clairvoyant gaze, a large rock is a world full of beings, crowded into matter (Figure 22). These are the earth spirits in their fantastic variety.

From the same little mere near Tongeren where Annie Gerding met Yodokus, three strange water nymphs suddenly appeared.

> They were covered in veils and long robes swirling round them. The robes seemed made of thousands of strips and streaks of light, transparent, phosphorescent. They themselves seemed made of light-filled streaks of the most beautiful shades of yellow and green. They seemed wholly insubstantial, just bundles of vibrating colours, lighting up. Everything about them was movement, like rippling water. They were transparent like coloured glass, and the colours kept changing. They spread a haze of whitish-green light about them. It surrounded them so that it looked as though a spotlight lit them up from deep under the water!
>
> The most amazing thing about them was that they had triangular heads and angular bodies, as Picasso might paint a woman! They had long, spindly arms. They were certainly not sweet and beautiful as elves sometimes are. Their movements were graceful and fascinating. They swayed slowly over the water and reminded me of waterplants floating along with the tide. On the crown of their peculiarly formed heads was a sort of mitre, like a bishop's mitre. Was it the shape of that ancient symbol, a fish's head? They were the most peculiar beings I had ever seen.

The salamander, the fire spirit, is at home in that most mobile, volatile element, fire:

> He is hard to describe. He had a mobile little face and his expression kept changing. He wore a pointy hat, with playful little flames darting from its sides. His feet were small and pointy, he had pointy elfin ears and quite a pronounced nose, as most of these creatures have.
>
> As far as I could see his eyes were strangely radiant, sapphire-blue with green flashes; they seemed like precious

Figure 23. Annie Gerding, Water-nymphs, Tongeren.

Figure 24. Annie Gerding, Fire spirit.

stones reflecting the light. They were hard, glistening eyes,
frightening by their fierceness and their fixed gaze. You could
feel them, rather than discern them clearly.

He seemed to be enjoying himself there, in the middle of
the fire. Sometimes he dissolved into his surroundings and
vanished, at other times he'd blossom up like some fiery flower
or a dancing flame, transparent as glass, but visible through his
colours: orange, yellowish-green and fiery-red.

It was as if he radiated these colours. They surrounded
him like an aura. Sometimes he seemed caught in a radiating
cocoon.

Figure 25. Geoffrey Hodson, Lord of the tree ferns.

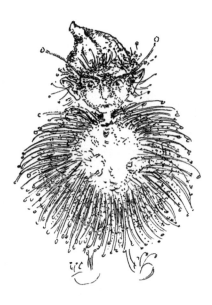

Figure 26. Annie Gerding, The very small elf of a linden (lime) tree, 1978.

Apart from the four elements, each of which is connected with a group of beings, there are countless nature beings connected to specific plants and trees. Something of the characteristics of that tree or plant can be recognized in their shape.

The devas, who guide species of plants and trees, form lines and patterns too, which are reproduced in the forms of leaves and stems. In his book *The Kingdom of Gods,* Geoffrey Hodson portrayed different devas, which form the foundation of certain species of plant and tree. Thus the fern is inspired by a deva who creates the spiral form of its unfurling leaves (Figure 25). But nature beings looking after an individual tree or plant, also form in the world of life forces what later manifests itself in the physical. Long before a magnolia opens its flowers, the buds of the shrub are surrounded by beings creating the imaginations of the flowers. These nature beings are already actively imagining in autumn: future events casting their shadows ahead.

In lime trees live little beings which bring into appearance something of the future flowers with their remarkably shaped stamens.

In the interplay between nature beings there is a harmony making larger patterns visible. All beings nurturing and maintaining nature are guided by hierarchical beings, who give them a meaningful place

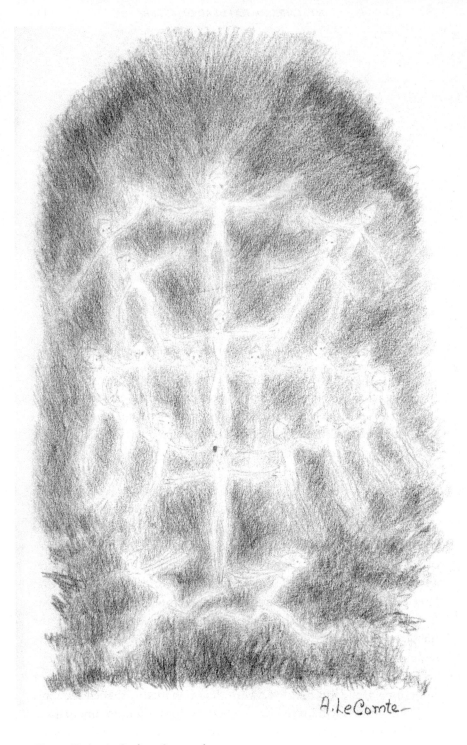

Figure 27. Annie Gerding, Summerdance.

in the whole. The drawing 'Summerdance' (Figure 27) shows how nature beings combine into a pattern where they can serve a greater whole.

Anyone looking at nature with different eyes can have the most extraordinary experiences observing even the simplest plants. It is an art, even for a schooled clairvoyant, to remain firm and steadfast amidst the endless variety of forms and beings, while being looked and stared at from all directions. Anyone entering this realm without the right preparation runs the risk of losing themselves in this world.

# 12 Elemental Beings in Art and Technology

American playwright Thornton Wilder (1897–1975) uses a very special expression to indicate that in art and technology we are working on a new creation. One of his works is called *The Eighth Day*. The seven days of creation are behind us. We human beings stand at the beginning of the eighth day, to bring a new creation into being by our own deeds. This creation does not – like Genesis – happen above or outside us, it has to do with ourselves.

In Jewish tradition too, the human being is destined to become co-creator. This task does not commence at the beginning of the eighth day of creation, but immediately. The founder of Hasidic Judaism, Rabbi Ba'al Shem Tov (1700–1760) once said,

> What was God thinking of when he said, 'Let us make human beings in our image and likeness?' Who was he addressing? He was talking to us. You and me, let us make the human being together, for without your help I cannot make you into a true human being.

From the very beginning, the creation of the human being is an appeal, 'Let us make human beings in our image and likeness.' In the Hasidic view the word 'us' indicates not only God, but also the human being.

It can sometimes seem as if creation in its natural state is perfect. Nevertheless there is something missing in the edifice of creation if we do not transform its building blocks into something new. Every tiny particle must be transformed. In a series of lectures, *The Temple Legend*, Rudolf Steiner speaks of the task to take every part of creation in hand:

We are now living in an epoch of evolution we may call the mineral epoch; and our task is to penetrate our mineral world through and through with our spirit. Please grasp fully what this signifies. You are building a house. You bring stones from a quarry. You cut them into shapes required for the house, and so on. What are you connecting this raw material to, obtained from the mineral kingdom? You are connecting raw material to human spirit. When you make a machine, you introduce your spirit into that machine. The actual machine does, of course, eventually break down and disintegrate. Not a trace of it will survive. But what you have done does not vanish without a trace, it passes into the very atoms. Every atom bears a trace of your spirit and will carry this trace with it. It is not a matter of indifference whether or not an atom has at some time been part of a machine. The atom itself has undergone change as a result of having once been in a machine, and this change you have wrought in the atom will never be lost to it.[1]

Some months later he continued this train of thought, opening up a perspective on a far and distant future:

The whole earth must be transformed into a work of art. That is the task of the human being for the future. As long as there is even one single atom left which human beings have not transformed with their forces, our task on earth has not been fulfilled. It is our task to transform dead physical matter into a great work of art. That is the reason why there have been works of art on earth, since long before Egyptian times. If you follow this thought through you will understand that our present time has the task to spiritualize the whole of mineral nature.[2]

In a distant future, when we have transformed the physical earth into a work of art, it will not be dead matter which we have to transform, but the realm of plants. In a distant future the human being will have to transform living nature into something higher too. At the end of this long path of the transformation of the earth, there will be a parting of the ways: one world will spiritualize itself, and another world of dead, untransformed matter will remain behind, as ash remains after a fire.

On the way to that far-off future we were given the capacities to build further on the foundations of creation by means of art and technology. Usually, when we think about art and technology, we obviously think of great artists and inventors. But even more important is for us to concentrate on what we can accomplish ourselves. Whether we want to or not, every human being creates a new, different world in his own environment, just by taking hold of matter. Even if only creating art and technology 'second hand' as it were, we are doing the same. The moment we absorb a work of art, listen to a composition, use technology, yes, even the moment we just become conscious of art and technology, we become co-workers in the transformation of the earth. It is not *what* that is decisive, but *how*. It is not terribly important what machine we use, what composition we listen to, but it is important how we look, how we listen, how we take hold of our machines and tools.

Having said that, it does not cheer you up to hear and read about what is summoned up in the world of technology. What does a trained clairvoyant see when he looks at a big industrial city? Rudolf Steiner describes the following:

> An industrial town is an ideal abode for all demons that want
> to make the human being forget he had a pre-birth existence
> in the spirit.[3]

We are up to our neck in a world of elemental beings who are in the service of certain opposition forces. What these beings want most of all is to make us forget we have a spiritual descent. Looking around in a big city, a crowded train, or at work, how many people do you see who are in a kind of cocoon? We are so absorbed in this hectic world we live in, that we forget where we come from, who we are, and where we are going. That does not mean avoiding all technology. The important thing is not that these demons – as Rudolf Steiner sometimes calls elemental beings in the service of Ahriman – are present everywhere, what matters is how we look at this world, how we think about it, how we deal with it. I have the feeling we can limit the damage caused by technology in this way. That gives us a key how to hold on to ourselves in this realm. We must be conscious of the fact that our machines are abodes for demons. We must also know how we can develop resistance against these demons. That alone will allow us to keep upright in this world, by recognizing these forces. Ahriman's activity becomes harmful to the degree we remain unconscious, by not knowing anything about him, or not wanting to know anything about him.

The key for dealing with this world is our consciousness of the forces that are active there. That is a task which will occupy us for centuries to come, until we see through and recognize the world of technology. For who really knows how the machines he uses work? Who is able to see behind the technology of a machine not only the way it works (a key in itself) but even more importantly the beings working in it? That is a huge task. In technical invention it is usually not logical or spiritual thinking that is decisive, but quite other forces. Often the semi-conscious and even the unconscious realms give clues to the right actions for making a certain discovery. Countless inventions throughout history came about through semi-conscious and unconscious promptings.

A well-known example is the invention of the sewing machine. For years the inventor had tried to find a method for mechanically threading the yarn through the cloth with a needle. Nothing seemed to work. When he was about to give up, he had the following dream: he saw a long row of men on horseback, clad in heavy armour and armed with long, sharp lances resting in their stirrups. Unusually, these lances very clearly had a hole near the point. When he woke up, the inventor knew he had the solution. Unlike in a normal needle, the needle for a sewing machine had to have a hole near the tip. Certain inventions are 'waiting to happen,' waiting for people with the intuitive and intellectual capacities to realize them.

The talents required for art and certain skills are formed in pre-birth existence. Just before birth, the elemental beings working in the realm of art and technology bestow special faculties in this field to an incarnating soul. Although these intuitive, semi-conscious capacities play a necessary part in creating and maintaining technology (someone has a 'feeling' for it), it is our task to gradually penetrate this area with our consciousness. Rudolf Steiner summed up this task succinctly: 'Anything we do not understand and master, will sooner or later turn against us.'

Where do we find elemental beings in our own environment that are connected to art and technology? We can begin at home, or in our workplace. These offer many opportunities for practising the ideas mentioned above. At home and in our workplace there are elemental beings of art and technology everywhere. You may encounter very little nature, but you are surrounded by a world of art, craft and technology.

At home there are countless opportunities to either cultivate the world or to leave it to its own devices. How do we deal with all the news and messages being delivered into our living room by television or computer. The misery of a whole evening of television can almost make us ill. Especially if we do not process it in some way. If we leave our television or radio on the whole day long, we cannot consciously absorb all this information. There is an overload, missing its target. That does not mean we should close ourselves off from those media. The question is, can I still absorb it all consciously, or does it bounce off? Am I so vulnerable and open that it rushes through me, am I overwhelmed by it? Or do I have the resilience to place my consciousness and insight over and against it?

So a right relation and interaction with technology requires consciousness of the way it works, but also self-knowledge: What can I absorb, what do I want to absorb, and what do I keep out? If we want to deal realistically with everything meeting us from our world, we must continually navigate between the extremes. Either we are overwhelmed by technology, the media, by everything that claims our attention – and we lose ourselves in an abundance – or we close ourselves off and lead a hermit's life. Sadly, these are not imaginary extremes, they occur quite often, because on the whole we are too unconscious of this aspect of our lives. We seldom realize we have a responsibility in this realm towards the invisible beings in our own environment.

Most countries and cultures acknowledged spirits of the home: the house gnomes, spiritual beings looking after the home as long as human beings looked after them. In ancient Rome for example, every home had an altar for the Lares, the gods of the home, where daily sacrifices were made. Besides gods of the home, protecting the family, there were spirits more like practical 'servants' of the house.

All these beings continually observe what human beings do in their environment, and especially *how* they do it. They give up on us when we neglect our surroundings. Even worse, in a chaotic household they can rebel. This was not only true in the past, you can still notice it today. In an unhappy home with many rows, the mood can feel so thick you could cut it with a knife. You can feel everything going wrong, going haywire. Nothing works as it should. As if even the everyday things refuse to function and don't to co-operate. Sometimes it feels as if the secretive world behind things announces, 'Do it yourself, we won't help anymore.' This is a realm which everybody can cultivate in their own surroundings. We can make a start with it even in the most modest of circumstances.

My first conscious experiences in this realm were in the vacations of our children. When I had the responsibility for the children and our house, I liked to 'keep house with Karlik,' as I called it. I began the day with quiet moments, where I tried to find an inner balance, to come to myself. If we begin things out of the peaceful mood arising from prayer or meditation, we do things differently. We can impart something of the peace we attained in meditation to our environment. We are all more or less aware of this. Just observe how people walk. Some people walk and every step is practically a kick. They go around the house kicking up dust and aggravation. Other people exude peace and quiet with every stap they take. We find this in the Bible, where it speaks of 'having shod your feet with the equipment of the gospel of peace,' and 'to guide our feet into the way of peace' (Eph.6:15, Luke 1:79).

Our feet can spread peace by the way we walk. Our gestures too can create disquiet and astral chaos, but can also spread peace and quiet. By taking our time and performing everyday tasks peacefully and with our whole attention, we can create a special mood. Our children clearly reacted to this. Young children are the best indicators for the atmosphere in a home. 'Keeping house with Karlik' in this way, we can impart the mood we create in meditation to our surroundings. Our surroundings actually begin with the air around us. That too is an endless realm for exploration. For instance, what happens to a space if we go around humming quietly? What happens if you sing a song, speak a poem or read a fairytale?

In *Karlik*, Ursula Burkhard sums it up in a single sentence. For years she lived with a nature being she called Karlik. They used to do the household chores together. Now and then he said to her: 'Take a chair, sit down and take delight in something!' That can often be enough. Don't hurry about like an ant, just sit down now and then and take delight in the small things of the day. Enjoy the sunrise when you open the curtains. Enjoy the smell of freshly baked bread. Take delight in birdsong. We can even enjoy that moment late at night when we have finished working and finally sit down, when the house is quiet and we let the events of the day sink in. Even in small events relating to technology we can practice this. Anyone who perceives the elemental beings behind technology sees an ugly, repulsive world – the important thing is how you deal with this. Ursula Burkhard wrote:

> For a while I made radio programmes for the blind for Radio Basle. The very first session I was quite frightened of the studio, which was accoustically dead. I felt totally deserted. After all, I could not see the engineers through the window of the recording booth, in the room next door. But I was not alone there. We are never alone by the way, we are always surrounded by invisible beings. There was a gnome-like being in the microphone, who looked at me in an insolent way. When I began to speak he grinned mockingly and confused me. Gnomes are wise, but the gnome-like machine creatures are too clever by half, cleverer than the cleverest gnome. They are so clever, they are chained by it in a pitiful way. 'Don't let him confuse you, speak in his direction.' I recognized my thought as wise advice coming from Karlik. After the recording, the director wanted to know how I was able to speak into the microphone, even though he had forgotten to point it out to me. That was a bit of a shock, because I was used to keeping my inner experiences quiet. 'It was ... it was ...' I stumbled, and was relieved when he answered himself: 'It was coincidence.'

What is the task of the elemental beings of technology? Rudolf Steiner says: The beings that are active in technology are the same beings that are active at birth and death. When a human being dies, when the physical sheath is broken down, destructive elemental beings are at work. These elemental beings are also connected to the world of technology. They are necessary; their task is to destroy the physical world. Steiner draws a shocking conclusion:

> By its very nature such a civilization [as ours] cannot serve
> the well-being of humanity in the physical world; it can only
> prove destructive to the human weal. The elemental spirits
> of birth and death are, of course, messengers of Ahriman.
> The iron necessity of world evolution forces the gods to use
> Ahriman's messengers to control birth and death ... But as
> civilization goes into its decline, from the fifth post-Atlantean
> period onwards, this element has to come in again, so that
> catastrophe may be brought about. Human beings must use
> these powers themselves. Ahriman's messengers are therefore
> an iron necessity; they have to bring about the destruction
> that will lead to the next step forward in civilization. This is
> a terrible truth, but it is so. And nothing will avail where this
> truth is concerned but to get to know it and to see it clearly.[4]

If we assume this point if view, we can see further, higher than the realm of the destructive forces.

The realm of technology is teeming with counterforces. Above these are the gods, spiritual beings guiding world evolution, who give these (Ahrimanic) forces the opportunity to connect themselves gradually with our outer culture, so that it can be destroyed in the end, in order that a new spiritual development may evolve from there. And above these hierarchies stands the 'Lord of the hierarchies' (the Old Testament calls him the Lord of Hosts), who carries creation. It is he who holds the angels of death, as the Apocalypse has it, 'ready for the hour, the day, the month, and the year' (Rev.9:15).

Someone with a sensitivity for future events, may at times recognize fragments of this future in his dreams. Someone with experiences in this realm once told me the following dream. He saw an image of an overcrowded city, with traffic, smoking factories and masses of people. Above it a dark sky with clouds gathering in spiralling forms. And fire was streaming from these clouds to the earth, on each side of this dream image. The fire crept like glowing lava over the earth, gradually covering the whole world. In spite of this the dreamer did not experience the slightest fear at seeing all this destruction. For above the spiralling clouds there stood vast angelic shapes, guiding and controlling this fire, the clouds and the elements. That was the certainty this dream brought him: above everything that perishes there stands a world which continues and leads us to the future.

All forms of art are also a matter of transforming the physical world and forming a new creation with its own character. The German poet Rainer Maria Rilke brought this task of art in connection with the transformation of the earth. 'I have,' wrote Rilke in his *Duino Elegies,* 'the task to internalize the world. All things in the world around me incline towards invisibility.'[5] They are not yet invisible, but they would like to be part of this future spiritual creation. The future the world will be all 'inner'; will have become 'world's interior.' Everything which is still outer world in the present, must be taken hold of and transformed by the I into a new creation.

Rilke's Ninth Duino Elegy concludes with this image of the future invisible world brought about by art, where the poet tells us that things hear and understand what we have to say. They entrust themselves to us to let us transform them into a new earth:

> These things that live in the temporal understand when you
> praise them: fleeting, they look for rescue through something
> in us, the most fleeting of all. Want us to change them
> entirely, within our invisible hearts, into—oh, endlessly—into
> ourselves! Whosoever we become.
>
> Earth, is this not what you want: an invisible re-arising
> in us? Is it not your dream to be one day invisible? Earth!
> Invisible! What, if not transformation, is your urgent
> command? Earth, dear Earth, I will!

The poet speaks to the earth as if addressing a being and saying, I want to transform you, I want to recall you to existence in the invisible heart.

Hidden behind the beauty of art there is an astonishing elemental world too. If we look beyond the work of art, and perceive the elemental beings which are drawn to it, we realize: the more beautiful the work of art, the more ugly and repulsive the spiritual beings connected to it. Beauty stands on the ground of the repulsive. The wife of a composer who had experiences in this realm once told me, 'You do not want to know what kind of revolting, spidery monsters dance around the platform during the most beautiful music!' It is not only Luciferic beings that make art possible, but also a world of repulsive elemental beings, which evoke interest in art, and inspiration for art. Rudolf Steiner said:

> These beings are deeply ugly. It is impossible to find anything more ugly, they are monstrous beings, archetypes of the repulsive. These are beings who live, like spiders, on the bottom of existence, so that humanity can learn to appreciate beauty out of this nadir of ugliness. They are always there when human beings enjoy beauty. Through ears and nostrils these repulsive creatures creep in and out. On the bottom of the repulsive the human enthusiasm for beauty comes into being.[6]

Looking at the struggle many artists have to go through, working on this lowest ground, this mysterious statement becomes somewhat comprehensible. A work of art must often go through a kind of death process to come to life. And artists must often go through crises and conflicts to really get to grips with their theme. Time and again we see that beauty arises out of its counter image. The Dutch poet J.C. Bloem (1887–1966) once wrote: 'Each new volume of poetry is a premature burial mound.' For an artist to create new life he must go through processes of death. For an artist to create harmony he must endure dissonance and disharmony.

The expressionist sculptor Ernst Barlach (1870–1938) described the creation of a work of art through crisis, the creation of beauty out of repulsiveness, several times in his own words. Shortly before the Second World War he created a series of monumental sculptures called *Die Lauschenden*. The German *lauschen* means far more than just hearing or listening, it is a deep, quiet listening. When the series of sculptures, in which all kinds of *lauschen* are depicted, was nearly finished, he suddenly found it impossible to continue.

Looking at the sculptures it struck him that they were beautiful, but too beautiful. Something was missing. A crisis hit him. He experienced deep despair, and out of this crisis he created a new

Figure 28. Ernst Barlach, *Blind Man* from the frieze *Die Lauschenden*.

sculpture, the *Blind Man.* The blind man stands there in his own world, supporting himself on two sticks, as if caught in some cocoon, but with an intently listening mood transcending and deepening everything else. When Barlach finished this last statue, he wrote to one of his friends, 'I once told you there was a law, stating that no work succeeds without being deepened and consecrated by a deep crisis. Judging by this criterion, my work is going well.

The same thing happened when he creates three sculptures for the Katharina Church in Lübeck. Between two lyrical statues called *Woman in the Wind* and *Singer,* Barlach placed a Beggar on Crutches. According to the commentary of a knowledgeable contemporary, 'This is the most beautiful sculpture, in which repulsiveness triumphs, and misery cries to high heaven.' In these words we can hear how close beauty and repulsiveness really are. When an artist connects and identifies himself deeply with what is ugly, beauty can truly come into its own.

# 13 The Role of the Hierarchies

This chapter begins and ends with the human being, who in a certain sense is the key to the realm of the hierarchies and of the counterforces. We usually picture the battle between the hierarchies and the counterforces as being waged over the human being: that they are fighting over us, tugging at us from above and below. Powerful images from cathedrals and paintings of the Middle Ages depict the dead as a plaything between demonic powers on the one hand and angels on the other.

But in principle we have the possibility of choice in this life. But life after death is the result of choices we made in life. Then these forces wage a battle over us. In life it is our task to fight our own battle and make our own choices.

Even this view is too limited to give a realistic idea of the battle being fought in creation. Our view is too limited if we think human beings are the only stake in this battle. Since ancient times the conflict was seen as a cosmic battle, as a struggle between superhuman and inhuman forces. The human soul is not the only battle ground of interest to these forces: creation too, nature and the elemental beings are at stake. But there is a difference with the first battle we mentioned. In principle we human beings can make our own choices, our own decisions. For nature beings this is not the case, they cannot choose for themselves. They are not directed by pure coincidence, to a large extent their fate is in our hands. Human beings are the decisive factor in the issue whether nature forces can again connect themselves to the hierarchies they originate from, or fall prey to the counterforces.

To gain a deeper understanding of this, we must turn again to our original task as stated in Genesis. Over the centuries this task gave rise to all kinds of misunderstanding. Even before God created the human being, the task is present in his intentions:

Let us make man in our image, after our likeness; and let them
have dominion over the fish of the sea, and over the birds of
the air, and over the cattle, and over all the earth, and over
every creeping thing (Gen.1:26).

The original Hebrew word *yered* is usually translated as 'to have
dominion over' or to rule over. When the divine decision has been
carried out, this word returns. '... fill the earth and subdue it, and
have dominion over the fish of the sea and over the birds of the air
and over every living thing' (Gen.1:28). The Hebrew word literally
means 'place your foot on it.' Of course God does not mean literally
that we should step on creatures with our feet or exterminate them.
On the contrary, when we place our feet upon the earth and walk
over the earth, we can impart something to creation, add something
to it. That is what Paul means in his Epistle to the Ephesians (6:15)
with the words: 'and having shod your feet with the equipment of the
gospel of peace.' Our feet can repel or nurture, trample on or care for
the earth beneath us.

A Jewish legend relates how Adam, expelled from Paradise, left a
dead trail behind everywhere: the grass withered under his feet. That
is the consequence of the Fall, that we have no peace in ourselves and
trample creation under foot.

The task that God gave Adam concerns the stewardship over the
earth. Even after the Fall, the word 'to rule' is used in a positive
sense, when God says to Eve, 'your desire shall be for your husband,
and he shall rule over you' (Gen.3:16). This is misused to the
present day. The Hebrew text here uses the word *mashal* for 'to
rule.' This can have more than one meaning. The noun of the word,
*mishlei*, means example, likeness, parable. The *Mishlei Shlomo* are
the parables of Solomon. Solomon gives his parables as examples
– perhaps one could say as archetypes of wisdom. Similarly the
Hebrew verb *mashal* means 'to be an example.' Adam is given the
task to lead an exemplary life and in doing so to precede, to go before
the woman. In later times the meaning of *mashal* shifted to 'rule,
regulate.' However, the human being – both male and female – has
the task to show the way to creation in all respects. Creation cannot
do that by itself.

This takes us back to our theme at the beginning of this chapter. We have the opportunity to choose between good and evil. Nature beings do not have that choice, they look to us for an example and must follow that. They are at our mercy, just like nature itself. The human being is the decisive factor in creation. We can observe this every day, all around us: we are being confronted with the consequences of our actions. This image of a creation disturbed by human beings has become so forceful that many are resigned to it. That is the origin of the cynicism in witticisms such as, 'We are heading for the abyss, but at least we are travelling first class!' Events seem to have overtaken us. Nevertheless this scenario of doom is not the whole picture, because it does not do justice to the spiritual reality which stands over and above it. If it is true that the human being is the decisive factor, one should not only conclude that some parts of nature have been irreparably damaged, but perhaps one can also say that some parts of nature have been unassailably liberated. There is not only a part of nature that has fallen prey to degenerative forces – in this context Rudolf Steiner speaks of nature beings that have become servants of Ahriman and Lucifer – but it is also possible to cultivate nature in such a way that the nature beings come into the service of the Christ, the Lord of the Elements. That is a field which must still be developed to a large extent. A task anyone can begin, wherever they are.

As always, saving the world begins at home. We can begin by cultivating this realm by our observation. It is not only a matter of spiritualizing our thinking and our actions, but it is of the greatest importance that our spirituality should be connected to physical reality by means of perception. Every observation – and I can even begin with the vase of flowers on my table – connects us with the spiritual reality behind physical appearances. The perception connects us, practically speaking, with the elemental being in the rose, in the stone wall, in the air, in everything which surrounds us and had been banished into it. The moment a spiritual reality becomes physical, elemental beings must be banished into this physicality, in order to create visible reality. The moment the human being becomes an example again for nature, in the sense of the original task he received at the beginning of creation, he weighs into the battle between superhuman and inhuman powers, in the battle between the Archangel Michael and the host of counterforces. How do we observe?

In a lecture series which Rudolf Steiner gave in Vienna he speaks of the importance of the intention with which we look at the world surrounding us.

> If we observe a plant in the usual way we do not in the least sense the presence of an elemental being dwelling in it, of something spiritual; we do not dream that every such plant harbours something which is not satisfied by having us look at it and form such abstract mental pictures as we commonly do of plants today. For in every plant there is concealed – under a spell, as it were – an elemental spiritual being; and really only he observes a plant in the right way who realizes that this loveliness is a sheath of a spiritual being enchanted in it – a relatively insignificant being, to be sure, in the great scale of cosmic interrelationship, but still a being intimately related to man ... And when we see the lily in the field, growing from the seed to the blossom, we must vividly imagine – though not personified – that this lily is awaiting something. (Again I must use human words as I did before to express another picture: they cannot quite cover the meaning, but they do express the realities inherent in things.) While unfolding its leaves, but especially its blossom, this lily is really expecting something. It says to itself: people will pass and look at me; and when a sufficient number of human eyes will have directed their gaze upon me – so speaks the spirit of the lily – I shall be disenchanted of my spell, and I shall be able to start on my way into spiritual worlds ... All about us are these elemental spirits begging us, in effect, do not look at the flowers so abstractly, nor form such abstract mental pictures of them: let rather your heart and your soul enter into what lives, as soul and spirit, in the flowers, for it is imploring you to break the spell. Human existence should really be a perpetual releasing of the elemental spirits lying enchanted in minerals, plants, and animals.[1]

A person who does not want to acknowledge this reality, who only looks at the plant as a thing, or as a product he can make money from, causes another reality to be realized by his intention, namely the intention of the counterforces to bind the elemental beings to them. Our intention can also cause the alliance between Ahriman and these nature beings to come about. It is as simple as that, how do I look at a human being, an animal, a plant or a mineral?

This other way of looking culminates in the statement: 'It is an absolute necessity that the human being should become as familiar with the nature spirits as with the minerals.' The theme of this book is not a luxury, it is a necessity: in our time we must begin – through our consciousness, through our soul moods – to come to the help of nature spirits. I offer three examples of ways in which we can make a beginning.

The first is from Albert Steffen, who quietly performed pioneering work in this field. In his memoirs and diaries we find impressive observations where he describes the spiritual reality in perceptions, starting from observations of a plant in his garden, or looking at the sky:

> You must realize that one can internalize the harmony
> streaming from the blue of the sky, by drinking in this blue,
> giving yourself over to it, and turning away from everything
> else. You might say: 'I did not drink enough blue today,'
> if you notice you are absent-minded and impatient. To
> overcome this, all you have to do is turn to the sky for a
> minute or so. When I have experienced a glowing sunset in
> a similar fashion, it always feels as if I have drunk wine. My
> courage has increased, my confidence too, and the flow of my
> thoughts is clearer. But it does not leave a hangover, like wine,
> and the effect is a lasting one.[2]

One of the people I regularly discuss this theme with, wrote down the following experience for me. Every year during her vacations she studies Rudolf Steiner's lectures on nature beings. She has studied these intensively, year in year out. She also practices observing nature. During one of these vacations she thought the following: 'Isn't it strange to work all your life trying to accomplish something with nature beings, and you never see them till you die.' This is perhaps the case for many of us; perhaps we are convinced they exist, but we are never sure of the results we achieve. In this case the woman heard a nature being responding. A gnome said the following to her: '... for the world is woven of love, and everywhere we do or perceive something else, we only see or create an increase of the intensity of the longing of the world for love – that is for God.' In one complicated sentence she heard what her task was. Gnomes still know that the world is woven out of love. Everything under our feet and in our hands, everything our eyes can see, is the result of love. Everywhere we do something other than imparting love, we are creating an increase of the longing for love; there this longing only increases. We could imagine that the moment we begin to observe with love, take hold of things with love, think about other people and phenomena with love, this mysterious process of the liberation of nature beings begins. This can begin on a very small scale.

I have had this experience myself, in my profession, where I regularly perform the sacraments – not always for large groups of people, but also on a very small scale. Sometimes the group where an Act of Consecration is celebrated, is so small that I ask myself whether it is quite right. During an Act of Consecration for just a handful of people, when I had this question half-consciously, during the raising of the bread and wine, the words *pars pro toto* (the part for the whole) were inwardly spoken to me. These words astonished me – not only because I hardly ever use this expression myself. With these words the insight came to me: what you perform here on a small scale, means something for all people and the whole of creation. This experience was even more convincing when I celebrated the Act of Consecration in quiet solitude. If possible I do this on a lonely spot in nature, where I am not disturbed while celebrating. After one of these Acts of Consecration in nature I wrote in my diary:

> Ever more strongly, sometimes overpoweringly so Christ
> penetrates the words of the sacred Act and communicates itself
> to nature. I gain a new feeling and consciousness for the fact
> that the human being is indispensable for the New Jerusalem.
> The earth is not surrendered to a blind fate, but to us. At the
> end of the Act of Consecration the impression arises: now
> something of this part of the earth may find its way to the
> New Jerusalem.

Of course at the same time there are much more striking and forcefully destructive powers, threatening nature on a huge scale. After all, nature is part of the apocalyptic battle, as we can read in the Revelation to St John. One of the characteristics of the counterforces is that they do everything in their power to intimidate the human being. These powers want to create the impression that they have us in their grip, and that all our efforts are in vain, but spiritual reality is different. Christ says of the opposing might: 'the ruler of this world is judged.' (John 16:11). Every day we can get the impression from the media, that this seemingly unequal battle is being won by the destructive forces. Hence the feelings of 'we are all doomed' and 'after us, the deluge.' In reality the positive forces by their very nature do not boast or shout from the rooftops, as the counterforces tend to do. Dutch poet Henriëtte Roland Holst (1869–1952) described this quiet battle impressively in her poem 'Ascent':

> The gentle forces will surely vanquish
> in the end – I hear this as a whispering
> in me: if silenced all light would darken
> all warmth in me would be extinguished.
>
> The forces still fettering love
> she will, gradually progressing, overcome
> then the great salvation may begin
> which, when we closely listen to our hearts,
>
> can hear in tender rustling
> as in little shells the greater sea.
> Love is the meaning of the life of planets
> and man and beasts. Nothing can disturb
> the rising up to her. This our certain knowing:
> to perfect Love does all ascend.

There are however certain strategies by which these quiet, modest forces can become more active. The most important aspect is that the work should be free from egoism and ambition. The more unselfishly someone works, the more effective (visible or invisible) the result will be. When over and above that people with the same intention can work together in freedom, the result will be more than the sum of the parts: the forces of individuals are multiplied by co-operation in harmony. This amplification does not only come about through common enthusiasm, but especially because the hierarchies connect themselves to the common labour. Then we can justifiably speak of the 'spirit of a community.'

The most concrete expression of this law we find in the Apocalypse, where John writes of the angel of the community. That is not a symbol or metaphor. Anyone who has capacities of observation can recognize that awe-inspiring angelic beings can connect themselves to certain groups of human beings and take such a community in their arms and maintain and guide it.

To conclude this chapter we must say something about the significance nature beings play in all this. From the descriptions so far one might have the impression that these beings are in a blank slate, awaiting their command. However, elemental beings are not ignorant and are no just the victims or helpers of human beings. Our age is in a way the culmination of a centuries-long battle, in which we are not alone. This culmination was prepared for a long time by the hierarchies, led by the archangel and time-spirit Michael. In the spiritual world, between death and rebirth, Michael prepares his followers for the culmination of this battle. Spiritual tradition calls this the School of Michael. Not only human beings took part in this preparation by Michael, but also groups of elemental beings.

Michael ... gathered his own around him: spiritual beings belonging to the supersensible worlds, a great host of elemental spirits, and many, many discarnate human souls who were longing for a renewal of Christianity.[3]

Anthroposophy – where people work selflessly for pedagogy, for the sick or handicapped, for plant or animal world, art or religion, natural science or in business – is not only a way to help human beings, but also to redeem nature beings. Everything accomplished in these fields is significant not only for 'Michael's host,' the hierarchies and humans trained in his school, but also for the 'host of nature beings' from the Michael School in the supersensible worlds.

Of course, selflessness is not a quality unique anthroposophy. It is a quality no single teaching, dogma or conviction has a monopoly on. Pupils of the School of Michael are not only to be found within the circles of anthroposophists (although Steiner does speak of anthroposophy as a stream originating in the School of Michael). Wherever people in our time place themselves selflessly at the service of other people, and take to heart the fate of the earth and humanity, the hierarchies and the elemental beings connected to them, can co-operate with them. Here too, forms of co-operation between people of different beliefs are necessary in our time.

# 14 New Developments and Experiences

In the final two chapters we will attempt to survey the present and the future. It may be relatively easy to write about the past (as far as it is historical), writing objectively about what happens in the present is quite difficult. We can only attempt to describe the drama of the elemental beings as we can see it from our own limited perspective. This does not of course allow the same distant perspective one has on the past. We are in the midst of things and must describe events from up close. In a couple of decades we will undoubtedly have a different view of the time we live in now. When you are in the middle of a certain development, you get a distorted view. Even more than in previous chapters I must stress that this work is by no means complete. It is an attempt to bring to attention an area which desperately needs our care. My descriptions are possible partly because for the past twenty-five years I have been in regular contact with people who have their own experiences in this realm, and who were willing to share them. In my pastoral work too I encounter supra-sensory perception more and more.

For a description of our own time, I will begin with a prelude to the drama. What is taking place in our times was something that in the Middle Ages Paracelsus wrote about in his work on nature beings. To my knowledge he was the first to predict what would happen in future in the realm of the elemental beings. This work gives the impression that Paracelsus had an overview of everything to come. He is of course quite an impressive personality. If we read the chapter Rudolf Steiner wrote on him we realize in what a high esteem Steiner held him.[1]

In his book, Paracelsus writes that there used to be friendship between elemental beings and humans. There was an intimate connection. Over the centuries, human beings turned away from their origins, from their Creator, and so have become estranged from nature. Paracelsus then describes how these spirit beings, the nature beings, withdraw more and more from the human being, although their fates are deeply interwoven. Especially since certain human beings have mocked and betrayed nature beings, they turn away from humans and only show themselves to children and to 'simple' people who are clairvoyant according to Paracelsus. Even if we are well disposed towards these beings, they may still mock or betray us, as if they want to revenge what has been inflicted on them collectively over the centuries. Those are the consequences of the estrangement.

This state, which was remarked upon in such a distant past, is noted again in the present by Ernst-Martin Krauss, who adds to the above description with the help of his own observations:

> If you direct your attention to nature beings nowadays, if you become sensitive to their mood, you will be sure to encounter despair occasionally. It is as if nature beings sometimes cry out: Is there really no one who listens to us?[2]

The nature beings are beginning to doubt the integrity of the human being. They are desperate about his interventions in nature.

In the Middle Ages certain individuals began to notice that nature beings were withdrawing more and more from the human world. The next step in the drama was that they also withdrew from nature and completely turned away from humans. The question now is, what will come in their place if nature beings no longer occupy their place.

It is only a small step from Paracelsus to the twentieth century, when Rudolf Steiner addressed this question of the exodus of nature beings in his Agriculture Course. When Steiner gave the course in 1924 he began by observing that nature was starting to degenerate. Nature was gradually being depopulated. Strangely enough, Steiner related this to the end of the Kali Yuga, the dark age. This era, during which, according to the ancient Indians, the heavens would remain closed, came to an end in 1899. You would expect that when it ends, it must surely be the beginning of a light-filled age. But it is just at this end of Kali Yuga, when the human being is furthest away from the spiritual world, that nature is left even more at the mercy of humans than before. From now on it will depend on the human being whether nature degenerates even further or not. That is the reason why Steiner communicates these matters.

As so often with Steiner, the Agriculture Course came about after a request. The farmers' request for a course came out of certain concerns. They had noted that even in their time, harvest yields were decreasing. Over the years the yield had decreased significantly. In the second lecture of the Agriculture Course Steiner says the following about this:

> This decline ... has to do with Kali Yuga coming to an end
> in recent decades and in those to come ... We are also faced
> with a great inner transformation in nature. The natural
> gifts, naturally inherited knowledge, traditional medicines,
> and so on that have been passed down from ancient times are
> all losing their value. We need to acquire new knowledge in
> order to be able to enter into all the interrelationships of these
> things. Humanity has only two choices: either to start once
> again, in every field of endeavor, to learn from the whole of
> nature, from the relationships within the whole cosmos, or to
> allow both nature and human life to degenerate and die off.
> There is no other choice. Today, no less than in ancient times,
> we are in need of knowledge that can really enter into the
> inner workings of nature.[3]

We have consumed our inheritance. We no longer have the instincts to interact with nature in a 'natural' way. Our traditional knowledge has been lost and there is nothing for it but to cultivate a new knowledge and an ability to bring about change.

Looking back to the situation at the beginning of the twentieth century it is easy to understand that some pioneers of biodynamic agriculture felt that although things were changing, surely they would not move so fast? Many of them hardly realized the severity of the situation and the scope of what they heard. I think that now, over eighty years later, we have a quite different perspective compared to that time. What was only a vague feeling then is now quite obvious to most people. It has become visible and demonstrable reality, and we can understand Steiner's words, which might have sounded incredible: 'A time will come when people will starve at tables groaning with food.' This time has come.

From 1924 we move to the present. I would like to describe from the 'outside' to the 'inside' what happens in nature and how the symptoms of degeneration are visible all around, not only in agriculture, but everywhere in nature. What is going on in nature at the moment? I refered earlier to a snapshot and inventory of nature worldwide. *National Geographic* published an issue in September 2004 called 'Threatened earth. The consequences of global warming.' The introduction had the title 'Beyond science fiction.' What in the previous decades had been depicted in fiction – in films and books which imagined the dramatic consequences of climate change – is now becoming reality: beyond science fiction. The article begins with the well-known fact that the temperature of the atmosphere of the earth has never risen so fast as in the past decades. We are looking at a global 'fever attack.' There have been climate changes in the past. Initially some scientists pointed to natural climate changes in earlier times, like the ice ages. This view is now considered outdated. According to biologists changes that used to occur over a whole geological era, are now happening within a few decades. In the past millennium, temperatures have never risen as fast as now. When we extrapolate this, the predictions are that over the coming hundred years, average temperatures worldwide will rise by 1.5 to 5.5°C (3.5–10°F). This may not sound very much, but such a rise in temperatures will have unprecedented consequences.

In the Netherlands at the end of 2005 an official report was published predicting that by the end of this century sea-levels will have risen by 20 to 110 cm (8–43 in). The uncertainty in this prediction indicates the uncertainties that face us in the coming decades. The report further predicts extremely hot and dry summers for the northwest Europe, but at the same time more and more violent rain storms. This will increase river-levels. It is expected that the consequences will become 'problematic' at the end of the twenty-first century. Because climate zones will move with an estimated 400 km (250 miles) per century, many plants and animals will not be able to adapt to the changes – and die out.

Professor Erkki Lähde, professor of forestry in Helsinki has for many years carried out research in the forests of Finland. In an interview he said, 'We found that over the past years, the green of plants and trees has literally changed colour, has bleached.'[4] This is caused by acid rain. Slowly but surely the colour of trees and plants changes from dark green to a lighter green. Erkki Lähde noticed another strange phenomenon, which gives pause for thought. He describes how in the last few years, the tops of fir trees have turned to face in the opposite direction. People in Finland knew that if you want to know where the south was, you looked at the tops of trees which grew in the direction of the scarce light. In the last few years the tops of trees in Finland have all turned north, away from the sunlight to protect themselves against an overdose of ultraviolet rays, coming through the ozone hole.

In Finland the leaves of aspen trees, which are dark green on top and light green underneath, have changed, so that now you see aspen leaves mostly with the light sides turned up. In the interview Professor Lähde said, 'These days we can't see the wood for the trees. We hardly know what kind of drama is playing out in our forests.'

In Scandinavia there are vast forests, where beard lichen *(Usnea)* grow on the trunks and branches of trees. These beard lichen can only survive in clean and healthy air. But now these beard lichen are slowly disappearing, making way for grey mildew. Sometimes, vast forests are draped in grey. This mould or mildew is a portent for tree diseases. They are a sign that the air is no longer clean and the vitality of trees, their power to regenerate is diminishing.

Forestry experts have observed an increase in a disease of noble firs *(Abies procera)*, where the needles begin to fall out and the green gets thinner. The trees weaken, become more prone to disease and have less regenerative forces.

So far I described several more or less random visible phenomena in nature. If we hear the experiences of those people who can 'look behind the scenes' things appear even more dramatic. Quite intimate experiences can speak volumes too. In 2005 Maria Thun told a remarkable story. A Catholic priest from Austria had contacted her, asking if she could provide healthy wheat. She recommended a nearby farmer working along biodynamic principles who provided the wheat. Several months later this priest invited Maria Thun to come and talk to his congregation about this special form of agriculture. When she asked why, he replied, 'For some time I had noticed during mass that at the transubstantiation, the consecrated host no longer had an aura. When I used the grain you provided, the aura reappeared.' That was why he had begun to look for different wheat, and now he wanted his congregation to know what the agricultural method was all about.

It is dangerous of course to draw general conclusions from this exceptional observation – for example that transubstantiation is dependent on the bread used at the altar. It is not like that. The process of transubstantiation is endlessly complicated and depends on many different factors. Not only on the nature of the substances used, but also on the attitude of the celebrating priest, the congregation, on the content and form of the sacramental words and actions.

Surveying these developments, we can have the firm impression that the invisible world behind nature is knocking on our door, trying to attract attention. Nature is totally dependent on human beings for her survival. The nature beings are asking for our attention, care and help. A well-known example of this new development can be found in the works of Verena Staël von Holstein. From childhood she had clairvoyant perceptions of nature. In an interview with Wolfgang Weirauch, she says:

> What is new here is the approach of elemental beings to
> humans because they have a longing to speak with them ...
> work together with humans in the future ... The present
> situation of the nature spirits can be compared to the work
> in a firm without a competent director at the head. Because
> the new management isn't aware of its task, it becomes even
> harder for the nature spirits to perform their tasks, for they
> are actually so structured that they want to be instructed. The
> nature spirits would like to know for sure if what they're doing
> is also right. They would like to know if their creative work
> is still able to sustain this world. And then the nature spirits
> come and ask, 'Am I doing it right, boss?' But the boss doesn't
> even know they exist.[5]

After this first publication there followed several more volumes of conversations with nature beings. (In Germany these publications gave rise to violent discussions: extreme supporters consult the books as if they were a new oracle, while extreme critics seem keen to throw away the baby with the bathwater; needless to say this polarization does the cause no good at all.) On careful reading one realizes that Verena Staël actually speaks in quite a differentiated and cautious way about the impressions she describes. In no way does she suggest hers are the last words on the subject.

In the first interview with Wolfgang Weirauch he asked, 'When you perceive one of these beings, couldn't it be that you're projecting the form of this being? ... Couldn't it be that this is just your subjective projection and another person would see him completely differently?'

Verena Staël replied, 'Obviously every person would see these beings differently, but not completely differently. ... Certain basic structures remain similar, others would be seen differently through the subjectivity of the person. The beings reflect the pictures that stream towards them from humans.'

She clearly puts her own statements in perspective. I do not get the impression that she wants these books to be seen as a new kind of authority.

Another worthwhile contemporary author is Tapio Kaitaharju from Finland, who published seven books on the interaction with nature and nature beings. After a life changing experience in the 1960s he came into contact with nature beings. He too describes how these beings have become ever more removed from human beings. They are disappointed in us. Kaitaharju is certain that in the coming decades, our one-sided thoughts and interventions in nature will have catastrophic results. These catastrophes, however, are also attemps by nature, to regain its equilibrium (as a fever is an attempt by an organism to regain its equilibrium). In spite of all this, nature beings are doing everything in their power to help human beings. When the catastrophes come there may be a willingness among certain groups of people to co-operate with them, rather than disturb the environment even further. Kaitaharju expects that in these extreme situations, new forms of community and new energy sources will be discovered:

> The nature spirits are prepared to help. We can be certain that
> during the coming catastrophes they will give human beings
> certain inspirations, on how human beings can survive and
> deal with them. Crises – both in individual biographies and
> in a wider context – serve a certain purpose. They make sure

that old, useless life forms are destroyed, so that new ones can come about. Every crisis can lead to positive results. We can begin a certain collaboration by tending nature with insight and care. When human beings are interested in their garden or a forest they walk in, nature beings begin to be interested in us. The first indication of this is that people who show an interest in nature, begins to get clear promptings, they acquire green fingers, or receive the right intuitions in dealing with nature. These are given to us by the 'little folk' in gratitude for the fact that we connect to them.[6]

Kaitaharju's advice is to try to find a place in nature where you feel at home. Start with a place where you have the impression something can flow to and fro. Take your time, sit down, listen to nature and above all be patient. By not forcing your way into nature in a hurry, but by patiently connecting to such a place, again and again, an interaction will gradually come about. The greatest danger is for someone who is very curious, to want to penetrate too soon into the secrets of nature. Kaitaharju says that if you try that, if you penetrate the world behind nature too quickly and unprepared, you create a disastrous confusion in yourself and in nature. You run the risk of falling prey to illusions. The risk that these nature beings conjure up illusions for you, because you penetrate their realm wrongfully.

I have encountered this in my pastoral work. If you engage with a certain theme for a long time, people who are dealing with it too, come towards you. In a recent conversation with a girl she told me how through certain practices of Wicca, a pagan religion focused around witchcraft, she had reached a state where impressions of nature overwhelmed and pursued her. She said: 'I have no peace or quiet anymore. I always see these eyes looking at me. Sometimes I ask: Can't it stop? But I can't get it to stop anymore.' In such cases you have the impression that someone has forced their way into contact with nature beings. Intensive pastoral-medical counselling is required to build up someone's defences against such impressions. Sometimes, if someone has been involved in such experiments for too long, the relation with everyday reality has been damaged to such an extent, that they are practically beyond help. Psychiatrist know the phenomenon of such people living totally in their own world – isolating themselves from society.

From experience I also know that when you approach the boundaries of invisible nature, you irrevocably meet your own boundaries, and you are sometimes drawn across these boundaries into an unknown and strange realm. You cannot remain a spectator when you form an intense connection with nature. You usually learn by trial and error where your boundaries are, and can feel: to here, and no further.

Someone who guards these transitions into the realm of invisible nature carefully and cautiously, and has thoroughly schooled his clairvoyant perception of nature is a German lawyer, Ernst-Martin Krauss. He prepared himself for impressions of nature by meditating one or two hours before going out. He then erased all meditative impressions. In taking the steps from imagination to inspiration and to intuition, various impressions must come to a complete halt before one can open oneself to the next step that comes to meet one from the spiritual world. The task is to meditate, to let go, and then to enter nature in a mood of strength and receptivity, and to ask questions. Ernst-Martin Krauss, speaking from his years of experience, said: 'When we start with this – even if we do not see anything for months or even years, – nature beings rejoice, because a human being is preparing himself for communion with nature.'[7]

It can be meaningful to give something to nature out of this mood. Someone who has instense experiences with nature noted down the following impressions for me. While her car was being repaired in a village in the south of Germany she went for a walk.

> I wanted to pray the Lords Prayer there, for the nature beings above and in the earth and I asked my angel to pray with me. I saw a large hollow space. Beings streamed towards it from all sides. It was a spiritual space I had created in my prayer.

She tells of another impression in Norway:

> The Hardangervidda lies north of the lake. There was the settlement where I was to spend Christmas. You can only reach it across the lake. For miles around there are only

footpaths. I had my own small log cabin, heated by a simple
wood-burning stove. It was extremely cold, the coldest night
was −30°C. One day I decided to go for a short walk in
the mountains. As soon as I had left the settlement, I felt a
long 'tail' of nature beings behind me. I thought, 'don't be
afraid,' and walked on for a bit. It wasn't comfortable and
I sensed: no, if I go on, I don't know what might happen. I
turned around, realizing it meant facing this tail of elemental
beings. But the tail swung round too and remained behind
me. I walked on calmly. 'Don't be afraid,' I said to myself.
They all suddenly disappeared within the enclosure of the
settlement. I crossed myself. I did not have the courage to say
the Lord's Prayer. The same happened the next time. I tried
going a little further, but felt it would be too risky. Walking
back I felt a hand on my shoulder. I managed to control my
fear and walked back, outwardly calm. When I reached the
settlement, the hand still on my shoulder, I quickly turned
round and made the sign of the cross in their direction. They
disappeared. Again I did not dare to say the Lord's Prayer,
because I knew you could be attacked. Much later I made
up for it. When praying, physical distance does not matter: I
could say it in their domain or somewhere else.'

Apparently the gulf between these nature beings and Christianity
was so wide that they experienced the Lord's Prayer as a threat. The
woman describing these experiences knew that in spite of this she
had to say the prayer for them: 'Much later I made up for it.' It is
not strictly necessary to be 'on the spot' to help nature beings. People
with experience and insight state that it is perfectly possible to help in
another place and time.

Nature not only tries to attract our attention, but also asks what
human beings can offer and contribute by their prayer, by their
intercession. Even the smallest attempt we make in this realm can
accomplish something. In this case the person has a first, vague
impression of what can happen: nature listens and absorbs the sign of
the cross.

Paracelsus goes further, saying everything we do for elemental
beings and nature will sooner or later accomplish these nature beings

progressing in their development and being nourished. The real, deeper reason why God created them is still hidden from us. It will only become apparent at the end of time. We must do something for them now, but what this accomplishes, and the actual reason behind the creation of these beings, must remain secret for now, according to Paracelsus.

Occasionally, a person at the end of their life may gain a clear impression of what they have achieved invisibly, imperceptibly. This can be seen with Alja Ackermans, who worked in the Netherlands developing biodynamic preparations for many years. Shortly before dying of cancer, she wrote a farewell message, which was published after her death.[8] She describes an imagination of her work, which she received shortly before her passing:

> I was standing at a kind of laboratory bench, with mortars, various rocks and substances. I was very concentrated, and at work. It was an artistic process, a dynamic creating, in which not only substances were metamorphosed, but I myself was refined too. For years I had been alone in this space, but in later years there had been an elemental being present and helping. There was always a dialogue, the elemental never leading: it co-operated. It was a very exciting process, a life's work. Each step in this process was related to inner steps, moral steps. A refinement, an inner schooling to attain purity. And it went well. It progressed until it was fulfilled. It touched me deeply, because it was gold. It was like the inner gold.

The fruits of her labour in agriculture become conscious for her in this imaginative picture language: working in a laboratory with substances; the lonely path she must go to purify the substances, to purify herself, to gradually come to the realization: I am not alone; there is a nature being accompanying me. Not directing, but accompanying me. Through this process the gold of the alchemists is created. The imagination continues in another realm.

> At once, eight angels appeared, and surrounded by eight angels, like an egg shape, I was carried off into the earth. I was allowed to see and get to know the earth from within.

The angels carried me to the depths of the earth, the centre, Shambhala. Here I encountered Christ and for a time we were together in the centre of the earth.

I cannot describe this experience further. Some time after, deeply moved, I was carried up again, by the same eight angelic beings, surrounded by them as if in an egg. They guided me through all the black, dark layers of the earth where demons reside. Between the wings of the angels, I could see the demons coming. They knew a human being was passing, but they also knew they could not do anything. I looked at the demons and felt totally safe between the wings of the angels.

They guided me back to the chamber in the tower and there was the same elemental being who had helped me all those years, the gold-being!

I wanted to thank him, but the being pretended not to understand, and danced about me. He tumbled and danced so comically, it made me laugh, and we both roared with laughter. But I still wanted to thank him.

'All right,' said the gold-being, 'if you want to thank, we will do that too.' Instantly, elemental beings approached from all sides, in a beautiful, colourful procession, in all kinds of forms and colours. They approached and showed me their gratitude in a very special way. They showed me the soil of the whole of Holland. I did not see any houses or roads, just the soil, the earth of Holland. In many places elemental beings were celebrating with whirling and dynamic dances. I saw elemental beings celebrating exuberantly. The gold-being said: 'Look at this, because we want to thank you for all your work on preparations. These are the places where, thanks to the preparations, the elemental beings can dance such a whirling dance of light.'

What begins as a lonely task, the difficult process of refining substances and preparations, communicates itself to the elemental being accompanying us our whole life, to the hierarchies, to the earth. Even if we seem to work on such a small scale, the elemental beings appreciate it nevertheless. If you cultivate the earth out of a selfless, spiritual or Christian impulse, it has far-reaching effects. People often denigrate these forms of agriculture: they are drop in the ocean compared to regular agriculture, they are marginal. But each and every patch of the earth which is cultivated in this way is invaluable to the nature beings and for the future of the earth.

I would like to conclude this chapter with the views of Ingeborg Lüdeling, who has been active for several decades in the spiritual care for nature. Together with her husband, Hartmut Lüdeling, she gives courses and she has published several books of her experiences. Preparing the present book, I asked her what the relationship is between nature spirits and the Christ, and what part we play in this connection. She wrote:

My reply is subjective, and is not applicable to all people or all nature beings. These are my experiences and my views: nature beings do not need us in a direct sense, they 'just' need our mindfulness and attention. They are there to help us in our process of becoming conscious, and we must ask them for this help. By the development of our own consciousness, we come closer to the heart of the Redeemer, because working on ourselves and on our souls will enrich and enlighten the cells and molecules of our body.

Thereby our radiance becomes lighter and finer, and thereby the human being begins to recognize the fine radiance of nature beings; he sees these beings and their concerns, can help them and let himself be helped by them. The eternal play of creation is a striving for balance. (In balancing the forces of Yin and Yang, there is always a process of give and take!) That is how nature beings and human beings can learn to live through insight: 'Help yourself, and God will help you,' as the saying goes. It is actually hard to separate these two, for we all carry a divine spark within us. But first we must become aware of this. A human being who has developed his consciousness in all areas, is freed from the conditioning of what binds him to the earth. Wagner, in his *Karfreitagszauber* wrote about nature: 'She cannot behold him on the cross: therefore she looks up to the redeemed human being.'

In my experience only a conscious, redeemed human being can offer help to the spirits of nature. A different vision and a different feeling are required for that. A 'normal' person too can have occasional, spontaneous contact with nature beings. But help them? I think more knowledge and insight is necessary for that. I would even go as far as to say that this consciousness also includes a consciousness of God. Redeemed, conscious human beings can help – in my experience – as follows: by prayer, as you do; by being attentive to their existence; by being conscious of our human needs. (How do I behave in nature? Do I really have to buy foods that are sprayed with chemicals? When do I really need to drive a car – we pollute not just the air, but also the living space of nature beings, etc.) There is so much to be done in this field! As you wrote yourself: there are more ways than you can see. But the ways you do see, you can follow!'

# 15 Elemental Beings and the Future

To gain an insight into the future we must consult people who are able to survey the future. I do not mean the indeterminate feelings many people have with regard to the future. As long as you still connect your own feelings and expectations with the future, you cannot form a clear, pure image. To gain a clear insight into the future a trained, schooled clairvoyance is required. And even more: the schooled person must have a 'genius' in the original sense of the word: inspiration by the genius, the guardian angel. For only when someone transcends their human limitations into the spiritual realm (devachan) that transcends the physical, etheric and astral realm, is he able to see the future clearly. In devachan the future is already present, and awaits recognition. This was expressed in a highly original way by the American playwright Thornton Wilder, who wrote some very short, powerful plays – 'three minute plays.'

In one of these, *Centaurs,* he described in a brilliant way how the future is being prepared in the spiritual world. I will describe the dialogue between Norwegian playwright Ibsen and English poet Shelley, who meet on stage, in spite of having lived at different times. Wilder did not want to portray a historical encounter, but he asked himself, what would have happened had these two met on earth. What do these two artists of genius talk about? The action takes place just before a performance of Ibsen's *Master Builder.*

Shelley goes onstage and addresses the audience, 'I must tell you of a peculiar feeling I have. The impression I have is that the play you are about to see performed, is actually mine.' Ibsen himself appears on stage too, and Shelley continues, 'Ladies and gentlemen, the day I drowned in the Mediterranean, I was full of a poem I would have called "The Death of a Centaur." But I had no time left to write it.'

Ibsen is furious: 'And I assert that I was the one who wrote it. The poem floated over the Mediterranean for a while, drifted over the Tirol to the north, and I received it and wrote it down, and it is called the "Master Builder".'

Ibsen is supported by his daughter Hilde, who tries to calm him. down. She says: 'We must look into this very carefully. In the first place, both poems are certainly about centaurs. What do you say, Shelley?'

Shelley replies, 'Well, it is not a strange or a new thought that the substance of masterworks floats freely in the atmosphere, awaiting expression in words. That is a truth Plato would have understood: the mere language, the words of a masterpiece are the least it has to offer. No, in the world we live in, languages are of no value. But the impulse, the idea for a work of art is a miracle, even in heaven. And never forget that fact, when you are feeling sad about all those works of art lost in wars. Every work that was not completed, still lives amongst you, and will certainly find its way into your life and that of your children.'

Ibsen replies: 'Enough, enough! If you are not careful, you will betray all the secrets! We have said enough to prove that the "Death of a Centaur" and the "Master Builder" are really one and the same work. Go inside, my children! Everything is ready for the play. Solness is seated with his head in his hands, the music of harps is floating through the air.'

Ibsen disappears behind the curtain. Shelley remains and Ibsen's daughter asks, 'What is the matter with you?'

Shelley replies: That reminds me of another poem ... I hadn't written it down either.'

In art and science the thought that an idea may be present before the work of art or the invention becomes physical reality, is not so strange. This principle applies to a high degree to the greatest work of art there is: the future of our humanity. This future is waiting to be recognized and expounded by geniuses, initiates who can perceive with the gaze of the genius. That is what happens to the first Christian initiate, John, who reveals this hidden future. The Greek word *apokalypsis* of course means 'revelation.' What in the future will become visible, audible and tangible reality, is revealed to John as a spiritual seeing (imagination), hearing (inspiration), and feeling (intuition). For John this is an extremely grave ordeal: he drops down as if dead at the feet of the Son of Man, who reveals the future to him. When he has come to himself again, the aural and visual impressions he is confronted with are overwhelming. The experience of the intuition is a 'bitter pill,' too for John: that is the little scroll he receives from the hands of the angel, which is sweet to the taste, but bitter in the stomach (Rev.10:10). He can bear this experience because he is a Christian initiate. He perceives future reality from the other side of the threshold.

Steiner has used the expression 'Initiation of Man' for the Apocalypse. What the author of the Apocalypse experiences as an individual, will become a collective experience for humanity in the future. Most of us have the wrong idea of what 'Apocalypse' actually means. An Apocalyptic vision has nothing to do with predictions of doom, with misery. Catastrophes are not the essence of the Apocalypse. The key to this work is given in the first sentence, *Apokalypsis Jesou Christou:* This is the revelation in which Jesus Christ reveals himself. The essence is that Jesus Christ reveals himself in all trials and catastrophes. He is the 'main character' in the work, but he is our future too. Everything belonging to the future rests in his hands. Which also means that in the future every human being will stand before him. John indicates this with the words: 'and every eye will see him, everyone who pierced him' (Rev.1:7). There will come a time in the future when every human being will come eye to eye with him, even those who turn against him, mistreat him, pierce him, will see him.

The Apocalypse, throughout the whole drama, shows that a part of reality has already been realized, that a part of the future is present in the spirit and that this future is still waiting for our initiatives and decisions. The Christ has a perfect consciousness of every person individually. He knows every human being through and through, not only throughout all their lives, from their furthest past, but he also knows their future potential. This has been the experience of people who have looked across the threshold of the spiritual world. For example when someone has a near-death experience and comes eye to eye with the Christ, this can be the most overwhelming experience: he knows me better than I know myself. He is my future.

Yolande van Eck described this dramatic encounter after her near-death experience:

Suddenly I found myself facing a man. He did not wear
modern clothes, but a long garment I could touch. My gaze
and his merged with one another. In these eyes I saw an
unconditional love and an immeasurable space. I read in
these eyes that this being knew absolutely everything about
my life. I could not hide even a minute of it. At the same
time I understood he did not wish to judge or condemn me.
While I stood before his greatness, it was I myself who passed
judgment on myself. I fell to my knees. That was the only
thing I could do at that moment, it was the only thing I could
offer ... I could only look at his eyes as long as he made me
understand he knew my whole life, as long as he gave me to
understand how much he loved me.[1]

That is the first, fundamental experience of overriding importance
someone has when they pass the threshold: the spiritual world has a
centre. Similar experiences can occur spontaneously in life too.

In one of the many Christ-experiences, collected in the 1970s by
a theological institute in Stockholm, a girl of nineteen describes this
encounter.

He looked at me. His gaze expressed nothing but
condemnation. I had never thought I might be guilty of
something. Of course I had learned all people are sinners
and that Jesus had taken all their sins on himself. I had not
sinned consciously. I knew of nothing extraordinary that I
should feel guilty about. But his gaze caused me to see myself
through his eyes. And now I realized: I was deeply sinful.
When I recognized my sins, and became conscious of the fact
that I needed his mercy, I sensed that all condemnation had
vanished. Now his eyes radiated a deep love, an immense sea
of love. I will never forget that gaze.[2]

Initially this second description seems to contradict the first.
But what begins as condemnation transforms into love. The author
describes the reason: she looks at herself with different eyes, from
outside, from a higher perspective. 'But his gaze caused me to see
myself through his eyes.' That is how this judgment comes about.

The future is here already. It is there in hidden form in the personality of Christ. However, there are certain pre-conditions before we can recognize something of this. The future waiting for us, is usually distorted by our own wishes, fears and cares. We must look from a different perspective than from the familiar, usual standpoint of our own self. The required perspective was once expressed in a conversation between Rudolf Steiner and Johanna von Keyserlingk, the lady who played such an important part in the foundation of biodynamic agriculture. She talked to Rudolf Steiner about her extraordinary experiences, which she could not understand. Rudolf Steiner explained to her what is was she was going through. It began when she was 27, when, in a crisis during an illness, she had a near-death experience. The physicians had almost given her up. She emerged from this near-death experience with the faculty of the new clairvoyance.

As we saw in Chapter 7, Steiner indicated this new clairvoyance with the words: 'You have the consciousness which will be customary in the third millennium.' This experience will become a reality for countless people as the new 'Damascus experience.' The way Paul experienced the overwhelming presence of Christ on the way to Damascus, in the middle of the day, is the way people in the future will experience the Christ during their lives. This experience is related to the imagination of the future, which was revealed to Johanna von Keyserlingk in the image of the Grail Castle. She could relate all her imaginations to Rudolf Steiner. In a memorable conversation, Steiner confirmed what she has seen and explained to her what it took to see so far into the future.

> For myself I did not need this confirmation of the truth, but I wanted to have it for the benefit of others, and so I asked Doctor Steiner: 'Can one believe, that the castle of the Holy Grail really is present in the ether world? People who penetrate into the spiritual world speak about this time and again: those who tell the Grail saga and the author of the Chymical Wedding. Is there really a castle which one can reach in the spiritual world?'
>
> Reply: 'Yes it is indeed present.'
>
> 'Is this Grail Castle one reaches the same sacred edifice which the Bible calls the New Jerusalem?'

Reply: 'The New Jerusalem the Bible speaks of, is the eternal archetype, as it will be in future.'

'And the Grail Castle is as it is now in the spiritual world? So then the Grail Castle is really present in the spiritual world?'

Reply: 'Yes that is so. One only reaches the Grail Castle, when one beholds oneself in occult vision from the outside, when one has freed onself from oneself. After one's fortieth year one can go back in life. When one does that and beholds oneself from outside until the moment one is born, one enters the Grail Castle.'

'And does one then experience in imaginations the images of the Grail Castle?'

Reply: 'Yes, one does.'[3]

This is a crucial condition, which is also a response to the question: How do I gain insight into the future in such a way that my own wishes, expectations, fears, illusions and cares are not mixed up in it? One can only manage this when one has freed oneself from oneself. When one steps outside of one's ego and looks at oneself in the strictest objectivity. The German poet Christian Morgenstern (1871–1914) expresses that experience as follows, 'My I looks at me.' That is the perspective required to gain insight into the future, from the spiritual world.

When crossing this threshold one has the same experience one has when entering the Grail Castle. Wagner describes this experience in his *Parsifal*. When Parsifal enters the Grail Castle he does not understand what is happening and says, 'I hardly walk and yet it seems I have gone very far.' The Grail Knight replies, 'You see, my son, here time turns into space.' That is the experience of crossing the threshold: time turns into space. We see this too in the near-death experience, where everything which was behind us, was our past during our life, actually becomes space. The Greek word *pan-horama* literally means: seeing everything. Then time becomes space.

Now let us look at what people say who are able to recognize what the future of the earth is like. Not just the individual human being and the whole of humanity have a future: the elements and nature realms, stone, plant and animal have a future too. What we human beings do, has consequences for other realms of nature. There are three realms which are inextricably interconnected, which are in a certain sense condemned to each other. These three realms are indicated in a sentence of the Creed of the Christian Community. This sentence speaks of the dying earth existence. A time has come in the biography of our earth where we are compelled to speak of the dying earth existence (which is not to be confused with the rapacious way we treat the earth at the moment). The impulse for the course Rudolf Steiner gave on agriculture, was the fact that harvests at the beginning of the twentieth century were declining. Farmers noticed that the earth yielded less than before, in spite of putting the same energy an dedication into their work. What was the cause of this? That was the question leading to the course on biodynamic agriculture. The earth is growing old, gradually loses her life-forces and goes through a process of dying. This process is intensified by the countless ways we maltreat the earth.

In the above-mentioned sentence of the Creed, we see the three realms which are dependent on each other for the future. 'Christ through whom human beings attain the re-enlivening of the dying earth-existence, is to this divine being as the Son, born in eternity.'

In this dying earth, which is irrevocably heading for death, works the Son who is born in eternity. He bestows his life-forces, his resurrection-forces, on the dying earth existence and on the human being. The image is complete: Christ – human being – earth existence. This is a new Trinity, forming a unity: three entities inextricably linked. In these words of the Creed we see a dimension reappear which for centuries has been pushed to the background, was even largely forgotten. These words do justice to the cosmic and earthly meaning of Christianity. Christianity has meaning not only for the individual – as Luther said, 'How can I find a merciful God?' Christ not only connects himself with all human beings, but also with the dying earth existence and with the heavens. We can only become Christian if we transcend ourselves towards the earth and towards the cosmos. The Nicene Creed of the Catholic and Orthodox church says: *Crucifixus pro nobis sub Pontio Pilato:* 'Christ was crucified *for us* under Pontius Pilate.' The Apocalypse goes beyond this traditional conception. Christ did not only die and resurrect only for us, but for the whole of creation. In the New Jerusalem, the whole of creation will be spiritualized. Stone, plant, animal and human being will form part of a new earth.

To understand how the physical world will be transubstantiated in the future creation, we need an occult mineralogy. Friedrich Benesch made that his life's work. His book on the Apocalypse is an occult mineralogy, where he describes the twelve foundations of the heavenly Jerusalem, and explains how these minerals represent certain qualities. The earth is spiritualized and can become the foundation of a new creation.

The plant world too is represented there, by the tree of life. From the animal world the twelve pearls each form a gate, an entry into the New Jerusalem. A precious quintessence from the animal world forms the portal to the future creation. And finally the new and future humanity is represented.

This future is not just imaginatively present. It is the elemental beings who have the capacity to prepare the future, although they are dependent for this on human beings for help. The elemental beings have a infallible consciousness – we can hardly imagine what this is like – of our morality. I will put into my own words what Rudolf Steiner said about the spiritualization of creation. The moment we look at a stone, a plant, an animal, the air, or some other phenomenon of nature, an interaction with the elemental beings occurs. Through our perception countless elemental beings enter the human being. They unite themselves with him. All these beings are at present banished into the physical world.

In this moment, if our looking is not conscious, if we do not think or feel anything, these beings, whether they want to or not, are nevertheless moved into the human being. They remain unredeemed, if we do not impart to them something of our thinking, our inner warmth and our ideals. When we die, they return into the elemental world, but are doomed to reappear on the physical plane at our next incarnation, to become chained to matter once more. However, if we show an interest when we look and form ideas about what we see, or admire the beauty of nature, and gradually spirtualize these impressions, we redeem the nature beings which enter into us in the moment of observation. Although they accompany us until our death, if during our life we have observed actively in this way, we are able to redeem and liberate countless of these elemental beings from their banishment. After our death they are spiritualized and are able to help prepare a new, spiritualized creation.

Anthroposophy is even more concrete, more practical about the role of the human being in the future creation, and about the responsibility we have for it. In our breathing out, three elements play a major part: our bodily warmth, the air we breathe, and water in the form of moisture. Our astral forces and ether forces connect themselves to these three elements (fire, air and water). Thereby we call up a future spiritual reality. Rudolf Steiner said about this:

> Deeds which arise out of love show something quite different from deeds which are done out of enthusiasm, a creative urge or the urge for perfection, for instance. But in every case the form in the breath reminds one of beings that do not exist on earth at all as yet. These beings [that appear through the forms in our out-breath] are a preparation for the ones that will reach their human stage on Jupiter [the distant future state]. Their forms are very changeable and will pass through further changes in the future, for these beings are the first advance shadow images of the beings who will reach the human level on Jupiter.[4]

On our out-breath, we continually create spiritual beings, which bear in them the seed of what will become reality in the New Jerusalem. Steiner makes a comparison with the moment the human being originated from the breath of God. Likewise, in the breath of each individual human being, in a small way, a future creation comes about. It is not only in our morality, in our thoughts, words and deeds, that a New Jerusalem is being prepared, but in our inhumanity too, in the amorality, an anti-creation is being prepared. Steiner continues:

> What about immoral behaviour? Immoral behaviour also comes to expression in the formation of the breath. But immoral behaviour imprints a demonic form on it. Demons are born through man's immoral conduct.

The three realms which are indispensable for the future, are also inextricably linked to each other. The elemental beings cannot realize the future without the help of human beings. We human beings cannot do our work without the help of Christ. The work we do is continually strengthened and carried by elemental beings, as long as we act morally. But even Christ, who embodies the beginning of the new creation, cannot help us if he is not helped in turn.

This fact is rendered in a deeply meaningful way in two scenes of Wagner's *Parsifal*. In these the trinity – human, unredeemed nature, Christ – is portrayed in its interrelation. Each of these three can only help if, in turn, it is helped. After years of wandering, Parsifal returns to the Grail territory. There is an enchanted mood in nature. Parsifal notices this enchantment, but does not recognize what is happening. Gurnemanz, the eldest knight of the Grail, tells him that the enchantment of Good Friday pervades nature. On this extraordinary day of the year, the Redeemer leaves his imprint on nature. The creation rejoices in him, but cannot behold the Crucified one. For this nature must look up at the redeemed human being. Why is it that the human being is redeemed on this day? Because on Good Friday, God himself has redeemed the human being through his sacrifice of love.

In this brief scene is rendered the inseparable trinity of the Redeemer, the redeemed human being, and nature absolved from all its sins, as Wagner calls it:

Thus all creation gives thanks,
All that here blooms and soon fades,
Now that nature, absolved from sin,
Today gains its day of innocence.

Unredeemed nature returns to her state of innocence through the Redeemer and the redeemed human being.

In the final scene of Wagner's *Parsifal* this interaction culminates in the words, 'The redemption of our Redeemer.' The Redeemer is redeemed by the human being helping him. Nowhere is this fact rendered so explicitly as here by Wagner. But we get an inkling of this in several psalms, singing of the future. In the language of the Old Testament this is called 'the new song' – the sound of the new creation – for the new song too communicates itself out of the spiritual world to the world of human beings, and from there to the creation. In Psalm 29 the new song is sung by 'heavenly beings.' The Hebrew text speaks of *Ben Elim,* literally the sons of the gods. These are the angels, singing the new song. They call up the future creation in the spiritual world.

In later psalms, such as Psalm 96, it is human beings singing this new song. To the song of the creation of the future human beings add their own voice, their entelechy, the full realization of their essence. And finally it is not only human beings, but also the sea, rivers and mountains joining in with the symphony of creation:

O sing to the LORD a new song,
for he has done marvellous things! ...
Make a joyful noise to the LORD, all the earth;
break forth into joyous song and sing praises!
Sing praises to the LORD with the lyre,
with the lyre and the sound of melody!
With the trumpets and the sound of the horn
make a joyful noise before the King, the LORD!
Let the sea roar, and all that fills it;
the world and those who dwell in it!
Let the floods clap their hands;
let the hills sing for joy together
before the LORD, for he comes to judge the earth. (Psalm 98:1,4–9)

Even less obvious, less self-evident in these connections between the divine world, the world of human beings and nature is the help Christ needs from nature.

We find it difficult to imagine that the Redeemer, who himself renews creation, could be in any way dependent on his creation. But he is not a 'Lord' in the normal sense of the word, not a Lord who stands above his slaves – but, as the Lord of the heavenly forces on earth, he lives and suffers along with his creatures. Everything we inflict on the earth, we inflict on him. Perhaps we must expand the parable of his return, to everything he created – and not apply it only to the human being: 'as you did it to one of the least of these my brethren, you did it to me' (Matt.25:40). His bretheren – might these not be the elements too? Some experiences of people who recognize the earth as a living being point in this direction.

Irene Johanson for example describes an extraordinary experience which was told her during her pastoral work. A man named Emanuel was given some money for his sixtieth birthday, for a trip to Israel. He travelled to the Holy Land to visit all the places where Christ lived. When he got there he could hardly recognize any traces that Christ might have left on the land. He was disappointed and left the crowded tourist traps, and journeyed along the River Jordan, from its sources to the Dead Sea.

> He travelled a path which told him more about Christ than all other places where people hoped to find some trace of him, but he realized that he had to go where other people were, for Christ went to the people, after all. So the man went to Jerusalem. He found a place to stay in the heart of the old town, and in the evening walked out of St Stephen's Gate. He walked in the Arab cemetery. There he stood between the tombstones and looked at the Garden of Gethsemane with its olive trees and dark cypresses. Dusk was falling. Suddenly he was overwhelmed by an intense emotion. He did not know what was happening to him. He knelt down and experienced how Christ spoke to him from the Garden of Gethsemane – as he had once spoken to the three disciples who were present when he fought death. 'Can you not wake with me for an hour?' he said. 'Look: the whole earth is my body – and she is dying before I can fulfil my task, love, in this body. Wake with me! The earth must not be allowed to die before I have made her into a star of love, through you human beings! Wake and pray with me.'
>
> Emanuel knelt down between the stones and the graves opposite Gethsemane. Tears streamed down his face. He had abandoned God throughout his whole life. He had been asleep, instead of waking with him. Every hour Christ was close to human beings, but which human being lived with him? Who let him be present in his speaking, in his actions? 'Help me Lord,' he prayed, 'let me never lose you, let me always feel you in our midst, that I may wake and pray with you, so that the earth, your body does not die, but becomes a star of love. Help me!'

Emanuel got up. There was no one he could to talk to about what he had experienced. He would have liked to return home straight away. But he stayed. Some days later he heard that on the day of his experience, far away in Chernobyl a nuclear reactor had sent out its destructive rays and badly damaged the earth, the air, water, people and animals, and all living things.[5]

The future has long since begun. It has been prepared for eons by the 'heavenly beings.' It is high time for us to take our responsibility in this process and join in with the new song. But the future will only become full reality when the earth too, which has carried us for many centuries, becomes a star of love and sings the song of creation with us.

# Notes

## 1 What is Matter?

1 Heisenberg, *Physics and Philosophy*, Chapter X: 'Language and Reality in Modern Physics.'
2 Matthew uses the word *seismos,* the same word used for earthquake.
3 John van Schaik, *Unde malum?*
4 Classical Greek also had a word for remaining outwardly silent, or not being able to find the words for something: *siopao.* When they used *sigao* they meant the sacred silence: the silence preceding the divine speaking, preceding the creative word.

## 2 The Path Through the Elements in the Mysteries

1 Persephone, daughter of Zeus and Demeter, was abducted by Hades and made queen of the underworld. During winter, when Demeter searches for Persephone in the underworld, nothing grows on the earth.
2 *Faust,* translation by Charles T. Brooks.
3 This and following quotes from Somé, *Of Water and the Spirit,* pp. 208f, 220f, 260–62.
4 Julius, *Sound Between Matter and Spirit.* There is also an article by Julius 'Nature-Spirits,' in *The Golden Blade 1971,* London 1970.

## 3 The Lord of the Elements

1 Carmichael, *Carmina Gadelica,* No. 56.
2 An impressive description of such rituals, performed to this day, can be found in Doug Boyd, *Rolling Thunder.*
3 Steiner, *Menschheits-Entwicklung und Christus-Erkenntnis,* lecture of Nov 22, 1907.
4 Steiner, *The Spiritual Guidance of the Individual and of Humanity* (Chapter 3).

5   Schroeder, *Von der Wiederkunft Christi heute*, (chapter 'Leben mit dem Jahreslauf').
6   A description of this nature study was given by Erna van Deventer in Keyserlingk, *The Birth of a New Agriculture*. This path of development was described systematically by Steiner in *The Boundaries of Natural Science*, lecture of Oct 3, 1920.
7   Richard Wagner, *My Life*, Vol. 3.

## 4   Elemental Beings

1   See Steiner, *Harmony of the Creative Word*.
2   Steiner, *Spiritual Beings in the Heavenly Bodies*, lecture of April 3, 1912.
3   Zoeteman, *Over moeder aarde*.

## 5   Genesis and the four elements

1   Steiner, *Genesis: Secrets of Creation*, lecture of Aug 17, 1910.
2   Steiner, *An Outline of Esoteric Science*, chapter 'Cosmic Evolution and the Human Being' (also published as *Occult Science: An Outline*).
3   See Waters, *Masked Gods*, part 2 'The beginning.'
4   Gorion, *Sagen der Juden*, I, 37.
5   Steiner, *An Outline of Esoteric Science*, chapter 'Cosmic Evolution and the Human Being'.

## 6   The elements in the New Testament

1   Our word 'idiot' is derived from the Greek *idia:* someone who has become so individualized that he has become estranged from his origin.
2   William Wordsworth, 'Ode: Intimations of Immortality.'
3   Steiner, *Approaching the Mystery of Golgotha*.
4   Emmerich, *Das bittere Leiden unseres Herrn Jesu Christi*.

## 7   St John the alchemist

1   Silesius, *Der cherubinische Wandersmann*.
2   Described in *The Golden Legend (Legenda Aurea)*, chapter 'John the Evangelist.'
3   Stracke, *Geheime Figuren der Rosenkreuzer*.
4   Keyserlingk, A. von, *The Birth of a New Agriculture*.
5   Keyserlingk, J. von, *Erlöste Elemente*.
6   Teilhard de, Chardin, *Hymn of the Universe*, p. 6.

## 8  Alchemy and Christianity

1   Steiner, *The Apocalypse of St John,* lecture of June 23, 1908.
2   Novalis, *Fragmente und Studien,* probably part of *Novalis: Philosophical Writings.*
3   This and the following two quotations are from Steiner, *Esoteric Christianity and the Mission of Christian Rosenkreutz,* lecture of Sep 28, 1911.

## 9  Elemental Beings and the Sacraments

1   Steiner, *Supersensible Influences in the History of Mankind,* lecture of Sep 29, 1922.
2   Mentioned by Alexander Count von Keyserlingk, in Keyserlingk, *The Birth of a New Agriculture,* p. 104.
3   Grosse, *The Christmas Foundation.*
4   Manen, *Sophia und Persephone.*
5   Burkhard, *Karlik.* Karlik is the Russian word for gnome.
6   Steiner, *Karmic Relationships,* Vol. 2, lecture of June 27, 1924.

## 10  The School of Chartres and the Goddess Natura

1   Julius Caesar, *De Bello Gallico, (The Gallic Wars),* VI.13.
2   Sharp, *Bride of the Isles,* Edinburgh, 1914 . (William Sharp also wrote under the pseudonym of Fiona Macleod.)

## 11  Elemental Beings in Nature

1   Steiner, *Karmic Relationships,* Vol 4, lecture of Sep 10, 1924.
2   Wegener, *Blick in eine andere Welt,* Stuttgart 1997.
3   Steiner, *The Spiritual Hierarchies and the Physical World,* lecture of April 14, 1909.

## Intermezzo: Natural Disasters

1   Steiner, *From Mammoths to Mediums,* lecture of Sep 11, 1923.
2   Gerding, *Kabouters, Gnomen en Fantomen.*
3   Weirauch & Staël von Holstein, *Neue Gespräche mit den Naturgeistern.*
4   This and the following quotes are from Gerding, *Kabouters, Gnomen en Fantomen.*
5   Rudolf Steiner describes at some length the antipathy the gnomes feel for frogs and toads. *Harmony of the Creative Word,* lecture of Nov 2, 1923.
6   Part of a verse beginning 'Seek the truly practical life ...' in Steiner, *Wahrspruchworte.*

## 12 Elemental Beings in Art and Technology

1   Steiner, *The Temple Legend,* lecture of Dec 23, 1904.
2   Steiner, *Ursprung und Ziel des Menschen,* lecture of March 30, 1905.
3   Steiner, *Lebendiges Naturerkennen,* lecture of Jan 19, 1923.
4   Steiner, *The Fall of the Spirit of Darkness,* lecture of Oct 6, 1917.
5   Rilke, *The Duino Elegies,* translated by J.B. Leishman and Stephen Spender.
6   Steiner, *Man and the World of the Stars,* lecture of Dec 16, 1922.

## 13 The role of the hierarchies

1   Steiner, *Michaelmas and the Soul-Forces of Man,* lecture of Sep 28, 1923.
2   Steffen, *Pilgerfahrt zum Lebensbaum.*
3   Steiner, *Karmic Relationships,* Vol. 8, lecture of Aug 21, 1924.

## 14 New Developments and Experiences

1   Steiner, *Mystics after Modernism,* chapter 'Agrippa von Nettesheim and Theophrastus Paracelsus.'
2   Krauss, *Holzwege, Steinwege.* See also interview with Ernst-Martin Krauss in Weirauch, *Naturgeister.*
3   Steiner, *Agriculture: Spiritual Foundations,* lecture of June 10, 1924, p. 40.
4   Erkki Lähde, interview by Jussi Tuuri and Wolfgang Weirauch in Weirauch, *Naturgeister.*
5   Wolfgang Weirauch, *Nature Spirits and What They Say,* pp. 10, 32; second quotation from p. 23.
6   Tapio Kaitaharju, interview by Wolfgang Weirauch in Weirauch, *Naturgeister.*
7   Ernst-Martin Krauss, interview by Wolfgang Weirauch in Weirauch, *Naturgeister.*
8   Alja Ackermans, 'Afscheidsgroet,' *Dynamisch Perspectief,* (Netherlands) March /April 2005.

## 15 Elemental Beings and the Future

1   Yolande van Eck, 'Im Anblick des Lichtwesens,' interview in Weirauch, *Nah-Todes Erfahrungen.*
2   Hillerdal & Gustafsson, *De såg och hörde Jesus.* (In German translation: *Sie erlebten Christus.*)
3   Keyserlingk, J. von, *Erlöste Elemente,* 'Gespräch mit Dr Steiner.'
4   Steiner, *Art as Seen in the Light of the Mystery Wisdom,* lecture of Jan 3, 1915.
5   Johanson, *Jeder Mensch birgt sein Geheimnis,* chapter 'Erlebnisse im Heiligen Land.'

# Further Reading

## On Christianity and nature

Alfons Rosenberg, *Der Christ und die Erde.*
Friedrich Benesch, *Apokalypse. Die Verwandlung der Erde.*
—, *Leben mit der Erde.*
—, *Christliche Feste.*
—, *Christus in der Gegenwart.*
—, *Das verborgene Gottesreich auf Erden.*
—, *Zur Äthergeographie der Erde.*
Barbara Nordmeyer, *Erde – Stern des Christus.*
Johannes Hemleben, *Urbeginn und Ziel.*

## On the earth as organism

Walther Cloos, *Das Jahr der Erde.*
Helmut Knauer, *Erdenantlitz und Erdenstoffe.*
Guenther Wachsmuth, *Erde und Mensch.*
Kees Zoeteman, *Gaia-Sophia.*

## On nature beings

Gerhard Joedicke, *Liebe zu einem Baum.*
Dirk Kruse, *Seelisches Beobachten in der Natur.*
Geoffrey Hodson, *Faeries at Work and at Play.*
—, *The Kingdom of Faerie.*
—, *The Kingdom of the Gods.*
Dora van Gelder, *The Real World of Fairies.*
Nancy Arrowsmith, *A Field Guide to the Little People,* (with an extensive list of
    nature myths, legends and fairytales).
Annie Gerding-Le Comte, *Kabouters, gnomen en fantomen.*
Ernst-Martin Krauss, *Holzwege, Steinwege. Erlebnisse mit Elementarwesen.*
Ingeborg Lüdeling, *Steine, Bäume, Menschenträume.*
—, *Zeitnischen.*

Marko Pogacnik, *Nature Spirits and Elemental Beings.*
—, *Healing the Heart of the Earth.*
Dick van Romunde, *Planten waarnemen: elementenwezens ervaren,* (English ebook:
    *Perceiving Plants: Experiencing Elemental Beings.)*
—, *Over vormende krachten in de plantenwereld,* (English ebook: *About Formative
    Forces in the Plant World.)*
Henriëtte Gorter, *Op zoek naar mensen die kabouters zien.*
Wolfgang von Goethe, *The Metamorphosis of Plants.*
Frits Julius, *Metamorfose. Ontwikkeling bij plant en mens.*
—, *Sound Between Matter and Spirit.*
Ursula Burkhard, *Auch die Stille hat eine Sprache.*
—, *Elementarwesen. Bild und Wirklichkeit.*
—, *Karlik.*
—, *Steinäckerchen.*
Sigrid Lechner-Knecht, *Die Hüter der Elemente.*

## Anthroposophy

Ernst Marti, *The Four Ethers.*
Jochen Bockemühl, *Erscheinungsformen des Ätherischen.*
Jochen Bockemühl, *Toward a Phenomenology of the Etheric World.*
Ernst Hagemann, *World Ether, Elemental Beings, Kingdoms of Nature.*
Hans Peter van Manen, *Sophia und Persephone.*
Maximilian Rebholz, *Studien zur Geisteswissenschaft,*(the chapters 'Über die
    Elementarreiche' & 'Über die Elementenwesen')
Wolfgang Weirauch & Verena Staël von Holstein, *Nature Spirits and What they
    Say,* Floris Books, UK 2004.
Weirauch & Holstein, *Nature Spirits of the Trees,* Floris Books, UK 2004.
Weirauch & Holstein, *Thoughts that Shine Like the Stars.*
Weirauch & Holstein, *Neue Gespräche mit den Naturgeistern.*
Wolfgang Weirauch, *Naturgeister 3.*
Wolfgang Weirauch, *Naturgeister 4.*
Verena Staël von Holstein and Friedrich Pfannenschmidt, *Gespräche mit Müller.*

## Nature beings in Ireland

Tanis Helliwell, *Summer with the Leprechauns.*
Diarmuid McManus, *The Middle Kingdom.*
Grimm, *Irische Elfenmärchen.*
Frederik Hetmann, *Die Reise in die Anderwelt.*
W.B. Yeats, *Irish Folk Stories and Fairy Tales.*

## *Lectures by Rudolf Steiner*

### Elements

—, *Universe, Earth and Man* (lecture of Aug 7, 1908, how the angels, archangels and archai work in the water, air, and warmth element of the earth).

—, *Genesis: Secrets of Creation* (lectures of Aug 22 & 23, 1910, The elemental world and the spiritual beings active within it; the work of the elemental world in the organs of the human being).

—, *Der Zusammenhang des Menschen mit der elementarischen Welt* (lectures of Nov 9, 14 & 15, 1914, the connection between the human being and the elemental world).

—, *The Connection between the Living and the Dead* (lecture of Nov 9, 1916, the influence of the elemental world on the physical life of the human being).

—, *The Light Course* (lecture of Dec 30, 1919, three phases in the connection of the human being with the world in light, warmth and air).

—, *Mystery of the Universe* (lecture of April 17, 1920, organs and elements).

—, *Education for Adolescents* (lecture of June 17, 1921, the Greeks and the four elements).

—, *Menschenwerden, Weltenseele und Weltengeist: Erster Teil* (lecture of June 26, 1921, the human being and the elements).

—, *Old and New Methods of Initiation* (lecture of Feb 19, 1922, the threefold human being in relation to the elements).

—, *Origins of Natural Science* (lecture of Jan 2, 1923, the four elements and the four bodily fluids according to Galen).

—, *World History and the Mysteries* (lectures of Dec 27 & 30, 1923, Aristotle on the relationship between the human being and the elements, and his connection to the earth; the transformation of the elements by absorbing them into the human 'I').

—, *Karmic Relationships*, Vol. 3 (July 13, 1924, ideas on the life of the elements up to the fifteenth century).

### Events in the elemental realms

—, *Manifestations of Karma* (lecture of May 22, 1910, events in the elemental realms in relationship to karma).

—, *Karmic Relationships*, Vol. 2 (June 29, 1924, elemental events).

### Elemental spirits

—, *Das Geheimnis der Trinität* (lecture of Aug 9, 1922, the working of particular elemental beings since the sixteenth century).

—, *World History and the Mysteries* (lecture of Dec 25, 1923, experiencing elemental spirits).

## Elemental world

—, *A Way of Self-Knowledge* (Part I, Ch. 3 The human's etheric body and the elemental world; Ch. 9 'I'-feeling and the human soul's capacity to love; Part II, Ch. 3 Clairvoyant cognition of the elemental world).

—, *Rosicrucian Wisdom* (lecture of May 26, 1907, the elemental world and the heavenly world).

—, *Secrets of the Threshold* (lecture of Aug 26, 1913, experiences of the soul in the elemental world).

—, *Die Sendung Michaels* (lecture of Dec 6, 1919, the activity of the elemental world in human destiny).

—, *The Human Soul in Relation to World Evolution* (lecture of May 28, 1922, acquiring knowledge of the elemental world).

## Elemental realms

—, *Mitteleuropa zwischen Ost und West* (lecture of May 2, 1918, the working of folk souls in different elemental realms).

## Elemental beings

—, *Foundations of Esotericism* (lectures of Oct 1, 17, 28 & 30, 1905, elemental beings; elemental beings in the astral realm, natural and artificial elemental beings; elemental beings in Atlantean times; elemental beings).

—, *An Esoteric Cosmology* (lecture of Feb 26, 1906, good and evil elemental beings).

—, *Das Hereinwirken geistiger Wesenheiten* (lectures of May 16, June 1 & 4, 1908, the nature and origin of different elemental beings; modern science and elemental beings; elemental beings); lectures of May 16 and June 4 included in *Nature Spirits*.

—, *Spiritual Beings in the Heavenly Bodies* (lectures of April 3 & 4, 1912, elemental beings of the earth and water; of fire and air).

—, *The Riddle of Humanity* (lecture of Aug 6, 1916, the human being and elemental beings).

—, *The Fall of the Spirit of Darkness* (lecture of Oct 6, 1917, task of elemental beings who are opposed to life).

—, *Secret Brotherhoods* (lecture of Nov 19, 1917, elemental beings).

—, *The New Spirituality and the Christ Experience* (lecture of Oct 22, 1920, elemental beings in east and west who oppose the idea of threefoldness).

—, *The Human Soul in Relation to World Evolution* (lecture of May 28, 1922, higher elemental beings).

—, *Man and the World of the Stars* (lecture of Dec 16, 1922, relationships of elemental beings to truth, beauty and goodness).

—, *The Cycle of the Year* (lecture of April 2, 1923, elemental beings in the cycle of the year).

—, *Harmony of the Creative Word* (lecture of Nov 3, 1923, evil and good elemental beings).

—, *Colour* (lecture of Jan 4, 1924, forming of rainbows by elemental beings).

—, *True and False Paths* (lecture of Aug 19, 1924, on possession, Ahrimanic elemental beings).

## Lecture cycles on nature beings

—, *Natur- und Geistwesen*, Dornach 1996.

—, *The Spiritual Hierarchies and the Physical World.*

—, *Harmony of the Creative Word.*

—, *Spiritual Beings in the Heavenly Bodies.*

—, *Nature Spirits.*

## Gnomes

—, *Nature Spirits* (lecture of May 16, 1908).

—, *Chance, Providence, and Necessity* (lecture of Sep 4, 1915, thoughts become living beings which are related to gnomes; gnomes in their relationship to the physical world).

—, *The Human Soul in Relation to World Evolution* (lecture of May 28, 1922, the realm of gnomes and the world of number).

—, *Harmony of the Creative Word* (lecture of Nov 3, 1923, root elemental beings, antipathy of gnomes toward lower beings).

## Salamanders

—, *Nature Spirits* (lecture of May 16, 1908).

—, *Harmony of the Creative Word* (lecture of Nov 2, 1923, fire spirits as complementary to the nature of butterflies).

## Sylphs, spirits of the air

—, *Nature Spirits* (lecture of May 16, 1908).

—, *Das Hereinwirken geistiger Wesenheiten* (lecture of June 1, 1908, bees and sylphs).

—, *The Human Soul in Relation to World Evolution* (lecture of May 28, 1922, spirits of the air and the human soul).

—, *Harmony of the Creative Word* (lecture of Nov 2, 1923, spirits of the air; sylphs as complementary to the world of birds).

## Undines, water-beings

—, *Nature Spirits* (lecture of May 16, 1908).

—, *Das Hereinwirken geistiger Wesenheiten* (lecture of June 1, 1908).

—, *Chance, Providence, and Necessity* (lecture of Sep 4, 1915, With undines we are in a very mobile world).

—, *The Human Soul in Relation to World Evolution* (lecture of May 28, 1922, the watery element and the emotional experiencing of the world).

—, *Harmony of the Creative Word* (lectures of Nov 2 & 3, 1923, undines as complementary to the world of fishes and the higher amphibians).

# Bibliography

Arrowsmith, Nancy, *A Field Guide to the Little People*, New York 1977 (with an extensive list of nature myths, legends and fairytales).

*Aurea Catena Homeri. Beschreibung von dem Ursprung der Natur und natürlichen Dingen*, Leipzig 1728.

Benesch, Friedrich, *Apokalypse, Die Verwandlung der Erde: Eine okkulte Mineralogie*, Stuttgart 1981.

—, *Christliche Feste* (2 vols), Stuttgart 1993, 1994.

—, *Christus in der Gegenwart*, Stuttgart 1995.

—, *Leben mit der Erde*, Stuttgart 1993.

—, *Das verborgene Gottesreich auf Erden*, Stuttgart 1996.

—, *Zur Äthergeographie der Erde*, Stuttgart 2000.

Bockemühl, Jochen, *Erscheinungsformen des Ätherischen*, Stuttgart 1985.

—, *Toward a Phenomenology of the Etheric World*, Anthroposophic Press, USA 1985.

Boyd, Doug. *Rolling Thunder*, New York 1974.

Burkhard, Ursula *Auch die Stille hat eine Sprache. Innere Bilder*, Dornach 2002.

—, *Elementarwesen. Bild und Wirklichkeit*, Dornach 1998.

—, *Karlik*, Werkgemeinschaft Kunst und Heilpädagogik, Germany 1987.

—, *Steinäckerchen*, Werkgemeinschaft Kunst und Heilpädagogik, Germany 1987.

Carmichael, Alexander, *Carmina Gadelica, Hymns and Incantation*, Floris Books 1992.

Cloos, Walther, *Das Jahr der Erde. Von der Alchymie der Jahreszeiten*, Stuttgart 1986.

Dionysius, *Celestial Hierarchies*, London 1894.

Emmerich, Anne Catherine, *Das bittere Leiden unseres Herrn Jesu Christi*, Stein am Rhein 1996.

Gelder, Dora van, *The Real World of Fairies*, Wheaton, USA 1977.

Gerding-Le Comte, Annie, *Kabouters, Gnomen en Fantomen. Ontmoetingen met Natuurwezens*, Rotterdam 1979.

Goethe, Wolfgang von, *Faust* (tr. Charles T. Brooks) Boston, 1868.

—, *The Metamorphosis of Plants*, (Tr. Douglas Miller) MIT 2009.

Gorion, Micha Josef bin, *Sagen der Juden*, Leipzig 1978.

Gorter, Henriëtte, *Op zoek naar mensen die kabouters zien,* Epe 1988.

Grimm, *Irische Elfenmärchen,* Stuttgart 1984.

Grosse, Rudolf, *The Christmas Foundation: Beginning of a New Cosmic Age,* Steiner Book Centre, Canada 1984.

Hagemann, Ernst, *World Ether, Elemental Beings, Kingdoms of Nature,* Mercury Press, 1996.

Heisenberg, Werner, *Physics and Philosophy: the Revolution in Modern Science,* Harper, 2007.

Helliwell, Tanis, *Summer with the Leprechauns,* Blue Dolphin Publishing 1997.

Hemleben, Johannes, *Urbeginn und Ziel,* Stuttgart 1976.

Hetmann, Frederik, *Die Reise in die Anderwelt. Elfengeschichten und Feenglaube in Irland,* Köln 1981.

Hillerdal, Gunnar, & Berndt Gustafsson, *De såg och hörde Jesus: Krustusuppenbarelser I vår tid,* Verbum, Sweden 1978.

—, *Sie erlebten Christus,* Pforte, Basel 1980.

Hodson, Geoffrey, *Faeries at Work and at Play,* 1925.

—, *The Kingdom of Faerie,* 1927.

—, *The Kingdom of the Gods,* Quest Books, USA 1987.

Holstein, Verena Staël von & Friedrich Pfannenschmidt, *Gespräche mit Müller – Feinstofflicher Austausch mit Geistwesenheiten,* Flensburg 2003.

—, *see also* Weirauch, Wolfgang

Joedicke, Gerhard, *Liebe zu einem Baum. Eine Chronik in Gedichten und Tagebuch-Notizen,* Borchen 2005.

Johanson, Irene, *Jeder Mensch birgt sein Geheimnis,* Stuttgart 1991.

Julius, Frits, *Metamorfose. Ontwikkeling bij plant en mens,* Zeist 1999.

—, *Sound Between Matter and Spirit,* Mercury Press, USA 2005.

Keyserlingk, Adalbert Graf von, *The Birth of a New Agriculture: Koberwitz 1924 and the Introduction of Biodynamics,* Temple Lodge Publishing, UK 1999.

Keyserlingk, Johanna von, *Erlöste Elemente: Aus dem Nachlass der Gräfin Johanna von Keyserlingk,* Mellinger, Stuttgart 1991.

Knauer, Helmut, *Erdenantlitz und Erdenstoffe,* Dornach 1961.

Krauss, Ernst-Martin, *Holzwege, Steinwege. Erlebnisse mit Elementarwesen,* Flensburg 1992.

Kruse, Dirk, *Seelisches Beobachten in der Natur* (Privately published).

Lechner-Knecht, Sigrid, *Die Hüter der Elemente. Das geheimnisvolle Reich,* Berlin 1989.

Lüdeling, Ingeborg, *Steine, Bäume, Menschenträume. Ein spirituelles Erlebnisbuch,* Freiburg 1997.

—, *Zeitnischen. Das verborgene Wissen der Externsteine,* Nienburg 1998.

Macleod, Fiona *see* Sharp, William

McManus, Diarmuid, *The Middle Kingdom. The Faerie world of Ireland,* Colin Smythe 1974.

Manen, Hans Peter van, *Sophia und Persephone – Anthroposophische Impulse in der Umweltschutzbewegung,* Dornach 1989.

Marti, Ernst, *The Four Ethers,* Schaumberg, USA 1984.

Nordmeyer, Barbara, *Erde – Stern des Christus,* Stuttgart 1965.

Novalis (pseudonym of Friedrich von Hardenberg), *Fragmente und Studien.*

—, *Philosophical Writings,* State University of New York Press 2007.

Pogacnik, Marko, *Nature Spirits and Elemental Beings: Working with the Intelligence in Nature,* Forres, UK 2010.

—, *Healing the Heart of the Earth: Restoring the Subtle Levels of Life,* Forres, UK 1998

Rebholz, Maximilian, *Studien zur Geisteswissenschaft,* Freiburg 1957.

Rilke, Rainer Maria, *The Duino Elegies,* (tr. by J.B. Leishman and Stephen Spender) Chatto & Windus, London 1975.

Romunde, Dick van, *Planten waarnemen: elementenwezens ervaren,* Zeist 1988; available as ebook in English: *Perceiving Plants: Experiencing Elemental Beings,* 2012.

—, *Over vormende krachten in de plantenwereld,* Driebergen 2000; available as ebook in English: *About Formative Forces in the Plant World,* 2012.

Rosenberg, Alfons, *Der Christ und die Erde,* Freiburg 1953.

Schaik, John van, *Unde malum? Een vergelijkende studie tussen het dualisme van de Manicheeërs en de Katharen,* Kampen 2004.

Schroeder, Hans-Werner, *Von der Wiederkunft Christi heute,* Stuttgart 1991.

Sharp, William, *Bride of the Isles,* Edinburgh, 1914.

Silesius, Angelus, *Der cherubinische Wandersmann,* Forgotten Books 2007.

Somé, Malidoma Patrice, *Of Water and the Spirit: Ritual Magic and Initiation in the Life of an African Shaman,* Tarcher, New York 1994.

Steffen, Albert, *Pilgerfahrt zum Lebensbaum,* Dornach 1982.

Steiner, Rudolf. Volume Nos refer to the Collected Works (CW), or to the German Gesamtausgabe (GA).

—, *Agriculture Course: The Birth of the Biodynamic Method,* CW 327, Rudolf Steiner Press, UK 2005.

—, *Agriculture: Spiritual Foundations for the Renewal of Agriculture,* CW 327, Biodynamic Farming and Gardening Association, USA 1993.

—, *Anthroposophical Leading Thoughts: Anthroposophy as a Path of Knowledge,* Rudolf Steiner Press, UK 1998.

—, *The Apocalypse of St John: Lectures on the Book of Revelation,* CW 104, Anthroposophic Press, USA 1993.

—, *Approaching the Mystery of Golgotha,* CW 152, SteinerBooks, USA 2006.

—, *Art as Seen in the Light of the Mystery Wisdom,* CW 275, Rudolf Steiner Press, UK 2010.

—, *The Boundaries of Natural Science,* CW 322, Anthroposophic Press, USA 1983.

—, *Chance, Providence, and Necessity,* CW 163, Rudolf Steiner Press, UK 1988.

—, *Colour,* CW 291, Rudolf Steiner Press, UK 2005.

—, *The Connection between the Living and the Dead,* CW 168, SteinerBooks, USA 2013.

—, *The Cycle of the Year as Breathing Process of the Earth,* CW 223, Anthroposophic Press, USA 1988.

—, *Education for Adolescents,* CW 302, SteinerBooks, USA 1996.

—, *Esoteric Christianity and the Mission of Christian Rosenkreutz,* CW 130, Rudolf Steiner Press, UK 2005.

—, *An Esoteric Cosmology: Evolution, Christ and Modern Spirituality,* CW 94, SteinerBooks, USA 2008.

—, *The Fall of the Spirit of Darkness,* CW 177, Rudolf Steiner Press, UK 2008.

—, *Foundations of Esotericism,* CW 93a, Rudolf Steiner Press, UK 1983.

—, *From Mammoths to Mediums: Answers to Questions,* CW 350, lecture of Sep 11, 1923.

—, *Das Geheimnis der Trinität,* GA 214, Dornach 1999.

—, *Genesis: Secrets of Creation,* CW 122, Rudolf Steiner Press, UK 2002.

—, *Harmony of the Creative Word,* CW 230, Rudolf Steiner Press, UK 2001.

—, *Das Hereinwirken geistiger Wesenheiten in den Menschen,* GA 102, Dornach 2001.

—, *The Human Soul in Relation to World Evolution,* CW 212, Rudolf Steiner Press, UK 1985.

—, *Karmic Relationships: Esoteric Studies,* Vol. 2, CW 236, Rudolf Steiner Press, UK 1997.

—, *Karmic Relationships: Esoteric Studies,* Vol. 3, CW 237, Rudolf Steiner Press, UK 2009.

—, *Karmic Relationships: Esoteric Studies,* Vol 4, CW 238, Rudolf Steiner Press, UK 1997.

—, *Karmic Relationships: Esoteric Studies,* Vol. 8, CW 240, Rudolf Steiner Press, UK 1975.

—, *Lebendiges Naturerkennen, Intellektueller Sündenfall und spiritueller Sündenerhebung,* GA 220, Dornach 1982.

—, *The Light Course: Towards the Development of a New Physics,* CW 320, SteinerBooks, USA 2001.

—, *Man and the World of the Stars: The Spiritual Communion of Mankind,* CW 219, Anthroposophic Press, USA 1963.

—, *Manifestations of Karma,* CW 120, Rudolf Steiner Press, UK 2000.

—, *Menschheits-Entwicklung und Christus-Erkenntnis,* GA 100, Dornach 1981.

—, *Menschenwerden, Weltenseele und Weltengeist: Erster Teil – Der Mensch als leiblich-seelische Wesenheit in seinem Verhältnis zur Welt,* GA 205, Dornach 1987.

—, *Michaelmas and the Soul-Forces of Man,* (part of CW 223), Anthroposophic Press, USA 1982.

—, *Mitteleuropa zwischen Ost und West,* GA 174a, Dornach 1982.

—, *Mystery of the Universe: The Human Being, Model of Creation,* CW 201, Rudolf Steiner Press, UK 2001.

—, *Mystics after Modernism: Discovering the Seeds of a New Science in the Renaissance,* CW 7, Anthroposophic Press, USA 2000.

—, *Natur- und Geistwesen – Ihr Wirken in unserer sichtbarer Welt,* GA 98, Dornach 1996.

—, *Nature Spirits* (selected lectures) Rudolf Steiner Press, UK 2003.

—, *The New Spirituality and the Christ Experience of the Twentieth Century*, CW 200, Anthroposophic Press, USA 1988.

—, *Occult Science: An Outline*, CW 13, Rudolf Steiner Press, UK 2005.

—, *Old and New Methods of Initiation*, CW 210, Rudolf Steiner Press, UK 1991.

—, *Origins of Natural Science*, CW 326, Anthroposophic Press, USA 1985.

—, *An Outline of Esoteric Science*, CW 13, Anthroposophic Press, USA 1997.

—, *The Philosophy of Freedom: the Basis of a Modern World Conception*, CW 4, Rudolf Steiner Press, UK 2012.

—, *The Riddle of Humanity*, CW 170, Rudolf Steiner Press, UK 1990.

—, *Rosicrucian Wisdom: An Introduction*, CW 99, Rudolf Steiner Press, UK 2000.

—, *Secret Brotherhoods and the Mystery of the Human Double*, CW 178, Rudolf Steiner Press, UK 2004.

—, *Secrets of the Threshold*, CW 147, SteinerBooks, USA 2007.

—, *Die Sendung Michaels*, GA 194, Dornach 1994.

—, *Spiritual Beings in the Heavenly Bodies and in the Kingdoms of Nature*, CW 136, SteinerBooks, USA 2012.

—, *The Spiritual Guidance of the Individual and of Humanity*, CW 15, Anthroposophic Press, USA 1991.

—, *The Spiritual Hierarchies and the Physical World: Zodiac, Planets, and Cosmos*, CW 110 SteinerBooks, USA 2008.

—, *Supersensible Influences in the History of Mankind*, CW 216, Rudolf Steiner Publishing Co, London 1956.

—, *The Temple Legend: Freemasonry and Related Occult Movements: From the Contents of the Esoteric School*, CW 93, Rudolf Steiner Press, UK 2002.

—, *True and False Paths in Spiritual Investigation*, CW 243, Anthroposophic Press, USA 1985.

—, *Universe, Earth and Man*, CW 105, Rudolf Steiner Press, UK 1987.

—, *Ursprung und Ziel des Menschen*, GA 53, lecture of March 30, 1905, Dornach 1981.

—, *Wahrspruchworte*, GA 40. Dornach 1991.

—, *A Way of Self-Knowledge: And the Threshold of the Spiritual World*, CW 16/17, SteinerBooks, USA 2006.

—, *World History and the Mysteries in the Light of Anthroposophy*, CW 233, Rudolf Steiner Press, UK 1977.

—, *Der Zusammenhang des Menschen mit der elementarischen Welt*, GA 158, Dornach 1993.

Stracke, Viktor, *Geheime Figuren der Rosenkreuzer – Das Geistgebäude der Rosenkreuzer – Wie kann man die Figuren der Rosenkreuzer heute verstehen?* Dornach 1993.

Teilhard de, Chardin Pierre *Hymn of the Universe*. Harper & Row 1961.

Wachsmuth, Günther, *Erde und Mensch*, Dornach 1965.

Wagner, Richard, *My Life*, Vol. 3.

Waters, Frank , *Masked Gods, Navaho and Pueblo Ceremonialism*, New York 1970.

Wegener, Dagny, *Blick in eine andere Welt. Begegnung mit Verstorbenen und geistigen Wesen*, Stuttgart 1997.

Weirauch, Wolfgang, *Nah-Todes Erfahrungen: Flensburger Hefte*, No. 51, Flensburg 1995.

—, *Naturgeister, Flensburger Hefte*, No. 55, Flensburg 2000.

—, *Naturgeister 3 — Von Rauchwesen, Wiesenwesen, Torfwesen und Machinenwesen*, Flensburger Hefte No. 21, 2004.

—, *Naturgeister 4, Fragenkompendium*, Flensburger Hefte No. 22, 2004.

Weirauch, Wolfgang & Verena Staël von Holstein, *Nature Spirits and What they Say*, Floris Books, UK 2004.

—, *Nature Spirits of the Trees*, Floris Books, UK 2004.

—, *Neue Gespräche mit den Naturgeistern*, Flensburger Hefte No. 80, 2003.

—, *Thoughts that Shine Like the Stars: Further Conversations with Nature Spirits*, Mill Press, Germany 2012.

Wilder, Thornton, *The Eighth Day*, London 1967.

Yeats, W.B. *Irish Folk Stories and Fairy Tales*.

Zoeteman, Kees, *Gaia-Sophia; Our Changing Relationship to the Earth*, Edinburgh 1991.

—, *Over moeder aarde: Dertien spirituele visies op de mens*, Rotterdam 1996.

# Index

# BOOKS BY BASTIAAN BAAN

*The Chymical Wedding of Christian Rosenkreutz:*
*A Commentary on a Christian Path of Initiation*

*Lord of the Elements:*
*Interweaving Christianity and Nature*

*Old and New Mysteries:*
*From Trials to Initiation*

*Sources of Christianity:*
*Peter, Paul and John*

*Sources of Religious Worship:*
*A History of Ritual from the Stone Age to the Present Day*

*Ways into Christian Meditation*

# Sources of Christianity
## Peter, Paul and John

Bastiaan Baan, Christine Gruwez, and John van Schaik

'The three authors combine academic thoroughness with a lively capacity to enter imaginatively into their theme.'
– *Camphill Correspondence*

This fascinating book paints a vivid picture of the three apostles, exploring their similarities as well as their significant differences, and demonstrating their continuing relevance today. Beginning with a discussion of the pre-Christian context, the authors conclude by tracing the esoteric streams of Petrine, Pauline and Johannine Christianity in the first few centuries after Christ. Crucially, they demonstrate how all three apostles are equally essential in order to truly approach the reality of Jesus Christ.

florisbooks.co.uk

# Old and New Mysteries

## From Trials to Initiation

Bastiaan Baan

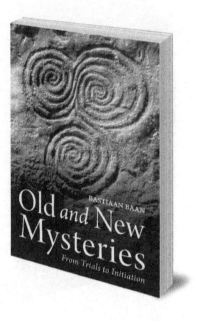

'Rich in references, rich in illustrations,
rich in knowledge and practical advice.'
– *New View*

This fascinating book compares and contrasts the trials
and rites that historically took place in the mystery centres
of antiquity with the modern-day experience of initiation.
Baan suggests that life itself, rather than a 'hierophant',
or guide, tests us and that this can lead to deeper spiritual
experiences between Christianity and the natural world.

florisbooks.co.uk

# Ways Into
# Christian Meditation

Bastiaan Baan

Meditation has long been a path to self-awareness, as well as a way of consciously building a bridge into the spiritual world. Many of the most popular techniques originated in eastern traditions, but this book describes a decades-old approach that comes from western Christianity.

florisbooks.co.uk

# The Chymical Wedding of Christian Rosenkreutz

## A Commentary on a Christian Path of Initiation

Bastiaan Baan

Containing the complete text of *The Chymical Wedding*, this timeless book explores the inner transformation of the soul. Baan's insightful interpretation and commentary makes this work accessible to modern readers. He uncovers the original significance, combining images and concepts from alchemy with insights from Rudolf Steiner's teachings.

florisbooks.co.uk

# Sources of Religious Worship
## A History of Ritual from the Stone Age to the Present Day

Bastiaan Baan

Different forms of religious worship and ritual are present throughout the development of human beings, from early stone-age ritual, nature religion and ancestor worship, to faiths from which Christianity and the Eucharist emerge. Baan traces the origins and metamorphosis of human religion in historical, theological and humanistic terms, examining its significance for human life on earth and in the spiritual world.

florisbooks.co.uk

# Free From Dogma
## Theological Reflections in The Christian Community

Tom Ravetz

One way in which The Christian Community differs from other churches is that it does not demand adherence to any creed or view of the world from its members. Nevertheless, spiritual, philosophical and religious questions arise, and by thinking about and discussing them, members can become part of the spiritual conversation that has been underway for the last 2000 years.

This book, the first of its kind to explore the theology of The Christian Community in a systematic way, asks such questions and offers many insights into religious life and experience.

florisbooks.co.uk

# Karlik

## Encounters with Elemental Beings

Ursula Burkhard

Elemental beings such as gnomes and fairies exist in many folk and spiritual traditions, and their significance to our world was of great interest to Rudolf Steiner. The ability to engage, and even communicate, with elementals is found in just a few people.

Ursula Burkhard was one such person. Blind from birth, she experienced gnomes and other elementals from early childhood.

In this readable little book, Ursula describes her remarkable experiences and in particular her relationship with a special gnome, Karlik.

florisbooks.co.uk